A READER'S GUIDE TO P
IN SEARCH OF LOST

Proust's *A la recherche du temps perdu* (*In Search of Lost Time*) is many things at once: a novel of education, a portrait of French society during the Third Republic, a masterful psychological analysis of love, a reflection on homosexuality, an essay in moral and aesthetic theory, and, above all, one of the great literary achievements of the twentieth century. This *Reader's Guide* analyzes each volume of the *Recherche* in order and in detail. Without jargon or technical language, David Ellison leads the reader through the work, clarifying but not oversimplifying the intricate beauty of Proust's imaginary universe. Focused both on large themes and on narrative and stylistic particularities, Ellison's readings expand our understanding and appreciation of the work and provide tools for the further study of Proust. All extracts in French are translated, making this an ideal guide for students of comparative literature as well as of French.

DAVID ELLISON is Distinguished Professor in the Humanities at the University of Miami, Florida.

A READER'S GUIDE TO PROUST'S *IN SEARCH OF LOST TIME*

DAVID ELLISON

University of Miami

CAMBRIDGE UNIVERSITY PRESS
Cambridge, New York, Melbourne, Madrid, Cape Town, Singapore,
São Paulo, Delhi, Dubai, Tokyo

Cambridge University Press
The Edinburgh Building, Cambridge CB2 8RU, UK

Published in the United States of America by Cambridge University Press, New York

www.cambridge.org
Information on this title: www.cambridge.org/9780521720069

First published 2010

Printed in the United Kingdom at the University Press, Cambridge

A catalogue record for this publication is available from the British Library

Library of Congress Cataloguing in Publication data
Ellison, David R.
A reader's guide to Proust's In search of lost time / David Ellison.
p. cm.
ISBN 978-0-521-89577-4 (hardback) – ISBN 978-0-521-72006-9 (pbk.)
1. Proust, Marcel, 1871–1922. @ la recherche du temps perdu–Handbooks,
manuals, etc. I. Title.
PQ2631.R63A78723 2010
843'.912–dc22
2009050375

ISBN 978-0-521-89577-4 Hardback
ISBN 978-0-521-72006-9 Paperback

Pour la famille nombreuse

Contents

Illustrations

Preface

This *Reader's Guide* to Marcel Proust's 3,000-page magnum opus, *A la recherche du temps perdu* [*In Search of Lost Time*], is intended not only for advanced undergraduates and graduate students in the humanities, but also for the intellectually curious reader who has heard of Proust's remarkable literary achievement but has not had the time, the courage, or the discipline to undertake a reading project of rather considerable scope. My purpose has been to analyze and to clarify Proust's text without having recourse to specialized vocabulary and without engaging at great length in dialogue with those critics who, from the early twentieth century until the present moment, have enriched our understanding of a beautiful but complex work. From Ernst Robert Curtius, Walter Benjamin, and Samuel Beckett to Antoine Compagnon, Julia Kristeva, and Malcolm Bowie, passing through stages of progressive insight brought to us by readers such as Germaine Brée, Georges Poulet, Jean-Pierre Richard, Gérard Genette, Gilles Deleuze, Roger Shattuck, Jean-Yves Tadié, and many others, Proust's text has been a testing ground for critical and theoretical meditation, an unavoidable point of reference for any serious reflection on literary modernity. It is incumbent upon the contemporary critic doing conceptually or philologically rigorous work on Proust to place his or her own thoughts within the large perspective opened up by these distinguished readers and the questions they have posed.

The present study is more modest: its focus is on the immediate experience of reading Proust, word by word, line by line. Whatever else Proust may have intended his work to be, it is first and foremost a novel, a long narrative composed of multiple intersecting and divergent threads. The role of the reader is, at first, simply to follow these threads and to see where they lead. For this reason, after an introductory chapter devoted to Proust's life, his literary career, and his early writings, I have followed the sequential movement of the novel, from its first to its seventh and final volume, devoting individual chapters to the volumes as they unfold in the forward thrust of the narrative (the exception being Chapter 5, which covers two volumes). My method has been that of close reading, and I have quite consciously chosen to have Proust "speak" as much as I do, which explains why this book contains many quoted passages from the *Recherche* (both in the original French and in English translation, so that the text can be accessible to a broad readership). My goal has been to accompany Proust, to remain within the imaginary universe he has created, and not to cast my own shadow over this universe. If a *Reader's Guide* is to succeed as an invitation to reading, it seems to me that the guide himself should emulate Virgil to his reader's Dante, and disappear once he has pointed out salient areas of the landscape, leaving the more arduous, but also more rewarding stages of the peregrination to the literary pilgrim, who must necessarily make the essential choices and discoveries individually. That pilgrim, dear reader, is you. It is for you that I have written what follows.

Acknowledgements

I am grateful to Linda Bree and to Cambridge University Press for having entrusted this volume on Proust to me. After some years of nomadic wandering away from Proust's universe, I was enticed to return to its charms by the late Richard Bales, who asked me to contribute an essay to *The Cambridge Companion to Proust* (2001). I have based both the Chronology and the Select bibliography in the present study on those provided for the *Cambridge Companion* by Professor Bales, whose erudition in all matters Proustian was exemplary.

I am also indebted to the University of Miami, and in particular to Michael Halleran, Dean of Arts and Sciences, for having granted me a semester's leave for the completion of the project. My thanks go to the Richter Library, and in particular, to Mr. Kyle Rimkus for his help in securing permissions for the photographs and other illustrative material in this book. For her unfailing technical and humanistic support, I would like to express my appreciation to Greta West. And last but certainly not least, I am happy to take this opportunity to state my gratitude to those colleagues and graduate students who have listened, read, and responded to early versions of this work.

Chronology

1871	July 10: birth, at Auteuil in the Paris suburbs, of Marcel Valentin Louis Eugène Georges Proust, son of Adrien Proust, a distinguished professor of medicine, and Jeanne-Clémence Weil. The father is Catholic, the mother Jewish.
1872	The Proust family takes up residence in the fashionable boulevard Malesherbes (Paris 8e). Proust will always live in this area, except at the end of his life.
1878–86	Family holidays at Illiers (now Illiers-Combray) in the *département* of Eure-et-Loir.
1882–89	Attends the Lycée Fontanes (renamed Lycée Condorcet in 1883); poor health often keeps him absent.
1888	Proust is strongly influenced by his philosophy teacher, Alphonse Darlu.
1889–90	Proust performs his military service at Orléans.
1890–95	Student years (law and political science). *Licence en droit* (1893); *licence ès lettres* (1895).
1891	Co-founds a short-lived journal, *Le Banquet.* Is an active contributor to this and other journals.
1894	Beginning of the Dreyfus Affair.
1895	Begins a novel, *Jean Santeuil* (unfinished).
1896	Publication of *Les Plaisirs et les jours*, a collection of stories, essays, and miscellaneous pieces.
1897	Proust begins to read the works of the English writer John Ruskin.
1898	Publication of Zola's "J'accuse." Proust rallies to the Dreyfus cause.
1900	Death of Ruskin. Proust devotes the next few years to translating and annotating selected works of Ruskin's. Two trips to Venice. The family moves to the rue de Courcelles.

1902	Artistic pilgrimages to Belgium and Holland; sees Vermeer's *View of Delft*.
1903	Death of Proust's father.
1904	*La Bible d'Amiens*, translation of Ruskin.
1905	Death of Proust's mother.
1906	Proust moves to 102, boulevard Haussmann. *Sésame et les lys*, translation of Ruskin.
1907–14	Summer holidays at Cabourg, on the Normandy coast.
1908	Writes *Pastiches* of other authors, based on an amusing extortion racket known as "L'Affaire Lemoine." Begins what is now known as *Contre Sainte-Beuve*, an essay.
1909	The essay transforms itself into a novel; it will eventually become *A la recherche du temps perdu*.
1910	Goes to see the *Ballets russes*. Has his bedroom lined with cork, because of building work in an adjoining apartment.
1911	The novel's title at this time is *Les Intermittences du coeur*. Proust employs a secretary to type up his work, more than 700 pages to date.
1912	Proust seeks a publisher, in vain.
1913	*Du Côté de chez Swann* is published by Grasset, at Proust's own expense. The general title of the novel is changed to *A la recherche du temps perdu*.
1914	The second volume of the novel as it then existed is being set up in proof when the outbreak of war stops the printing presses.
1914–18	During the war, with no possibility of publication, Proust vastly expands his novel, notably amplifying the role of the character Albertine.
1916	Publication rights are transferred from Grasset to Gallimard.
1918	Publication of *A l'Ombre des jeunes filles en fleurs*.
1919	Proust is forced to move from 102, boulevard Haussmann, first to the rue Laurent-Pichat, then to what will turn out to be his final residence, 44, rue Hamelin. He is controversially awarded the *Prix Goncourt*, France's premier literary prize, for the publication of *A l'ombre des jeunes filles en fleurs*.
1920	Proust is named Chevalier de la Légion d'Honneur. Publication of *Le Côté de Guermantes I*.
1921	Extracts from the novel are regularly published in journals, mainly *La Nouvelle Revue française*, continuing into 1922. Proust visits an exhibition of Dutch paintings at the

	Orangerie in May: he sees the *View of Delft* again. *Le Côté de Guermantes II – Sodome et Gomorrhe I* is published.
1922	*Sodome et Gomorrhe II* is published. Proust develops bronchitis, then pneumonia, and dies on November 18. He is buried in Père Lachaise cemetery on November 22.
1923	Publication of *Sodome et Gomorrhe III – La Prisonnière.*
1924	Publication of *Albertine disparue.*
1927	Publication of *Le Temps retrouvé.*
1952	Publication of *Jean Santeuil.*
1954	Publication of a version of *Contre Sainte-Beuve.*
1954	Publication of *A la recherche du temps perdu* in the first Gallimard-Pléiade edition (three volumes), Pierre Clarac and André Ferré editors.
1987–89	Publication of *A la recherche du temps perdu* in the second Gallimard-Pléiade edition (four volumes), Jean-Yves Tadié *et. al.* editors.

Introduction: At the threshold of Proust's novel

APPRECIATING PROUST'S STYLE

Marcel Proust's vast novel of recollected human experience, *A la recherche du temps perdu* [*In Search of Lost Time*] (1913–27), has enjoyed the esteem of writers and literary scholars for many years. After an initial period of incomprehension in France (Proust's sentences seemed too long, the narrative line of his story too slow to unfold), the *Recherche* gained an international reputation as one of the masterpieces of modernism, largely thanks to a discerning foreign audience. Toward the end of Proust's life, and in the two decades following his death in 1922 at the age of fifty-one, European writers from a wide variety of backgrounds and nationalities acknowledged their debt to the French writer, indicating in their statements of admiration and affiliation the degree to which their own texts could not have been possible without their discovery of Proust's beautiful but strange fictional universe. Although many examples of such statements could be brought forward, I would like to cite three writers who had very little in common with each other, but for whom the act of reading Proust constituted an event in their lives and in the development of their own writing styles.

The first quotation is from Virginia Woolf (1882–1941), author of *Mrs Dalloway*, *To the Lighthouse*, *The Waves*, *Orlando*, *A Room of One's Own*, and other important works of fiction and essayistic prose, whose life overlapped with that of Proust, and who read him with discernment from the very beginning of his career as a novelist. The second is from Walter Benjamin (1892–1940), the German-Jewish essayist, translator, and philosopher, author of the vast *Arcades* project, and the reader who best understood the importance of Charles Baudelaire for the nineteenth century. The third is from Jean Genet (1910–86), the thief-turned-writer whose prose style is perhaps second only in importance and distinctiveness to that of Proust for twentieth-century France, and whose florid metaphorical discourse owes much to his predecessor.

1 Marcel Proust, twenty years old, with his mother and his brother, Robert

Virginia Woolf, writing in May 1922, six months before Proust's death:

Proust so titillates my own desire for expression that I can hardly set out the sentence. Oh, if I could write like that! I cry. And at the moment such is the astonishing vibration and saturation and intensification that he procures – theres [*sic*] something sexual in it – that I feel I *can* write like that, and seize my pen and then I *can't* write like that. Scarcely anyone so stimulates the nerves of language in me; it becomes an obsession.[1]

Walter Benjamin, writing in 1929:

The thirteen volumes of Marcel Proust's *A la recherche du temps perdu* are the result of an unconstruable synthesis in which the absorption of a mystic, the art of a prose writer, the verve of a satirist, the erudition of a scholar, and the self-consciousness of a monomaniac have combined in an autobiographical work. It has rightly been said that all great works of literature establish a genre or dissolve one – that they are, in other words, special cases. Among these cases, this is one of the most unfathomable. From its structure, which is at once fiction, autobiography, and commentary, to the syntax of boundless sentences (the Nile of language, which here overflows and fructifies the plains of truth), everything transcends the norm.[2]

Jean Genet, in an interview from 1975:

I read *Within a Budding Grove* [*A l'Ombre des jeunes filles en fleurs*] in prison, the first volume. We were in the prison yard trading books on the sly. It was during the war [World War II], and since I wasn't very concerned about books, I was one of the last and someone says to me, "Hey, you can take that," and I see Marcel Proust. And I said to myself: "That should be a pain in the butt" … I read the first sentence of *Within a Budding Grove* which is when Monsieur de Norpois is introduced at a dinner at the home of Proust's – or rather the narrator's – father and mother. And it's a very long sentence. And when I'd finished the sentence, I closed the book and said to myself, "Now I'm calm, I know I'm going to go from one marvel to another."[3]

Although Woolf, Benjamin, and Genet appear to be sensitive to quite different aspects of the *Recherche*, and although the rhetorical tone of their declarations cannot be said to resemble each other in the least, there are nevertheless some common threads that run through their reactions to Proust's particular mode of writing. Foremost among these, for want of a better word, is *style*. For Woolf, style is Proust's signature, the fact of his individuality, the way he writes, "like that": it is something intensely physical, even sexual, which has the effect of fueling her own desire to write. For Benjamin, the *Recherche*, like all great works of literature, breaks previously established molds and structures, and does so, in large part, through style – especially Proust's notoriously long sentences, his convoluted syntax, which Benjamin compares, quite strikingly, to the overflowing "Nile of language." For Genet, style as apprehended by the reader of Proust has a double effect: it is, at first, surprising (one's initial expectation was that the book would be "a pain in the butt," yet, to use Benjamin's language, it "transcends" that expectation); and then, precisely through the meandering of its long sentence structure, it produces "calm." It is this calm that makes possible the reader's capacity to open him- or herself to the Proustian text and to "go from marvel to marvel."

In the pages that follow, I shall be taking quite seriously the centrality of Proust's style – understood in the broadest sense, as his quite personal and particular use of grammar, of syntax, and of figural language (especially metaphor, about which Proust theorized at great length). According to Proust himself, it is only the greatest attentiveness to the individualized style of a writer that allows the reader access to the essential literary contribution of that writer's work. In one of his late essays, entitled "A propos du 'style' de Flaubert" (1920), Proust penned a rejoinder to an article by the noted critic Albert Thibaudet, who had written that the author of *Madame Bovary* "was not a born writer; verbal mastery in its very nature had not been granted him."[4] In Proust's view, not only was Flaubert's style revolutionary for the history of French literature in its often unusual use of the imperfect (*imparfait*) verb tense, but his quite original manipulations and occasional distortions of the laws of grammar, while stylistic in origin, in fact implied a new *vision*. Proust contends that Flaubert's "completely new and personal use ... of the imperfect, the preterit, the present participle, certain pronouns and certain prepositions, *has renewed our vision of things* nearly as radically as Kant, with his Categories, his theories of Knowledge and of the Reality of the exterior world."[5] What Proust is saying here is not that literature is to be confused with philosophy (which some literary critics have done in attempting to reduce Proust to one or another philosophical position, or in linking his thought with excessive facility to that of Schopenhauer or Nietzsche), but rather, that literary language is deserving of the same level of scrupulous analysis as is the conceptual discourse of philosophy.

In practical terms, as far as this *Reader's Guide* is concerned, in order to remain as close as possible to the specificity of Proust's novel, that is, its stylistic particularity, I shall be as attentive as possible to the novelist's use of language. Quoted passages will appear first in the original French,[6] then in English.[7] Each chapter will begin with a brief plot summary as well as an indication of the general interpretative and narrative issues that will confront the reader in the course of his or her perusal of the text; but the bulk of each chapter will consist of close readings of specific episodes along with commentary concerning the ways in which episodes relate to each other, not only within one of the novel's seven volumes, but also from one volume to another. In the analysis of any novel, there is a built-in tension between the particular and the general, the microcosm and the macrocosm. This tension is exacerbated in a novel possessing the bulk of the *Recherche*, which, occupying some 3,000 pages, is approximately twice the length of Tolstoy's *War and Peace* (1865–69). An understandable temptation on the part of the critic would be to emphasize the macrocosm at the expense of the microcosm, simply in order to respect the overall design of a highly structured text. I shall attempt not to succumb to that temptation, and, in spending time on detailed readings of shorter sections of the novel, shall attempt to respect, and in some ways, to recreate, the word-by-word, sentence-by-sentence experience we all have as readers of Proust.

PROUST'S LIFE AND ITS SIGNIFICANCE FOR HIS LITERARY WORK

In his monumental account of Proust's life and work, *Marcel Proust: Biographie*, Jean-Yves Tadié lists not only sixteen formal biographies that have preceded his, but also fifty-two volumes of informal "remembrances" or "souvenirs" written by friends and acquaintances of Proust. Even if one were to limit oneself to the very best recent biographies of Proust for detailed information on the writer, it would be necessary to take into account not only Tadié's contribution (generally considered to be definitive in its scope and in the power of its overall argument), but what should be called the earliest "modern" Proust biography, G.D. Painter's two-volume *Marcel Proust: A Biography*, as well as the scrupulously well-documented and readable *Marcel Proust: A Life* by William C. Carter, and Edmund White's concise and witty *Marcel Proust*, which has a strong focus on Proust's homosexuality. When one adds to this vast library of information and speculation about Proust's life the existence of a treasure trove of letters – the twenty-one-volume *Correspondance de Marcel Proust* scrupulously edited and annotated by the late Philip Kolb – it becomes difficult not to see Proust as a thoroughly examined, if not dissected, individual about whom everything essential has been said, recast, repeated, and submitted to the utmost scrutiny.

The reasons for this intense interest are fairly obvious. Although born in the upper middle-class, Proust circulated easily in Parisian aristocratic circles; many of his readers are interested in gaining access, however indirectly, to the rituals and social codes of these circles. Proust was born of a Catholic father and a Jewish mother; this double origin, in and of itself, exercises a certain fascination. And, perhaps most importantly, Proust was homosexual, at a time when the stark alternative of living within or coming out of the "closet" was no simple matter. The discomfort that he endured as a practicing-but-at-the-same-time-closeted homosexual in the late nineteenth and early twentieth centuries is of inevitable interest to twenty-first-century readers living in an era characterized by the recent development of gender and queer studies.

This being said, there is a delicious irony in the obsessive interest in Proust the man (whether Proust the social climber, Proust the ambivalent figure caught between two religions, or Proust the active but melancholy homosexual), considering that Proust himself, in the period immediately preceding the composition of the *Recherche*, had developed a coherently articulated theory directed *against* the excessive interest in writers' lives (as opposed to their works). Proust located this tendency to overvalue the possible impact or "influence" of an author's life on his writings in the work of Charles-Augustin Sainte-Beuve (1804–69), the greatest of France's nineteenth-century critics, whose massive influence on the *homme et oeuvre* approach to literature lasted well into the mid-twentieth century.[8] In the fragmentary series of essays and novelistic sketches that prefigure the earliest stages of the *Recherche* and which have been published under the title *Contre Sainte-Beuve* [*Against Sainte-Beuve*], Proust establishes his critical position in contradistinction to that of his nineteenth-century predecessor. Sainte-Beuve had written:

> Literature is not for me distinct or separate from the individual and his constitution [i.e., personality, temperament] ... One should not hesitate to approach a man from various angles to understand him, that is, as something other than a pure spirit ... What were his opinions on religion? How was he affected by the spectacle of nature? What were his relationships with women, with money? Was he rich, poor; what was his daily routine? What were his vices, his weaknesses? None of the responses to these questions is indifferent if one wishes to judge the author of a book and the book itself, if this book is not a treatise of pure geometry, if it is essentially a literary work. ("La Méthode de Sainte-Beuve," *Contre Sainte-Beuve*, 221; my translation)

Proust, on the other hand, in an assertion that would be difficult to interpret otherwise than as a warning against the excesses of biographical reductionism, after criticizing Sainte-Beuve for getting lost in a sea of documents surrounding the writer he is studying, states:

> This method [that of Sainte-Beuve] ignores what our own insight into ourselves teaches us: that a book is the product of another self than that which we manifest in our habits, in society, in our vices. If we wish to locate and understand that deeper self, we must seek to recreate it within ourselves. ("La Méthode de Sainte-Beuve," 221–22; my translation)

Much could be written about these two countervailing critical views, each of which represents an extreme position on a continuum. Sainte-Beuve's emphasis on the study of all aspects of the writer's life could easily lead to confusion between knowledge of him or her as a human being and purported knowledge of the work in question. Proust's absolute division between two completely separate selves might be a clever ploy on the part of a writer who, for strategic reasons, would prefer to keep his compulsive social aspirations and homosexual identity out of view. At the very least, however, Proust's theory can serve as a warning to us as we stand at the threshold of his novel. An over-emphasis on establishing one-to-one correspondences between what we know of Proust's life and what we read in his fiction is an act of reduction and of impoverishment. At the same time, however, whereas in "La Méthode de Sainte-Beuve" Proust simply dismisses the Beuvian critical method out of hand in an intellectual argument, he will reinscribe his debate with Sainte-Beuve within the pages of his novel and will allow it to unfold in a narrative evolution.

Some of the most fascinating of Proust's fictional characters will incorporate and enact the tendency to confuse man and work, superficial and deep or authentic self. The strange and outrageous Baron de Charlus, one of the three or four most developed characters in the novel, is guilty, on a constant basis, of the fall into that confusion. The fact that Charlus is, at one level, a rather transparent caricature of one of Proust's closest friends, the poet and dandy Robert de Montesquiou (1855–1921), further complicates the question of the relation between the individual human in his or her lived existence and the transposition of that human into a fictional "equivalent." Is it really possible for the informed reader to set aside his or her knowledge of the writer and of the real background of that writer's fictional characters, in an effort to focus exclusively on the "deep self"? Whatever the answer to this question, it is clear that in moving from the form of critical essay to that of the novel, Proust was able to present his intellectual disagreement with Sainte-Beuve not as a Manichean choice, but rather as the narration of a temptation, of a seduction. We know better than to confuse a person with his or her work, reality with fiction, but it is that very confusion that generates the psychodrama through which one large strand of Proust's narrative is woven.

As I move now to a brief overview of the salient events in Proust's life and career, it is with the preliminary understanding that knowledge of these facts and factors is important but not sufficient for an understanding of the work itself. For purposes of clarity and practicality, I shall divide my biographical sketch into six parts: 1. Childhood; 2. Adolescence and early adulthood; 3. Early writings; 4. Proust as translator; 5. The *Recherche* from its inception until World War I; 6. The *Recherche* after World War I.

CHILDHOOD

Marcel Proust was born on July 10, 1871, shortly after the conclusion of the Franco-Prussian War and at the very beginning of the Third Republic. Proust was to live most of his life during the so-called "belle époque" or "golden era," so designated because of the relative political stability that prevailed in Europe between 1871 and 1914, and because of the combined developments of the sciences, technology, and the arts. The flourishing of the Impressionist aesthetic during this period, featured in large sections of Proust's novel, seemed, on the surface at least, to liberate the arts from realism and from the depiction of an often violent political and social reality, and to open up new perspectives for formal experimentation. Proust grew up during what was, for the upper bourgeoisie, a happy phase of the late nineteenth century. His family was not rich, but was very comfortable financially, and its values expressed themselves both in a certain middle-class social conformity, and also in a profound interest for culture – literature, music, fine art, dance, and theater. But among these, literature and music were dominant. It was Proust's mother, Mme Adrien Proust, née Jeanne Weil (1849–1905), who inculcated in her son a love for literature and a strong sense of aesthetic appreciation.

Although little is known of Proust's childhood, if we allow ourselves for a moment the luxury of establishing the kind of link between life and work that Proust himself refused to admit, we can surmise that the young Marcel's life was characterized essentially by happiness and tranquility. It is the pages of *Combray*, the first of the three parts of *Du Côté de chez Swann* [*The Way by Swann's*], which in their depiction of a stable, regular, sun-infused universe tempt us to draw this conclusion. Although not devoid of drama and of the fears a child would have in facing the world, the universe depicted in *Combray* is one of familial stability, of witty conversation, of the joys of reading, and of an incipient artistic apprenticeship. In real life, however, there is one event that interrupts this happy picture, tingeing it with a somber tone: Marcel's first asthma attack, in 1881, at the age of nine. Proust was to suffer from respiratory problems, at times severe, throughout his adult life. His complaints about these problems, which punctuate his Correspondence, need to be taken seriously, not as the sign of hypochondria, as some skeptical readers have surmised. Asthma and its attendant complications kept Proust out of school during fairly large stretches of his childhood and adolescence, but did not hinder him from developing, from an early age, an obvious talent as a writer.

ADOLESCENCE AND EARLY ADULTHOOD

The turning-point in Proust's life – the moment at which he discovered his vocation as a writer and his homosexual identity – occurred in the autumn of 1887, when he was sixteen years old. His first infatuations, including that for Jacques Bizet, the son of Georges Bizet (1838–75), the composer of *Carmen*, were largely "literary" in that they consisted for the most part of letters and of declarations rather than of concrete actions. But from year to year there was a procession of young men whom Marcel pursued, at times quite aggressively, with varying degrees of success and of reciprocity. Marcel's leanings were not only displeasing to his parents; they were the subject of heated debate in his home, and of much anguish for Marcel, who, as of 1888, tried unsuccessfully to resist them. There was a scene with his mother when Marcel showed her a photograph, now frequently reproduced in illustrated biographies of Proust, with the future writer seated in front of his two close friends, Lucien Daudet and Robert de Flers. Daudet, his right arm leaning on Marcel's left shoulder, directs his attention toward the object of his admiration in a way that was unambiguous to Mme Proust (see illustration 2). There were also moments which seem appalling to a modern sensibility, in which Proust's father, the distinguished pathologist and epidemiologist Adrien Proust (1834–1903), sent Marcel along to a local brothel in order to give him experience with women and to "cure" him of his homosexual inclinations.

Proust was not to be "cured," however, and as he progressed from adolescence to early adulthood, continued to pursue love with the young men he encountered, either in the context of his studies, or in the artistic circles he had begun to frequent. Perhaps the longest and most important of his early liaisons was with the talented musician Reynaldo Hahn (1875–1947), who was his lover from 1894 until 1896, and a lifetime friend after their physical relationship had ended. Half-Jewish like Marcel (Hahn's father was of German-Jewish extraction, while his mother, a Venezuelan, was of Basque origin), Reynaldo developed from child prodigy pianist to composer, conductor, and music critic. He was especially known as a composer of songs, as a brilliant conversationalist, and as an eloquent writer. He was a major influence (and became, barely disguised, a major character) in Marcel's first, abortive novel, *Jean Santeuil*, written from 1895 until 1899 but not published in Proust's lifetime. The letters between Reynaldo and Marcel which we do possess (others have been lost or have been withheld from publication) betray a passionate relationship, with Marcel often in the role of jealous lover. Until the much later relationship between the by then well-known novelist Marcel Proust and his chauffeur Alfred Agostinelli in 1913–14, Marcel was not to know a love as deep or as developed in its genuine reciprocity of feelings as that with Reynaldo.

EARLY WRITINGS

The decade stretching from 1889 until 1899 was a long but enriching transitional period for Proust. In 1889–90 he successfully completed his military service at the Coligny Caserne in the city of Orléans – an experience which formed the basis of an episode in *Le Côté de Guermantes* [*The Guermantes Way*], the third volume of the *Recherche*. Between 1890 and 1895 he pursued advanced study in the fields of law and political science, obtaining the degrees of *licence en droit* in 1893 and *licence ès lettres* in 1895. In order to placate his parents, who were concerned that, despite these intellectual efforts and achievements, Proust had no particular career in mind, he obtained a volunteer position at the Bibliothèque Mazarine in Paris in 1896. To say that Proust had no vocation as librarian or archivist is an understatement: he expended considerable time and energy avoiding his job, and managed, in the end, to obtain an extended sick leave.[9] He was never to have a job or exercise a profession in the conventional sense. Rather, he was beginning to develop his talents as a writer and to become known both in high society and among the literary and artistic élite.

Proust's problem was not that he was a dilettante, as many of his contemporaries assumed during this period, but that he was unable to focus his many talents as social observer, essayist, critic, and burgeoning creator of prose fiction on any one object or project. Until the turn of the century, it could have appeared that Proust was on his way to becoming a French Oscar Wilde – a master of the *bon mot*, social butterfly, very talented but undisciplined writer, polymorphous polymath, a person more memorable as a *raconteur* than as the creator of new and challenging artistic forms. Appearances, in this case, were more than deceiving. Underneath the brilliant but somewhat vapid surface of things, Proust was discovering the social and psychological underpinnings of his future novel, and he was gaining in the life experience from which he was to draw many of his acute political and moral observations.

The use of the term "political" in conjunction with Marcel Proust may seem odd to readers who associate the writer with introspection and an idiosyncratic, isolated existence (most notably, the cork-lined room full of anti-asthma fumigations in which he wrote the bulk of the *Recherche*). This particular image of Proust, which has obtained an iconic status in popular representations of him, is, like all caricatures, based upon a fragment of truth which has been so distorted as to obscure the complexity of the figure it purports to evoke.[10] Although Proust's aesthetic is certainly far removed from the kind of adherence to social and political reality advocated either by socialist realism or by the didactic form of *littérature engagée* (engaged, or committed literature) as practiced by some French existentialists in the decades following his death, it is important to keep in mind that Proust was an active observer of and occasional participant in the political events of his day. The most important of these was the so-called "Dreyfus Affair," a protracted and divisive crisis in French society which, at first crystallizing around the single figure of one military officer and his falsely alleged treasonous acts, eventually became a social drama in multiple, mutually contradictory episodes.

Alfred Dreyfus (1859–1935), suspected of passing on French military secrets to the Germans, was arrested for treason on October 15, 1894. On January 5, 1895, he was convicted in a court martial and sentenced to life imprisonment on Devil's Island in French Guiana. But in August 1896, a newly appointed head of French military intelligence, Lieutenant Colonel Georges Picquart (1854–1914), determined that the real traitor was a certain Major Ferdinand Walsin Esterhazy (1847–1923). During the three subsequent years, French public opinion was buffeted in a storm of claims and counter-claims concerning the innocence or guilt of Dreyfus, and many intellectuals, including Marcel Proust, took determined stands on the issue. As of 1897 Proust was convinced of Dreyfus's innocence, and was active in obtaining signatures from prominent political and artistic figures in petitions to the government for the liberation of the imprisoned and disgraced former soldier.

As was the case throughout France, Proust's own family was split on the matter. Dr. Adrien Proust, very much the conservative, remained convinced of Dreyfus's guilt, whereas Marcel, his mother, and his brother, Robert (1873–1935), were *dreyfusards*, or pro-Dreyfus. What made matters extraordinarily complicated, and politically poisonous, was the fact that Dreyfus was Jewish, in a time characterized by often virulent anti-Semitism. What we know from Proust's Correspondence and from the letters, newspaper articles, and other publications of his contemporaries, is that Proust, who did not consider himself to be Jewish, did not identify with Dreyfus for religious or cultural reasons, but rather defended and supported him for general ethical reasons: justice had been perverted; justice needed to be restored. The naturalist novelist Emile Zola (1840–1902) came to the aid of Dreyfus's defenders when, on January 13, 1898, he issued his famous open letter to France's President Félix Faure (1841–99) entitled "J'accuse." Published in the widely circulated Paris daily *L'Aurore*, the letter accused the French Army of obstruction of justice and of anti-Semitism. Just a few days later, a literary journal called *La Revue blanche*, with which Proust had been associated in his formative years, published a strong denunciation of what it called the "occult power of the military bureaucracy," which, in its view, had duped the public and fostered a "fanatical and anti-Jewish outcry."[11]

Proust's association with the pro-Dreyfus contingent was sufficiently visible and appreciated to warrant his formal introduction to Colonel Picquart, most likely in early 1898. Dreyfus was pardoned in 1899, but had to wait until 1906 to be fully exonerated. The "Affair," which had lasted more than eleven years from initial accusation until final exoneration, left its marks on the *Recherche*, notably in those passages in which questions of race, of Jewish identity, and of anti-Semitism emerge, in the actions and in the linguistic habits of the novel's characters.

The decade 1889–99 was a time of literary initiation and experimentation for Proust, with some successes and some equally significant failures. Having begun to contribute short pieces to the literary magazines *La Revue verte* and *La Revue lilas* while at school (the names of these reviews deriving from the color of their respective jacket covers), beginning in 1890–91, Proust published a regular social column in the journal *Le Mensuel*, and in 1892 was a co-founder of *Le Banquet*. For the next several years he wrote both for this review and for the more widely circulated and better known *La Revue blanche*. Several of the texts initially published in these venues were chosen and somewhat arbitrarily stitched together to form Proust's first book, *Les Plaisirs et les jours* (1896). This expensive, *fin-de-siècle* volume contained illustrations by the society painter and watercolorist Madeleine Lemaire (1845–1928) and an introduction by the then celebrated Anatole France (1844–1924). A writer who has faded from view as his style and aesthetic have been largely superseded (first by Proust himself), France, in his lifetime, was sufficiently famous to have merited a state funeral whose magnitude and pomp rivaled that of Victor Hugo (1802–85) four decades earlier.

It is generally agreed that Anatole France is the principal model of Proust's fictional character Bergotte, who plays the same mentoring role in the *Recherche* as France did in Proust's life. Madeleine Lemaire would seem to be one of several possible models for Mme Verdurin, the comical and cruel society matron, or "*Patronne*" of *Un Amour de Swann* [*A Love of Swann's*], the second section of the novel's first volume. *Les Plaisirs et les jours*, somewhat cheekily titled after Hesiod's poem *Works and Days* [*Les Travaux et les jours* in French], a work written *c.* 700 BC containing much praise of honest labor and a polemic against idleness (certainly an interesting choice of title for a young man considered uselessly idle by his parents and a superficial snob by many of his contemporaries), contains a number of themes that Proust will develop later in his novel, especially those of memory and of jealousy. Yet the impression one has on reading the collection is one of structural fragmentation and dispersed talent rather than of compositional solidity or artistic achievement.

The period from 1895 until 1899 saw both Proust's disengagement from his passion for Reynaldo Hahn and the writing of a substantial quasi-novel posthumously titled *Jean Santeuil*. The manuscript of this unfinished and undisciplined work – some seventy notebooks and several boxes of shuffled papers – was fortuitously found by a young Proust scholar, Bernard de Fallois, in 1954, among the deceased writer's abandoned belongings. References to *Jean Santeuil* in Proust's Correspondence are few and cryptic. We can only surmise that, despite the substantial volume of the text (some 700 pages in published form), and despite his obvious efforts to make of it a polished work of fiction, Proust himself realized that his text was not publishable, and decided, literally, to "shelve" it. Several years later, when he had begun the *Recherche*, Proust would often return to the pages of *Jean Santeuil* and choose passages and episodes from it for inclusion in his novel, sometimes as almost direct quotations, sometimes in severely modified form.

Another factor that may have played a part in Proust's decision not to publish the abortive fictional work from 1895–99 was his discovery, during that period, of the writings of Ralph Waldo Emerson (1803–82), the American essayist, philosopher, and leader of the Transcendentalist movement; Thomas Carlyle (1795–1881), the Scottish essayist, satirist, and historian; and, especially, John Ruskin (1819–1900), the art critic and social critic, who, like Carlyle, was central to the development of a morally anchored aesthetics and the practical enactment of a strong social conscience during the Victorian period. During the final years of the nineteenth century, it would appear that there were two essential strains in Proust's thought: on the one hand, an interest in social mores and in psychological observation that led him to explore fictional forms; on the other hand, an increasing intellectual involvement with moral philosophy, literary criticism, and aesthetic theory. As of 1900, Proust was to temporarily abandon the first strand in favor of the second, and to devote himself to the detailed study and translation of works by John Ruskin. It is only after he had completed this phase that he was able to find a way to combine the two in one coherent textual web, *A la recherche du temps perdu.*

PROUST AS TRANSLATOR

The six-year period from 1900 to 1906 constitutes one of the most important phases in the maturation of Proust as writer and as human being. At the experiential level, this was a time of separation, loss, grief, and feelings of abandonment. Three events stand out: the marriage of his brother, Robert, on February 2, 1903; the death of his father on November 26 of that same year; and the death of his mother, the one person he loved most in his life, on September 26, 1905. Although Robert, a well-regarded practitioner and published author in the field of urology, was to remain close to his brother for the entirety of their lives, providing editorial as well as moral support during Marcel's final years, his marriage signified a break in the unified family of four. The wedding ceremony itself took place on a wintry day and was suffused with gloom. Mme Proust was so ill that she had to be taken to the church of Saint-Augustin by ambulance. Marcel attended the mass, but was so physically and emotionally drained by the experience that he took to bed for the following two weeks. With the subsequent deaths of both his father and mother, Proust had to learn to live alone and to pursue his literary projects in increasing solitude.

Before he began to close the doors to the outside world, however, he experienced an intellectual awakening which motivated him to undertake two extended artistic pilgrimages: the first, to Venice in 1900; the second, to Belgium and Holland in 1902 (there was also a second voyage to Venice in late 1900, but it was of shorter duration, and we know neither whether Proust travelled alone or accompanied, nor what his itinerary was). Both of the longer voyages were to leave textual traces in the *Recherche* – the first, in the truncated and symbolically complex Venice episode of the novel's penultimate volume, *Albertine disparue* [*The Fugitive*]; the second, in the numerous allusions to Flemish and Dutch art which punctuate the novel, and in particular, the celebrated passage describing Bergotte's death in *La Prisonnière* [*The Prisoner*], set against an aesthetic meditation on the *View of Delft* by Johannes Vermeer (1632–75). Although both of these travel experiences contributed to the innovative ways in which Proust was to link text to image in his novel, it is the first of these, the sojourn in Venice, which constituted a turning-point in Proust's career.

In the happy company of his mother, Reynaldo Hahn, and Reynaldo's English cousin, Marie Nordlinger (1876–1961), Proust visited the churches, palaces, squares, and museums of Venice, as well as the Arena Chapel at Padua (to see the frescoes by the Italian Renaissance painter and sculptor, Giotto [*c.* 1267–1337]). This was, in fact, a Ruskinian pilgrimage. Proust brought with him numerous volumes written by Ruskin, including the three-volume treatise, *The Stones of Venice* (1851–53), which depicted the artistic glories of the City of the Doges as well as its decline and fall. Perhaps of greatest significance to us as readers of Proust is that this voyage can be considered an initiation to the act of reading, in the broadest sense of that term. What Ruskin as mentor had taught his disciple was the importance of deciphering the symbolic language which the artisans of the Middle Ages and Renaissance had inscribed into the stones of their buildings, especially the sacred edifices, which, enduring the fall of civilizations and the passing of Time, stood as monuments to the faith of their builders. For Proust, whose asthma and nervous constitution often hampered his ability to travel, the stay in Venice constituted an apprenticeship in which the increasingly knowledgeable student of Ruskin was able to verify the insights of his teacher by comparing what Ruskin had written to the aesthetic objects he had scrutinized. In so doing, Proust gradually began to distance himself from Ruskin's critical method, which he increasingly found to be flawed, especially in its intellectually suspect mixing of aesthetic and moral considerations.

Having read Ruskin's major works with care, Proust set out to translate two of them: *The Bible of Amiens* (1885), an act of interpretative reading focused particularly on the biblical figures carved in the west portal of Amiens cathedral, and *Sesame and Lilies* (1865), a two-part treatise containing Ruskin's ideas on universal education for the English people, and on appropriate objects of study and cultural activities for women. Since Proust's knowledge of English was rudimentary at best, he had his mother provide him with a first, word-by-word translation of the English text, which he then transformed into elegant French, often enlisting the support of friends and members of the Parisian intellectual community for help in cultural references and in matters of erudition. This method served him well for *La Bible d'Amiens*, which, shortly after its appearance in 1904, garnered significant praise, not only for the quality of the translation itself, but also for the notes and introductory material Proust had provided. When Mme Proust died in 1905, midway through the translation of *Sesame and Lilies*, Proust called upon Marie Nordlinger to do the first, rough translation, and to collaborate with him as he completed the project.

Although Proust specialists have found some errors in the translations, it is unanimously agreed that the future author of the *Recherche* managed to convey Ruskin's winding sentences and flowery Victorian prose in a fluent and readable French style. Remarkable in both *La Bible d'Amiens* and *Sésame et les lys* is the critical apparatus with which Proust surrounded Ruskin's text – lengthy footnotes, often extending to more than one page in small italics; allusions to other works by Ruskin which demonstrated Proust's keen sense of the thematic continuities that link together what was often considered to be a disparate body of work; and, most impressively, substantial introductory essays in which Proust established what amounted to a posthumous intellectual dialogue with the writer, who had died, after a decade of mental illness, on January 20, 1900. Two of these critical essays are important for the evolution of Proust's thought as aesthetic theorist and for the ways in which their central ideas were eventually transmuted into figures and episodes within the *Recherche*: "John Ruskin," the second half of the translator's introduction to *La Bible d'Amiens*, and "Sur la lecture" ["On Reading"], the prefatory essay to *Sésame et les lys*.

In "John Ruskin," Proust begins by establishing the centrality of religion in Ruskin's aesthetic philosophy, and by stating that the Beauty to which the English writer dedicated his life "was not conceived of by him as an object of enjoyment made to charm, but as a reality infinitely more important than life, for which he would have given his own life."[12] This statement, made in an absolute declarative tone, could also stand for *A la recherche du temps perdu*, a work for which Marcel Proust, in the most literal sense, gave his life. But early on in his essay, Proust notes that Ruskin's adoration of natural as well as man-made beauty is not "pure." We are not in a Kantian universe here, in which the aesthetic object appears, abstracted from its environment, to the disinterested observer. Rather, according to Proust: "Ruskin did not separate the beauty of the cathedrals from the charm of the regions from which they sprang, and which everyone who visits them still enjoys in the particular poetry of the region and in the remembrance of the misty or golden afternoon he spent there" ("John Ruskin," 42).

What we have here is a law of association that will function throughout the *Recherche*, at several levels. The characters in the novel not only associate works of art with people, but people with the places in which they initially appear, and even the most elementary sounds (vowels, consonants, phonemes, the "colors" of words) with the places they call forth in the active imagination of the day-dreaming subject. Throughout the *Recherche*, Proust will play with a fundamental dialectic of chance and necessity, as when a man meets a woman in a given place, a given aesthetic context. Although it is by pure chance that this woman happens to be in an aristocratic *salon* while a particular piece of music is being performed, because the man who notices her with increasing interest loves that piece of music, by association he will eventually love her. The music "is" her essence, she "is" the music, so that the woman and the music become necessarily linked (we will return to this pattern in our reading of *Un Amour de Swann* [*A Love of Swann's*] in Chapter 1 of this study).

Another theme that emerges in "John Ruskin" is the fundamental contrast, or even contradiction, between life and death on which many great works of art are built. Following Ruskin's lead, Proust admires the painstaking care with which the artisans of the Middle Ages crafted even the smallest of the figures that adorn the arched doors and windows of ancient cathedrals. The works left behind after the death of the artisan testify to his labor, and create an abiding presence of beauty that would seem to justify or vindicate his ephemeral existence, provided a reader of artistic signs such as John Ruskin comes along to restore life to the dormant statuary. In writing about one of the almost invisible figures on the west portal of Amiens cathedral, a mere ten centimeters in size, Proust asserts:

> The artist, who died centuries ago, left there, among thousands of others, this little person who dies a little more each day, and has been dead for a really long time, forever lost in the midst of the crowd. But he had put it there. One day, a man for whom there is no death [John Ruskin], for whom there is no material infinity, no oblivion, a man who, casting away from him that nothingness which oppresses us to follow purposes which dominate his life, purposes so numerous that he will not be able to attain them all, while we seemed to have none, this man came, and among those waves of stone where each lacelike effervescence seemed to resemble the others, seeing there all the laws of life, all the thoughts of the soul, naming them by their names, he said, "See it is this, it is that". As on the Day of Judgment, which is represented nearby, his words resound like the archangel's trumpet, and he says, "Those who have lived will live, matter is nothing." ("John Ruskin," 45–46)

It is this triumphant tone, and this dialectical movement whereby that which appears dead is raised up and reaches a level of existence beyond that of "material infinity" or "nothingness," which characterize the peroration of *Le Temps retrouvé* [*Finding Time Again*], the final volume of the *Recherche*, where Proust retroactively states the aesthetic theory upon which his novelistic enterprise will have based itself.

The final pages of "John Ruskin," appended as a "post-scriptum," provide an element of complexity to an essay which had appeared, through much of its development, to be essentially an act of intellectual admiration and of faithful discipleship. Whereas in an early section of the article,

Proust had mentioned in passing but judged as "not dangerous" a certain "fetishism" in the writing of Ruskin (39–40), in the "post-scriptum" he returns to this theme and subjects it to a thorough analysis. What Proust calls "fetishism" or also "idolatry" is Ruskin's tendency to confuse aesthetic with moral ideas, as when the Victorian essayist condemns the inhabitants of Venice for their decadence, painting their crimes in especially dark colors because these crimes were committed in the shadow of their marble churches. Proust notes that a crime is a crime, decadence is decadence; precisely where the heinous acts occur, in what aesthetic context, is of no moral significance. Proust's conclusion is particularly concise and well formulated, and contains one observation in particular that is of importance to the thematic orchestration of the *Recherche*:

> The doctrines he [Ruskin] professed were moral doctrines and not aesthetic doctrines, and yet he chose them for their beauty. And since he did not wish to present them as beautiful but as true, *he was forced to deceive himself* about the nature of the reasons that made him adopt them [*il était obligé de se mentir à lui-même* sur la nature des raisons qui les lui faisaient adopter]. Hence there was such a continual compromising of conscience, that immoral doctrines sincerely professed would perhaps have been less dangerous for the integrity of the mind than those moral doctrines in which affirmation is not absolutely sincere, as they are dictated by an unavowed aesthetic preference. (*Marcel Proust: On Reading Ruskin*, 51; *Contre Sainte-Beuve*, 130; my emphasis)

The question of "fetishism" or "idolatry," which Proust uncovers not only in the complex argumentation of Ruskin, but also in the actions and discourse of his outrageous aesthete friend, Robert de Montesquiou, emerges throughout the *Recherche* in the relations among the fictional characters, precisely as a form of self-deceit, or *lying to oneself*. As we shall see in subsequent chapters, the theme of lying is one of the most developed ones in the novel, especially in the context of love (a lover lies to his beloved in order to uncover the secrets of that part of her existence which is unknown or invisible to him; she lies in response to his lies, in order to protect that very existence). But the act or fact of lying to oneself poses the question of a subject's inner authenticity or inauthenticity, of the very ground on which he or she attempts to apprehend both the beauty of the world and the moral motivations underlying human consciousness. This lying to oneself, which appears in "John Ruskin" as a question of aesthetic and moral philosophy, becomes one of the motivating factors, one of the "motors" of the novel's narrative evolution.

A number of the more extended and analytical translator's notes to *Sésame et les lys* continue in the same vein as the "post-scriptum" to "John Ruskin." Looking this time at Ruskin's ideas on universal education and on the democratizing of cultural activity, Proust once again finds signs of intellectual insincerity vitiating the English writer's argument. However, the main thrust of Proust's criticism in this volume can be found not so much in a demystifying or deconstructive reading of Ruskin's more or less sincere or insincere rhetoric, as in a strong philosophical disagreement on the place, nature, or essence of the act of reading. In the first section of *Sesame and Lilies*, entitled "Of Kings' Treasuries," Ruskin compares reading to a conversation among friends. It is the translator's dislike for this conception of reading that fuels not only several critical footnotes to Ruskin's essay, but also the intricate and evocative essay by which Proust introduces his translated text – "Sur la lecture." In these pages we find a foretaste not only of a number of Proustian themes, but also the particular atmosphere, the magic, the charm, that characterize Proust's depiction of childhood in the first volume of his novel.

"Sur la lecture" is divided, rather cunningly, into two seemingly opposed parts. In the first pages, Proust recreates what one might call the scene of reading, relying on his own childhood memories to evoke the afternoons in which, oblivious to his surroundings, he entered the universe of the books he was reading. And yet, precisely in evoking these surroundings to us readers, with poetry and precision, Proust manages, quite consciously, to take us away from the books themselves toward their physical and imaginative contexts. In a passage that foreshadows the more developed and fictionalized scene of reading in *Combray*, Proust reminds us of the power of reading – the potential contained within this activity to cause us to forget our surroundings while we read, whereas years later, it is precisely the surroundings, in all their beauty, that remain accessible to our memory. Describing the act of reading as being solitary, anti-social, best accomplished in a protected setting, Proust writes:

> I would let the others finish eating at the lower end of the park, beside the swans, and I would run up the labyrinth as far as some hedge where I would sit, not to be found ... In this hedge, silence was profound, the risk of being discovered almost nil, safety made sweeter by the distant cries which, from below, called me in vain, sometimes even came nearer, climbed the first banks, searching everywhere, then returned, having found nothing; then no more noise; only from time to time the golden sound of the bells which in the distance, beyond the plains, seemed to toll behind the blue sky, could have warned me of the passing hour; but, surprised by its sweetness and disturbed by the profounder silence, emptied of its last sounds, which followed it, I was never sure of the number of strokes. (Preface to "On Reading," 107–08)

In an elaborate rewriting of this scene in *Combray*, Proust will return to the tolling of the bells and will link the reader's plunge into oblivion of time and space with the paradox underlying the grand theme of Memory: namely, that to remember the charm of those childhood afternoons, we must simultaneously forget the content of what we read and recall the surroundings in which we were reading. In "Sur la lecture," Proust begins to sound this theme, and makes use of it as a structural device for his essay. Before proceeding to the properly analytical section of his text, Proust evokes the "spell" cast by the act of reading on its initiates, stating that one must both succumb to it but then disengage oneself from it before any critical or theoretical considerations *about* reading can become possible. This double movement – submitting to the seductive powers of books and of other aesthetic objects, becoming absorbed in their enchantments, before stepping back to unravel their magical effects – weaves itself into the *Recherche* as one of the leitmotifs of the novel. In evoking the "charming childhood reading whose memory must remain a benediction to each one of us," Proust states:

I have not escaped its spell [*sortilège*]: wishing to speak about it, I have talked about everything but books, because it is not about them that this reading has spoken to me. But perhaps the memories which one after the other it has brought back to me will themselves have awakened some in the reader and will little by little have led him, all the while lingering in those flowery and out-of-the-way roads, to recreate in his mind the original psychological act called *Reading*, with enough force for him to be able to follow now, as if within himself, the few reflections I still have to offer. ("On Reading," 110–11; "Sur la lecture," 59; Proust's emphasis)

The "few reflections" that make up the second, analytical section of the essay, constitute a coherent theory of reading, which Proust sets up in opposition to Ruskin's ideas on the subject. According to Proust, Ruskin's major error consists in granting an excessive importance to reading. The entirety of Proust's counter-argument is based upon a careful delineation of the possibilities and limits of reading – what it can and cannot do. What differentiates Proust's perspective from that of Ruskin is that whereas the latter is concerned with a large social question – how to educate the working classes effectively – the former views reading from the standpoint of a would-be creator, of a potential artist who, through the act of reading, is preparing him- or herself to become a creative writer. The following is one of the key statements of the essay, which will become a cornerstone of the aesthetic theory undergirding the vast edifice of the *Recherche*:

And there, indeed, is one of the great and marvelous features of beautiful books (and one which will make us understand the role, at once essential and limited, that reading can play in our spiritual life) which for the author could be called

"Conclusions" and for the reader "Incitements." We feel quite truly that our wisdom begins where that of the author ends, and we would like to have him give us answers, when all he can do is give us desires. And these desires he can arouse in us only by making us contemplate the supreme beauty which the last effort of his art has permitted him to reach. But by a singular and, moreover providential law of mental optics (a law which perhaps signifies that we can receive the truth from nobody, and that we must create it ourselves), that which is the end of their wisdom appears to us as but the beginning of ours, so that it is at the moment when they have told us all they could tell us that they create in us the feeling that they have told us nothing yet. ("On Reading," 114–15)

From this large, general assertion flow several corollaries, which Proust develops in theme-and-variations style, and which, for purposes of economy, I shall list telegraphically:

- We readers cannot "receive" the truth from any exterior source, whether it be an aesthetic object or a human being; we must create the truth ourselves, from within ourselves (this point will be beautifully amplified in the *petite madeleine* scene of *Combray*, perhaps the most memorable episode of the novel, in which the narrator, in rediscovering the essence of his past, finds himself capable of creating the fictional universe of his novel).
- Reading is useful when it plays the limited role of "incitement," but can be dangerous to a person's aesthetic and moral development if it becomes a mere substitute for such development.
- Reading leads to knowledge, and knowledge leads to erudition. But mere erudition can produce effects of fetishism and idolatry, as when a literary scholar thinks that he or she possesses the "truth" about a given writer simply by locating, in an archive, this or that fact about that writer. The archival object then becomes a fetish-object, a mere substitute for the deeper lessons the scrutinized writer could yield to our inquiries.
- Whereas Ruskin had associated reading with friendship, with books being considered idealized "friends," Proust asserts that friendship is interwoven with mendacity: i.e., lying to others and lying to oneself inhabit friendship as socially sterile and superficial occupations. In this observation we have a foreshadowing of the major distinction Proust will make in his next literary project, *Contre Sainte-Beuve*, between the superficial self (the self that circulates in the world, among friends) and the deep self (the self that develops through reading and aesthetic creation), both of which inhabit all human beings, both of which make claims upon our attention and inflect the authenticity or inauthenticity of our actions.

With the publication, in May 1906, of *Sésame et les lys*, Proust had not only completed the phase of his discipleship to Ruskin and become one of France's preeminent specialists on the English writer's work, but he had begun to set forth the foundation for his own aesthetic theory. This theory was to be based on the redemptive power of art and the cultivation of the inner self through a process whereby a cultivated aesthetic receptiveness, as in "the original psychological act called *Reading*," gradually yields to or evolves into the originality of artistic creation. It is now time to proceed to the final two phases of Proust's development as writer.

THE *RECHERCHE* FROM ITS INCEPTION UNTIL WORLD WAR I

Between 1906 and 1909 Proust remained visible to the literary public by publishing a number of articles in the Parisian press, including several delightful stylistic imitations or "pastiches" having as their ostensible subject the "Lemoine Affair." Henri Lemoine, a French electrical engineer, had extorted £64,000 from Sir Julius Wernher, a banker and director of De Beers diamond mines, having convinced Wernher that he could produce synthetic diamonds. In 1908 Lemoine was indicted for fraud, but managed to flee the country before being judged in court. In 1908 and 1909 Proust wrote several accounts of this scandalous affair, adopting the styles of a heterogeneous group of writers. These included, among others, the novelists Honoré de Balzac (1799–1850) and Gustave Flaubert (1821–80), the eminent historian Jules Michelet (1798–1874), the philosopher and writer Ernest Renan (1823–92), celebrated for his *Vie de Jésus* (a biographical account of Jesus in which the Son of God is treated essentially as a human being, not as a divinity), and the Duc de Saint-Simon (1607–93), soldier, courtier, to whose influential *Mémoires* Proust was often to refer in the *Recherche*. Also included in the set was a wonderful Proustian imitation of Sainte-Beuve criticizing Flaubert's article on Lemoine, an impressive "pastiche" at double remove.

While Proust appeared to be amusing himself at Sainte-Beuve's expense, he was also working on a curious, hybrid project that eventually grew into *A la recherche du temps perdu* – a fragmented text, part essay, part fictional narrative, to which scholars have given the title *Contre Sainte-Beuve*. At first, Proust's idea was to compose a critical work in which he would establish his own ideas about literary creation in contradistinction to those of Sainte-Beuve. But as he began organizing this text, he thought it would be a good idea to frame it in a specific context and to give it the form of a Socratic dialogue, in which he would play the role of the philosopher, and his mother that of the interlocutor-disciple. But as he continued to elaborate this "Conversation avec Maman" ["Conversation with Mother"], the setting itself, initially merely a room, gradually began to expand, becoming part of a house, then of a village, which itself became populated with characters. Within a year, from 1907 to 1908, the treatise was on the way to becoming a novel. The setting, which was originally intended simply as a pleasant framework to contain an aesthetic theory, became the large vehicle for that theory, enclosing it within the narrative ramifications of a fictional development.

As of 1908, Proust would write to his friend Robert Dreyfus: "I have in progress: / a study on the nobility/ a Parisian novel / an essay on Sainte-Beuve and Flaubert / an essay on Women / an essay on Pederasty (not easy to publish) / a study on stained-glass windows / a study on tombstones / a study on the novel."[13] All of these strands were eventually to be woven into the *Recherche*. Some of them date from the Ruskin period, some from the current period of concentration on Sainte-Beuve, but others are, in fact, sketches or drafts for what will be large themes in the novel (Women, the nobility, and "Pederasty" – understood by Proust to mean not only homosexuality as erotic practice, but also homosexuality as system of signs expressed in a particular coded language, as set of social conventions, as mode of being).

Between 1909 and the end of 1911 Proust had written some 700 pages of a novel which had by now changed its title from *Contre Sainte-Beuve* to *Les Intermittences du coeur* (the heart's "intermittences" meaning here its fickle or changeable character). Rather than conclude with the "Conversation avec Maman," as was to be the case with *Contre Sainte-Beuve*, this new version included a final scene juxtaposing the passing of Time (the ageing of the fictional characters) with a discourse on the redemptive value of art, which was to remain, in modified form, in the final version of the *Recherche*. The novel of 1911 covered large sections of what eventually became the first two volumes of the definitive novel, *Du Côté de chez Swann* [*The Way by Swann's*] and *A l'Ombre des jeunes filles en fleurs* [*In the Shadow of Young Girls in Flower*], but it lacked one major character called Albertine – the young woman with whom the narrator would fall in love and who would become the object of his jealous and anxious investigations.

Confident in the literary value of his project, Proust submitted his manuscript in December 1912 to the most prestigious new publishing house in France, Éditions Gallimard, only to experience a curt refusal. Not to be deterred, in early 1913, he contacted one Alfred Humblot, director of the Ollendorff publishing company, only to receive the now famous (infamous) second refusal, formulated in unforgettable terms: "I may be as thick as two short planks, but I fail to understand why a chap should require thirty pages to describe how he tosses and turns in bed before falling asleep."[14] Success was finally achieved in the latter half of 1913, when the editor Grasset agreed to publish Proust's novel at the author's expense, in a projected three-volume series (the manuscript had grown by now to some 1,500 pages, and was to be divided into three more or less equal parts). The novel now had its definitive title, *A la recherche du temps perdu*; its first volume, *Du Côté de chez Swann*, finally appeared and was, for the most part, favorably reviewed, in the final months of 1913.

From the perspective of the evolving novel, the year 1913 could thus be viewed as a violent pendulum swing from disappointment and disenchantment to elation: in the arcane and ever-fickle world of publishing, one success erases two failures. However, two events were developing – one personal and the other international in scope – that were to change Proust's life and dramatically alter the shape of his novel. Between the summer and the end of 1913, Proust had been falling in love with a man called Alfred Agostinelli, whom he had met several years earlier at the Norman seaside resort of Cabourg and whose services he had employed as auto mechanic and chauffeur. Agostinelli, who was to be in his company not only in Cabourg during the summer of 1913 but also in Paris during that autumn (again, officially, as "chauffeur"), seems to have understood the arts of seduction, emotional blackmail, and extortion as well as anyone. Proust was constantly showering him and his wife, Anna, with gifts, in a desperate effort to keep them with him and to ensure that Alfred would not escape from his jealous clutches. To no avail: on December 1, 1913, the Agostinellis fled, sending Proust into a deep depression, just when he was receiving the first positive reviews of *Du Côté de chez Swann*. On April 30, 1914, Alfred, who had registered in an aviation school at Antibes under the pathetic name of "Marcel Swann," ignored the instructions of his instructor and flew out over the Mediterranean, where he plunged to his death.

The process of grief and mourning which Proust then endured no doubt found its way, fictionally transposed, into the final version of the novel, in the twin volumes *La Prisonnière* [*The Prisoner*] and *Albertine disparue* [*The Fugitive*]. Alfred Agostinelli was, in some ways and to a certain degree, the "model" for Albertine. To understand the penultimate volumes of the *Recherche*, it is important to know about this interesting life-to-art, male-to-female transformation. At the same time, Albertine is far more than a pale imitation of a life experience, as we shall see in subsequent chapters of this *Guide.*

The second event that was to transform and, like the Agostinelli drama, substantially enlarge the scope of the *Recherche* was the advent of World War I. On the one hand, the period 1914–18 brought with it considerable trauma and restrictions, not only bombings, scarcity of food, power outages, and so forth, but also the curtailing of paper supplies and of publishing activities. On the other, the war also became a subject to be explored novelistically. Between the appearance of *Du Côté de chez Swann* in 1913 and the publication of the second volume, *A l'Ombre des jeunes filles en fleurs,* in 1918, the novel had doubled in size, and was overflowing the tripartite scheme which Proust had originally planned for its structural organization. Albertine as character had begun to exercise a considerable influence on the overall design of the second volume, and the passionate and jealous relationship she was to have with the narrator in the later sections of the novel was to add nearly a thousand pages to the total between the years of 1919 and 1922. When Proust also added a section devoted specifically to wartime Paris to the beginning of *Le Temps retrouvé* [*Finding Time Again*], the result is an opus that, from its 700 pages in 1911 and its 1,500 pages in 1913, was to reach 3,000 by the time of the author's death on November 18, 1922.

THE *RECHERCHE* AFTER WORLD WAR I

The biography of Proust after World War I is largely the story of his novel's evolution. To deepen one's understanding of the writer during this time, one is better served by reading the second half of the *Recherche* than by examining the anecdotal evidence surrounding Marcel Proust's social activities. Although Proust's personal life was not without a certain intrinsic interest during this period, including new friendships and amorous relationships (notably a two-year liaison with a certain Henri Rochat, who is said to have "posed" for the Albertine of *La Prisonnière* as well as for the Baron de Charlus's lover, the violinist Morel), one has the sense that these developments were, for the writer, secondary to the all-consuming task of completing the *Recherche.* By 1919 Proust's novel was no longer merely a matter of curiosity for a small group of cognoscenti, but had become widely known and discussed among devoted readers of contemporary literature, both in France and abroad. Ever since 1916, when Proust was able to disengage himself from his contract with

Grasset, the *Recherche* was being published by Gallimard and serialized in Gallimard's prestigious literary journal, *La Nouvelle Revue française.* In 1919 *A l'Ombre des jeunes filles en fleurs* received the *Prix Goncourt*, arguably the most important award for literature in France. Although Proust was not elected to the Académie Française, he did attain the rank of "chevalier" in the Légion d'Honneur, in a ceremony presided over by his brother Robert on November 7, 1920. During this period he got to know a younger generation of writers, many of whom admired and understood the originality of his work, including the surrealist poet and theoretician André Breton (1896–1966), who corrected the proofs of the novel's third volume, *Le Côté de Guermantes* [*The Guermantes Way*], the playwright Jean Giraudoux (1882–1944), and the Nobel-prize-winning poet Alexis Saint-Léger Léger (pseudonym Saint-John Perse) (1887–1975). From 1919 until his death, Proust would be in regular contact with Sydney Schiff (1868–1944), an author of experimental fiction who published under the pseudonym Stephen Hudson and who befriended and supported many of the great modernist artists, including James Joyce (1882–1941) and the painter Wyndham Lewis (1882–1957). Schiff hosted a famous party in Paris on May 18, 1922, when Proust met Joyce (it would appear, from all accounts, that they had very little to say to one another, Joyce being inebriated upon arrival); other guests at the event not to be overlooked were the founder of the *Ballets russes*, Serge Diaghilev (1872–1929), Igor Stravinsky (1882–1971), and Pablo Picasso (1881–1972).

It is during the final years of his life that, with his increasing celebrity, Proust began to assume the traits of the strange and legendary phantom figure who, wrapped in his bulky overcoat, would invite his friends and hangers-on to the Ritz at all hours of the evening and into the early morning, quite probably using their poses, their mannerisms, and their language tics as material for his novel. The fact that, during this time, he was also taking drugs (veronal, opium) in combination with large amounts of caffeine and other stimulants, must have contributed to his unusual physical appearance and erratic behavior. Proust was now living solely for his work: he was keeping himself alive in order to write, and he was stretching his body's capacities to the limit of its endurance. Even among the most dedicated of writers, seldom has there been a case when life and work became so utterly merged as to be coterminous. When Proust died, he left behind him an unfinished monumental work, nearly one third of which was published posthumously, thanks in no small part to the unstinting efforts of Robert Proust, who had long recognized the genius of his unusual, complicated, hypersensitive, affectionate, and tenacious brother. What we read now as *A la recherche du temps perdu,* one of the most important and most beautiful of twentieth-century European novels, is the result of exceptional talent and also of immense labor. What one senses, in pages that by now have accrued the patina of Time, is a life's energy transmuted into art. It is time now to turn to that art.

CHAPTER I

Du Côté de chez Swann [The Way by Swann's]

A CURIOUS THREE-PART VOLUME

Shortly after the appearance of *Du Côté de chez Swann* in 1913,[1] Paul Souday, literary critic for *Le Temps*, expressed what must have been a widely shared opinion among Proust's first readers:

> It seems to me that the large volume by Marcel Proust is lacking in compositional unity, that it is as hyper-extended as it is chaotic, but that it contains precious elements from which the author could have formed an exquisite small book.[2]

Although in retrospect Souday's judgment may appear excessively harsh and off the mark, it must be conceded that the perplexed reviewer had a point. How can any reader, however perceptive, when confronted for the first time by this beautiful yet strange new fictional universe, locate a thread capable of unifying the volume's three quite distinct parts, which bear the titles: *Combray*, *Un Amour de Swann*, and *Noms de pays: le nom*? In *Combray*, after three introductory sections which function like three narrative false starts, we have an evocation of the small town in which the narrator spent his holidays as a child and the introduction of major characters and fundamental themes that will be developed as the novel evolves. In *Un Amour de Swann* we find the only sustained section of third-person narrative in the *Recherche* (the rest of the novel being organized around the reflective consciousness of an "I" or *je* who is both narrator and protagonist of his own story). This second section of the novel's first volume could easily stand alone, and is sometimes read in classrooms as a self-enclosed work of fiction. It functions, however, as an intercalated novella within the aesthetic whole of the *Recherche*. It is centered not on the narrator but on a character named Charles Swann and his love for a certain Odette de Crécy, its tightly organized story taking place one generation before the main action of the novel, at the very beginning of the *belle époque*. The brusque thrust backward in time from *Combray* to *Un Amour de Swann* might have seemed more jarring than aesthetically pleasing to

2 Marcel Proust, Robert de Flers, and Lucien Daudet

early readers, and the structural justification for the replacement of first- by third-person narration might not have been immediately obvious. The short final section, *Noms de pays: le nom* [*Place-names: The Name*], cannot be fully appreciated by itself, but needs to be read in tandem with *Noms de pays: le pays* [*Place-names: The Place*], an episode located in the second large section of the subsequent volume, *A l'Ombre des jeunes filles en fleurs* [*In the Shadow of Young Girls in Flower*], at an appreciable distance of some 250 pages.

Paul Souday's blindness to the structural articulations and architectonic unity of Proust's novel[3] is understandable, in that, in an important sense, the entirety of *Du Côté de chez Swann* is preparatory material for what follows, something like a vast cauldron of themes which invite infinite repetition. In a perverse or diabolical way, one could say that Proust rendered *Du Côté de chez Swann* unreadable on a first reading, that the initial volume presupposes a second reading in which its many links to the subsequent volumes of the novel will have become visible, decipherable. In the pages that follow, I shall indicate, sometimes only in passing, sometimes in more detail, the ways in which certain early sections of the first volume prefigure thematic material and entire episodes that occur later in the text. It is important, from the beginning, to be aware of the care with which Proust constructed the narrative whole of his novelistic project. Although this drive toward narrative wholeness or coherence in no way precludes fragmentation, although, as we shall see, the narrator's theories of aesthetic synthesis or completeness often conflict with the playful or even deconstructive force of his textual practice, it is crucial for the first-time reader of Proust to become aware of the effects of reflection, mirroring, symmetry, and repetition that make of the novel a complex system of articulated, varied, and evolving meanings.

COMBRAY

Between wakefulness and sleep, or the place of uncertainty
*(*R *I, 3–8;* S *1, 7–12)*

Like ancient epic poetry, *A la recherche du temps perdu* begins not at the chronological starting-point of its storyline, but *in medias res*, with a plunge into the midst of the events it will be recounting:

> Longtemps, je me suis couché de bonne heure. Parfois, à peine ma bougie éteinte, mes yeux se fermaient si vite que je n'avais pas le temps de me dire: "Je m'endors." Et, une demi-heure après, la pensée qu'il était temps de chercher le sommeil m'éveillait; je voulais poser le volume que je croyais avoir encore dans les mains et souffler ma lumière; je n'avais pas cessé en dormant de faire des réflexions sur ce que je venais de lire, mais ces réflexions avaient pris un tour un peu particulier; il me semblait que j'étais moi-même ce dont parlait l'ouvrage: une église, un quatuor, la rivalité de François Ier et de Charles Quint. (*R* I, 3)

For a long time, I went to bed early. Sometimes, my candle scarcely out, my eyes would close so quickly that I did not have time to say to myself: "I'm falling asleep." And, half an hour later, the thought that it was time to try to sleep would wake me; I wanted to put down the book I thought I still had in my hands and blow out my light; I had not ceased while sleeping to form reflections on what I had just read, but these reflections had taken a rather peculiar turn; it seemed to me that I myself was what the book was talking about: a church, a quartet, the rivalry between François I and Charles V. (*S* 1, 7.)

At the entryway to the novel we find uncertainty, hesitation, and paradox. The narrator is neither awake nor asleep, but in an in-between space where his mind and his body are playing a game of hide-and-seek characterized by humor and even a certain grotesque strangeness. In this scenario the intellect is not presented in isolation or abstracted from the body, but appears to be chasing after (and always late with respect to) the independent and unpredictable actions of the body. Thought by no means disappears from this semi-nocturnal scene, but it takes on "a rather peculiar turn" as it plunges into the unconscious, where it produces fanciful but telling images. When, at the conclusion of the short passage, the narrator tells us "it seemed to me that I myself was what the book was talking about: a church, a quartet, the rivalry between François I and Charles V," the significance of his statement is both incongruous and profound. Incongruous because it is indeed "peculiar" for a person to be metamorphosed into a religious edifice, a work of music, or especially an abstraction (the narrator does not become either François I or Charles V, but the rivalry that divides and defines them). Profound because, in the final analysis, the *Recherche* in its totality is about the narrator's search (for love, for aesthetic revelation, for the truth as enveloped in natural and cultural objects), so that the statement "it seemed to me that I myself was what the book was talking about" is an admirably concise definition of the novel-to-come.

The hesitation between sleep and wakefulness, between the body and the mind, and between conscious and unconscious modes of representation, takes place in a space that is at first without contour or borders and at a time that cannot be defined with precision. But as the six-page Overture to the novel develops, the narrator, and with him the reader, gain an increasingly clear notion of time and place, of location in every sense of that term. Uncertainty, hesitancy, and paradox gradually yield to certainty, logical resolution, and narrative clarity. The in-between space of the room without boundaries in which the narrator vacillates between wakefulness and sleep gives way to a particular room – "my room at Mme de Saint-Loup's" (*S* 1, 10) – which the first-time reader of the novel will not be able to locate, but which foreknowledge of the novel in its entirety allows Proust's ideal reader to situate: it is to be found near the end, but not at the very end, of the action, before the episode of the Baron de Charlus's experiences during World War I and before the aesthetic revelations which conclude the final volume of the *Recherche*. Later in the passage, that particular room gives way to the narrator's remembrance of several other geographically dispersed rooms and places he has inhabited earlier in his life – fictional sites we readers will visit as the narrative unfolds.

The gradual movement from uncertainty to certainty carries with it both a gain and a loss: what we gain in logical understanding and in intellectual reassurance entails a loss at the level of the creative imagination. We have all had the Proustian experience of waking up in a strange room and thinking that the bookcase or the chest of drawers or the writing desk are located in positions opposite to their actual location. When we realize where we are, we achieve a sense of calm as the room turns on its axis, so to speak, curtailing our sense of anxiety and vertigo. Yet the very moment of absolute uncertainty, where we have no notion of where we are, in causing intellectual hesitation and even fear, is also productive in that it can open up to us regions of our past experience analogous to our present, magical regions we visit all too seldom and whose disappearance marks the vanishing point of our childhood. It is these areas that Proust has explored with greater depth than any writer and that bear his unmistakable imprint within the broad territory of modern European literature.

At the conclusion of the Overture the reader of the *Recherche* has been initiated into a fictional universe which is constructed on the dialectical interplay of certainty and uncertainty, memory and forgetfulness, novelty and habit. The reader has glimpsed for the first time the places in which the action of the novel's seven volumes will transpire, which include not only Paris and the fictional town of Combray, but also the imaginary Norman seaside resort called Balbec, and places beyond France's borders – most notably Venice, which Proust inscribes into his novel as a homage to and dialogue with John Ruskin. What has not been revealed, however, is whether access to these places, and to the creative reimagining of one's past life, is a matter of pure chance and arbitrariness, or whether one might devise a method which would permit the regaining of all that is lost, on a daily basis, to the dullness of habitual actions and to the oblivion into which even the most memorable human actions tend to sink. It will take two more narrative false starts for Proust to arrive at this method, and for his novel to begin its long unfolding.

*The scene of the good-night kiss, or the primal scene of writing and reading (*R *I, 23–43;* S *1, 26–46)*

Immediately following the Overture is a short section in which the narrator begins to introduce some of the novel's main characters: notably his mother, father, grandmother, and grandfather, as well as the protagonist of the second part of the first volume, Charles Swann. Swann is the first in a procession of characters who play a mentoring role for the narrator. In giving the young boy photographs of Giotto's *Vices and Virtues* from the Arena Chapel in Padua, he opens up for the as yet unaware aspiring writer the world of symbolic expression and of artistic representation. Like a number of other figures in the *Recherche*, Swann also possesses, both for the protagonist and for his family, some enigmatic characteristics. On the one hand, his conversation is straightforward to the point of being bland and occasionally dismissive in its tone; on the other hand, as a member of the prestigious Jockey Club, Swann clearly has friends among the highest aristocratic circles and seems to prefer both hiding these connections and refusing to engage his interlocutors in any discussions that might contain a serious political, cultural, or artistic dimension. Swann is the first of many characters who exhibit what one might call an inauthentic mode of being: he never reveals his innermost thoughts or emotions. He also represents an obstacle to the immediate fulfillment of the narrator's desires in the early pages of *Combray*, in that his presence at the family dinner table stands in the way of the ritualistic good-night kiss bestowed each evening by the mother on her adoring and anxious son. Each time Swann comes to dinner, the narrator must eat early, climb the stairs, and go to his room without receiving this token of his mother's affection. The *Recherche* begins a second time with a twenty-page section devoted to the dramatic representation of the initial withholding, then final granting, of the kiss.

As is often the case in Proust's novel, a scene with serious psychological ramifications is related with considerable humor. The entirety of the episode is told from the perspective of the young protagonist, for whom all other worldly concerns fade into nothingness when compared with his overwhelming need to obtain the kiss. Having been banished from the dining area and sent upstairs to a "tomb"-like room by his uncomprehending father, his desperation turns into an interesting form of action:

Une fois dans ma chambre, il fallut boucher toutes les issues, fermer les volets, creuser mon propre tombeau, en défaisant mes couvertures, revêtir le suaire de ma chemise de nuit. Mais avant de m'ensevelir dans le lit de fer … j'eus un mouvement de révolte, je voulus essayer d'une ruse de condamné. J'écrivis à ma mère en la suppliant de monter pour une chose grave que je ne pouvais lui dire dans ma lettre … *Mais pour mettre une chance de mon côté, je n'hésitai pas à mentir* et à lui dire que ce n'était pas du tout moi qui avais voulu écrire à maman, mais que c'était maman qui, en me quittant, m'avait recommandé de ne pas oublier de lui envoyer une réponse relativement à un objet qu'elle m'avait prié de chercher; et elle serait certainement très fâchée si on ne lui remettait pas ce mot. (*R* I, 28–29; my emphasis)

Once in my room, I had to stop up all the exits, close the shutters, dig my own grave by undoing my covers, put on the shroud of my nightshirt. But before burying myself in the iron bed … I had a fit of rebelliousness, I wanted to attempt the ruse of a condemned man. I wrote to my mother begging her to come upstairs for something serious that I could not tell her in my letter … *But to give myself a better chance, I did not hesitate to lie* and tell her that it was not in the least I who had wanted to write to Mama, but that it was Mama who, as she said goodnight to me, had exhorted me not to forget to send her an answer concerning an object she had asked me to look for; and she would certainly be very annoyed if this note was not delivered to her. (*S* 1, 31–32; my emphasis)

Of primary importance here is the association of writing with lying. This is the first time that the act of writing appears explicitly as a theme in the novel, and it does not emerge in the isolated self-sufficiency of a pure aesthetic context, but in a complicated emotional and ethical entanglement. The narrator, through the force of his volition and the naïveté of his imagination, thinks of his letter as a performative assertion: according to his fantasy, his words will have the immediate effect of bringing his mother upstairs. The reality of the matter is quite different, however, since the narrator cannot deliver the letter himself, but must rely upon the family's maidservant, Françoise, a simple but wily peasant woman who probably does not believe his fabrication and who, "like those primitive men whose senses were so much more powerful than ours … could immediately discern, from signs imperceptible to us, any truth that we wanted to hide from her" (*S* 1, 32–33). Throughout the *Recherche* the narrator and several of the other characters dream of the possibility of an unmediated form of communication, a kind of "communion of souls," but this never occurs. For Proust language is always, from the beginning (from the earliest scene of all scenes), mediated. Messages are always deflected and deviated from their points of origin, and they are inevitably the product of a desire rather than the mere transcription of a thought. The goal of the letter is coercion and emotional blackmail; and the goal, despite the presence of some initial obstacles, is eventually achieved.

The second half of the scene is suffused with psychological intensity and seems to call for a psychoanalytical or "Freudian" reading (according to critical consensus, Proust never read Freud and Freud never read Proust, but it is abundantly clear to readers of both writers that they explored many of the same mental territories).[4] Whereas the narrator's mother initially refuses to come upstairs, she eventually does, not only granting him the good-night kiss, but spending the night with him, in his room, in a bed next to his. The father, who had regularly criticized his son for his nervous disposition and hypersensitivity, unexpectedly withdraws from the scene, in what could be interpreted as an abdication of his paternal responsibility. In Freudian terms, the Oedipal triangle of father–mother–son collapses with the disappearance of the father, allowing the son to usurp the father's role.

The theme of incest, which is adumbrated somewhat delicately in the physical presence of mother and son in the same room, is reinforced through a subtle but unmistakable literary reference. In her attempt to calm her son and facilitate his falling asleep, the narrator's mother resorts to the tactic of all parents – the bedtime story, in this case, the reading of carefully selected sections of a short fiction by the novelist George Sand (1804–76) entitled *François le Champi*. Chosen as a gift by his grandmother, who admires Sand's distinguished prose style, this particular text bears an uncanny resemblance to the narrator's own situation and, in an important sense, tells the story of a wish to which the son cannot give conscious expression. The protagonist of the story, François, is a foundling ("champi" in the regional dialect) who eventually marries his adoptive mother. The narrator, whose father has disappeared from the scene in the *chiaroscuro* flickering of light in the dim upstairs hallway, could very well see himself in François and wish for a similar but, given social constraints, impossible fate. The final moments of the scene depict the mother reading to her son, in a moment of near-perfect intimacy, a moment of tranquility and of emotional equilibrium which will never be recovered in the novel's following 3,000 pages. If one were to adopt a Freudian perspective on the episode as a whole, one would be tempted to say that all the narrator's subsequent love relations constitute attempts to recreate this primal scene, but that none of the women he will love (or rather, pursue in an attempt to love) can provide him with the unconditional affection possessed by his mother.

The rhetorical tone of the passage as a whole is mixed. On the one hand, there are unmistakable traces of melancholy tinged with culpability, as when the narrator, conscious of the "victory" he has obtained over his mother by forcing her to leave her guests and attend to his needs, notes ruefully:

Il me semblait que si je venais de remporter une victoire c'était contre elle [maman] que j'avais réussi comme auraient pu faire la maladie, des chagrins, ou l'âge, à détendre sa volonté, à faire fléchir sa raison et que cette soirée commençait une ère, resterait comme une triste date … [Il] me semblait que je venais d'une main impie et secrète de tracer dans son âme une première ride et d'y faire apparaître un premier cheveu blanc. (*R* I, 38)

It seemed to me that, if I had just gained a victory, it was over her [Mama] that I had succeeded, as illness, affliction, or age might have done, in slackening her will, in causing her judgment to weaken and that this evening was the beginning of a new era, would remain as a sad date … [It] seemed to me that with an impious and secret hand I had just traced in her soul a first wrinkle and caused a first white hair to appear. (*S* 1, 41)

On the other hand, the narrator is aware that the sheer intensity of this remembered moment causes it to stand out from its surroundings, to become detached from the shadowy past in which it might have been lost. Time passes and destroys people, places, and things. But the human consciousness, even in retrieving memories that contain a bitter substance and in reviving sad or tragic experiences, itself seems capable of recreating the essence of that very past and, in expressing that essence, infusing it with renewed aesthetic significance. Immediately after his painterly evocation of the father's disappearance into the night and before the scene of reading with the mother, there is a narrative pause in the unfolding of the episode, a pause that must certainly stand as one of the most beautiful passages in the *Recherche*, in its evocation of a different kind of "victory" than the one only temporarily achieved by the young boy: in this case, that of time regained over time lost.

Il y a bien des années de cela. La muraille de l'escalier, où je vis monter le reflet de sa bougie [celle de mon père] n'existe plus depuis longtemps … Il y a bien longtemps aussi que mon père a cessé de pouvoir dire à maman: "Va avec le petit." La possibilité de telles heures ne renaîtra jamais pour moi. Mais depuis peu de temps, je recommence à très bien percevoir si je prête l'oreille, les sanglots que j'eus la force de contenir devant mon père et qui n'éclatèrent que quand je me retrouvai seul avec maman. En réalité ils n'ont jamais cessé; et c'est seulement parce que la vie se tait maintenant davantage autour de moi que je les entends de nouveau, comme ces cloches de couvents que couvrent si bien les bruits de la ville pendant le jour qu'on les croirait arrêtées mais qui se remettent à sonner dans le silence du soir. (*R* I, 36–37)

This was many years ago. The staircase wall on which I saw the rising glimmer of his [my father's] candle has long since ceased to exist … It was a very long time ago, too, that my father ceased to be able to say to Mama: "Go with the boy." The possibility of such hours will never be reborn for me. But for a little while now, I have begun to hear again very clearly, if I take care to listen, the sobs I was strong enough to contain in front of my father and that did not burst out until I found myself alone again with Mama. They have never really stopped; and it is only because life is quieting down around me more and more now that I can hear them again, like those convent bells covered so well by the clamour of the town during the day that one would think they had ceased altogether but which begin sounding again in the silence of the evening. (*S* 1, 39–40)

If one listens well enough, one can perceive even the most distant echoes of the past. But do these resonances occur only fleetingly, only when life has "quieted down" sufficiently for the listener to become aware of their existence? Or could there be a way to search them out actively, to make of these barely perceptible sounds the retrieved meaning of a life and the raw material of a work of art? It is only in the novel's third beginning that this question receives its dramatic and literarily memorable response.

The miracle of involuntary memory; the petite madeleine *and the resuscitation of the past (*R *I, 43–47;* S *1, 46–50)*

At the beginning of the short passage on the *petite madeleine*, the little cake which unlocks the essence of the narrator's past in what has become the most celebrated episode of Proust's novel, the narrator laments the fact that his past remembrances appear in isolation as starkly illumined fragments of a largely unexamined life. When he summons up past thoughts and actions in his imagination, he sees nothing more than a barebones theatrical décor possessing neither depth nor detail. In short, the Combray from his childhood which he can retrieve upon conscious reflection is *without context*, or, in his words, "isolated from everything that might surround it" (*S* 1, 46). To re-experience the essence of the past, according to Proust, is to relocate past experience within the fullness of its contextual location, in space and in time. The narrator's explanation of the way in which this feat can be achieved has both a theoretical dimension and a metaphorical, mythical resonance.

The theoretical underpinning of the scene is the strong distinction the narrator makes between voluntary and involuntary memory. The former, also called "the memory of the intelligence," is capable only of furnishing information concerning the past, not the past's fundamental significance, whereas involuntary memory, which comes upon us unawares, can open up the gateway to those areas of human experience that otherwise would be lost to oblivion. To make his point, the narrator resorts to ancient Celtic mythology, and to an animistic or magical belief within that tradition. It is important to note that the narrator finds this belief, which modern science or rationality could easily brand as superstitious, "very reasonable" (*S* I, 47). The theoretical argument in favor of involuntary memory and against "the intelligence" will draw its weapons not from rational argument, but from the universe of folklore and figurative discourse, yet it will state, paradoxically, that its truth claims, however unreasonable in their appearance, should be taken as "reasonable" at a higher level – that of poetic persuasiveness. The episode of the *petite madeleine*, the quintessential moment of the cake dipped in tea which, like the Eiffel Tower for the city of Paris, has become *the* recognizable iconographic symbol of Proust's fictional universe as a whole, begins with an analogy founded upon a paradox:

Je trouve très raisonnable la croyance celtique que les âmes de ceux que nous avons perdus sont captives dans quelque être inférieur, dans une bête, un végétal, une chose inanimée, perdues en effet pour nous jusqu'au jour, qui pour beaucoup ne vient jamais, où nous nous trouvons passer près de l'arbre, entrer en possession de l'objet qui est leur prison, Alors elles tressaillent, nous appellent, et sitôt que nous les avons reconnues, l'enchantement est brisé. Délivrées par nous, elles ont vaincu la mort et reviennent vivre avec nous. (*R* I, 43–44)[5]

I find the Celtic belief very reasonable, that the souls of those we have lost are held captive in some inferior creature, in an animal, in a plant, in some inanimate thing, effectively lost to us until the day, which for many never comes, when we happen to pass close to the tree, come into possession of the object that is their prison. Then they quiver, they call out to us, and as soon as we have recognized them, the spell is broken. Delivered by us, they have overcome death and they return to live with us. (*S* I, 47)

The remainder of the passage is a slow description of the efforts made by the narrator one cold winter's day to retrieve a short moment of ecstatic joy he initially feels upon tasting a *petite madeleine* dipped in tea. Like the Overture of the novel, the scene as a whole centers on the problem of location: where does this sensation of unexplainable happiness originate? Is the cause of the powerful feeling to be found *in* the little cake, or is that feeling somehow merely linked to it? If this should be the case, what is the nature of that link? It is in the examination of these questions that the narrator reveals, with some subtlety, that the analogy between the Celtic myth and the scene of involuntary memory is good as far as it goes, but imperfect when pursued in detail. The difference between the two scenarios is that the souls of one's ancestors, according to legend, are to be found somewhere in the outside world, and, in being released, pass from that world into the human being who has apprehended their essence and their meaning. In the scene we are now witnessing, however, the truth being sought is not to be found in exterior space, but within the seeking consciousness itself. In the narrator's striking formulation, we read:

Il est clair que la vérité que je cherche n'est pas en lui [le breuvage, le thé], mais en moi ... Je pose la tasse et me tourne vers mon esprit. C'est à lui de trouver la vérité. Mais comment? Grave incertitude, toutes les fois que l'esprit se sent dépassé par lui-même; quand lui, le chercheur, est tout ensemble le pays obscur où il doit chercher et où tout son bagage ne lui sera de rien. Chercher? pas seulement: créer. Il est en face de quelque chose qui n'est pas encore et que seul il peut réaliser, puis faire entrer dans sa lumière. (*R* I, 45)

It is clear that the truth I am seeking is not in the drink, but in me ... I put down the cup and turn to my mind. It is up to my mind to find the truth. But how? What grave uncertainty, whenever the mind feels overtaken by itself; when it, the seeker, is also the obscure country where it must seek and where all its baggage will be nothing to it. Seek? Not only that: create. It is face to face with something that does not yet exist and that only it can accomplish, then bring into its light. (*S* 1, 48)

We find in this passage a central element of Proust's aesthetic philosophy and a defining feature of his fictional universe: namely, the primary importance of the reflective consciousness, or, stated differently, of the split within the consciousness which stands at the very origin of the novelistic project. It may be true that Proust examines, in the *Recherche*, a host of themes which are worldly in nature, which emanate from human and social relations (aspects of the political and social reality of Third Republic France; love and the attendant subthemes of anxiety, lying, and jealousy; homosexuality as semiotic system and mode of being; the ritualistic behavior of the aristocracy viewed through the lens of social satire, and so on). Yet the reader senses, at every turn of the novel, that even those characters and events which appear at the farthest remove from the narrator's scrutiny are subject to interiorization, to a kind of "digestion" within the self in its capacity as narrating voice.[6] In fact, the constitutive split that organizes the *Recherche* drives a wedge between what could be called a "narrating I" and a "narrated I" – both of whom use the same word, "I" (*je, moi*), but to designate different temporal and spatial locations of the same fictional being.[7] The "I" who says "For a long time, I went to bed early" is at the same time the "I" who utters that sentence from the perspective of a middle-aged man, and also the various incarnations of that "same" person at a number of earlier junctures in his life ("same" in scare quotes because one of Proust's preoccupations is with the impossibility of uniting the self through its temporally and spatially distant metamorphoses). The self who tells the story of the *Recherche* is also the object of the

Recherche, the seeker as well as that which is being sought, intuitively and painstakingly, throughout the novel's development.

In the end, the narrator is able to identify precisely the origin of his happiness when he realizes that the taste of the cake moistened in tea and served to him in his adult years by his mother is that of "the little piece of madeleine which on Sunday mornings at Combray (because that day I did not go out before it was time for Mass), when I went to say good morning to her in her bedroom, my Aunt Léonie would give me after dipping it in her infusion of tea or lime-blossom" (*S* 1, 49). The past rejoins the present through the sensation of taste; time is abolished by the congruence of past and present experience. The joy felt by the narrator throughout the scene is an intimation of immortality. Perhaps the strongest affirmative moment of a strongly affirmative passage is to be found in the artfully differed assertion:

> Mais, quand d'un passé ancien rien ne subsiste, après la mort des êtres, après la destruction des choses, seules, plus frêles mais plus vivaces, plus immatérielles, plus persistantes, plus fidèles, l'odeur et la saveur restent encore longtemps, comme des âmes, à se rappeler, à attendre, à espérer, sur la ruine de tout le reste, à porter sans fléchir, sur leur gouttelette presque impalpable, l'édifice immense du souvenir. (*R* I, 46)
>
> But when nothing subsists of an old past, after the death of people, after the destruction of things, alone, frailer but more enduring, more immaterial, more persistent, more faithful, smell and taste still remain for a long time, like souls, remembering, waiting, hoping, on the ruin of all the rest, bearing without giving way, on their almost impalpable droplet, the immense edifice of memory. (*S* 1, 49–50)

The final paragraph of the passage builds upon the contrast between the very small and the very large which is contained in the stark juxtaposition of the "almost impalpable droplet" and "the immense edifice of memory." Once the narrator has recognized the childhood origin of the *petite madeleine* dipped in tea, the entirety of Combray – its geographical detail, its inhabitants, the lived experience of the narrator within the small town – all people, places, and things emerge from the taste sensation and become deployed as the building blocks of a narration: "all of Combray and its surroundings, all of this which is assuming form and substance, emerged, town and gardens alike, from my cup of tea" (*S* 1, 50). The rhetorical device used here is a favorite one for Proust throughout the *Recherche*: it is an inversion of the container (*le contenant*) and the contained (*le contenu*). Whereas it is, of course, the town of Combray that contains the people, places, events, and things that exist within it (including cups of tea and people drinking this tea), the narrator is telling us, in his figurative language, that it is the cup of tea that "contains" Combray – i.e., it is the experience of involuntary memory which gives rise to the possibility of the fictional existence and to the very narrative possibility of Combray *as* location, as childhood space to be explored in the succeeding pages.

*Combray: characters, places, scenes (*R *I, 47–184;* S *1, 51–187)*

The section of the novel which follows immediately upon the scene of involuntary memory, called "Combray II" by the Pléiade editors, is a leisurely description of the town of Combray in its historical and geographical dimensions, as well as an exposition of the principal characters who inhabit it, some of whom will play a major role in the development of the novel. Based in large part on the small town of Illiers in which Proust spent his school holidays, located south of Paris in the Beauce region not far from the magnificent cathedral of Chartres, the fictionally transposed Combray is a quiet place whose inhabitants appear, at first glance, to be rather simple people, whom the narrator treats with affection tinged with gentle irony.

The narrator's Aunt Léonie, a hypochondriac addicted to gossip as well as dependent upon her various medications for the construction of a compulsive and highly ritualized existence, bears no small resemblance to the adult writer Marcel Proust, himself voluntarily enclosed in a cork-lined room thick with fumigations. Aunt Léonie, like the author of *A la recherche du temps perdu*, seeks to gain an understanding of the mysteries of the outside world through the reports of friends and acquaintances who circulate in an exterior space which, given her pessimistic assessment of her own health, is now off-limits. She apprehends the world through the eyes of her female friends, and thanks to the regular visits of the local vicar, or *curé*. One senses that Aunt Léonie, in her capacity as fictionalized authorial self-parody, needs to be taken more seriously as a character than her mannerisms and the vapid nature of her conversation would seem to merit. Yet Proust disposes of her by having her die quite early in the proceedings, within a remarkable parenthetical phrase interrupting a paragraph that had begun with a description of the narrator's walking habits:

> Si le temps était mauvais dès le matin, mes parents renonçaient à la promenade et je ne sortais pas. Mais je pris ensuite l'habitude d'aller, ces jours-là, marcher seul du côté de Méséglise-la-Vineuse, dans l'automne où nous dûmes venir à Combray pour la succession de ma tante Léonie, *car elle était enfin morte*, faisant triompher à la fois ceux qui prétendaient que son régime affaiblissant finirait par la tuer, et non moins les autres qui avaient toujours soutenu qu'elle souffrait d'une maladie non pas imaginaire mais organique. (*R* I, 151; my emphasis)

If the weather was bad in the morning, my parents would give up the walk and I would not go out. But I later acquired the habit of going out to walk alone on those days along the Méséglise-la-Vineuse way, during the autumn in which we had come to Combray to settle my aunt Léonie's estate, *because she had at last died*, proving correct both those who had claimed that her enfeebling regimen would end by killing her, and also those who had always maintained that she suffered from an illness that was not imaginary but organic. (*S* 1, 153–54; my emphasis)

Throughout the second section of *Combray*, the reader is struck by a peculiar combination of triviality and psychological depth that seems to inhabit the principal characters. The *curé* of Combray is quite tiresome in his display of regional historical erudition and in the lengthy etymological explanations he furnishes for the area's place names, but what he has to say about the place in which he lives provides an important historical resonance and serves to situate Combray within the evolution of France as a nation. The pages devoted to his visits to Aunt Léonie also serve to emphasize the role played by the Catholic Church in small French towns. In the case of Combray, not only is the church the central edifice around which the village organizes itself, but it represents, in the temporally distinct layers of its architecture, Time itself as a "fourth dimension." In a lyrical passage reminiscent of the sweeping descriptions in Ruskin's writings, the narrator describes the awe he feels upon entering a place that has witnessed and housed the passage of Time:

... je m'avançais dans l'église ... comme dans une vallée visitée des fées, où le paysan s'émerveille de voir dans un rocher, dans un arbre, dans une mare, la trace palpable de leur passage surnaturel, tout cela faisait d'elle pour moi quelque chose d'entièrement différent du reste de la ville: un édifice occupant, si l'on peut dire, un espace à quatre dimensions – la quatrième étant celle du Temps –, déployant à travers les siècles son vaisseau qui, de travée en travée, de chapelle en chapelle, semblait vaincre et franchir non pas seulement quelques mètres, mais des époques successives d'où il sortait victorieux. (*R* I, 60)

... I moved through the church ... as though through a valley visited by the fairies, in which a country person is amazed to see in a rock, a tree, a pool, the palpable trace of their supernatural passage, all this made it, for me, something entirely different from the rest of the town: an edifice occupying a space with, so to speak, four dimensions – the fourth being Time – extending over the centuries its nave which, from bay to bay, from chapel to chapel, seemed to vanquish and penetrate not only a few yards but epoch after epoch from which it emerged victorious. (*S* 1, 63–64)

Lest the reader be tempted to view the provincial cast of characters in *Combray* as being somehow less important, less substantial in their representative vices and virtues than the more elegant and sophisticated figures of the Parisian sections of the novel, the narrator has endowed several of them with the very same moral complexity that will inhabit the dukes and duchesses of the Faubourg Saint-Germain. A case in point is the engineer Legrandin, who, exercising his profession in Paris, gives free play to his apparent disdain for the arrogance of the aristocracy in high-flown tirades which he offers up, upon weekend visits, to the citizenry of Combray, but which the narrator's grandmother finds excessively well turned, lacking in the quality dearest to her, "naturalness" (*S* I, 70). What we learn, within a few pages of our first encounter with M. Legrandin, is that he is, in fact, the worst of snobs: that is, he is infected with the very vice that he has chosen to castigate. Legrandin is the relatively transparent vehicle used by Proust in the early pages of the text to introduce one of the large themes of the *Recherche* – that of social ambition, of social climbing as an exercise in posing, in hypocrisy, and in lying to oneself. In Freudian terms, Legrandin's speech is a prime example of *Verneinung* (in English, "negation," in French, *dénégation*), a linguistically symptomatic psychological phenomenon whereby a person reveals, within his criticism of a particular social or ethical infirmity, his own attachment to that very infirmity.[8] Without having read Freud, the narrator's grandmother had intuited the problem: "Worldly ambition was a sentiment that my grandmother was so incapable of feeling or even, almost, of understanding, that it seemed to her quite pointless to bring so much ardour to stigmatizing it" (*S* I, 70).

If one were to generalize to the extreme, one could say that the entirety of *Combray* is a delicate balancing act between the two traditional poles of nature (both nature as landscape and nature as the grandmother's ideal of human "naturalness") and culture (viewed both as a socially refined territory shared by the upper classes, and as the privileged domain of the arts). On the one hand, there are numerous, quite beautiful sections of *Combray* in which the reader is introduced to Proust's considerable talents as descriptive writer, sections which, in their controlled lyricism, sound like prose poetry (passages on the hawthorn flowers; the depiction of the contrast between the plain of Roussainville and the aquatic universe of the Vivonne; the evocation of the sunrise with which the narrator concludes the first volume). On the other hand, we have the narrator's love of the theater and of the celebrated actress, La Berma; the early encounter with the writer Bergotte, whom the narrator will admire and emulate in the first phase of his artistic apprenticeship; the enigmatic musician Vinteuil, a modest provincial piano teacher whose compositions will revolutionize French music.

Because Proust constructs his novel as an accumulation of discrete narrative blocks which, in most cases, can stand on their own as isolated and largely self-sufficient episodes, it could be tempting to the reader to separate, in his or her mind, the nature from the culture passages, and to view them as equally important yet intrinsically different in their emphases and in their thematic content. This would be a mistake, and an impoverishment of the textual complexity that characterizes the *Recherche*. One passage in particular, quite possibly the most controversial one in *Combray*, the one that shocked many early readers in its frank presentation of a sexual situation,[9] is based upon an intertwining of the nature and culture motifs and on a thought-provoking overlap of the aesthetic and ethical domains. As I conclude my discussion of *Combray*, I should like to look briefly at that pivotal scene and examine its implications for the novel as a whole.

Large sections of *Combray* are presented as mini-narratives of discovery, in which the young protagonist, taking walks in and around the small town, seeks to understand the people and places he encounters. Proust endows these excursions with a certain geographical symbolism, in that he has his narrator explain, midway through the first volume, that there are two (and apparently only two) "ways" in which one can go for a walk – "in such opposite directions that in fact we left our house by different doors when we wanted to go one way or the other: the Méséglise-la-Vineuse way, which we also called the way by Swann's because we passed in front of M. Swann's estate when we went in that direction, and the Guermantes way" (*S* I, 135). The way by Swann's is a plain, whereas the Guermantes way takes the narrator and his family by the Vivonne river. The differences that distinguish these two universes – in geographical particularity, in flora and fauna – appear absolute in the mind of the child, and make of them irreconcilable places between which it would be impossible to establish any lines of communication. Much later in the novel, the adult narrator discovers that the two "ways" are, in fact, amenable to being linked and bridged, and this discovery will form part of his reflections on the possibility of establishing an aesthetic unity for the apparently fragmented course of his life.

In the earliest moments of the text, however, the way by Swann's is an arid path in which the narrator discovers the frustrations and temporary ecstasy of sexual desire. It is in a walk in this direction on a particularly warm day that he witnesses an unexpected and peculiar scene (*R* I, 157–63; *S* I, 159–66) which is to have a major thematic resonance for the rest of the *Recherche*. In a rather brusque act of temporal foreshortening, the narrator informs his readers that this particular walk takes place "a few years later" (*S* 1, 159) in the scheme of things, and, in a repetition of the parenthetical device that had been used for Aunt Léonie, he lets us know, casually and in passing, that M. Vinteuil, into whose home we are about to peer voyeuristically, "had died a short time before" (*S* 1, 160). What we are about to witness is a strange ritual involving Vinteuil's daughter and her female friend, in which nature and culture wage a curious form of theatrical conflict before achieving a complex resolution.

To say that the narrator presents the scene theatrically is an understatement: the scene *is* pure theater, with the narrator occupying the place of the audience, hidden immediately outside the illuminated windows of the house, while the two young women enact a drama of their own making. There are two interrelated strands woven into the development of the episode: the nascent sexual desire of Mlle Vinteuil, the boyish daughter of the musician, for her more experienced lesbian friend; and the profanation ritual to which they submit M. Vinteuil, as they insult his memory and spit on his photograph. What is clear from the cautious words with which the narrator frames the scene is that the shock value of what he calls the young women's "liturgical" language (*S* 1, 163) and ritualistic actions should not be overestimated, but should be seen as a screen for more profound, tender emotions. The sheer evidence of cruelty and of sadistic theatrics masks a powerful love that has not found its mode of expression. The reason for the discrepancy between dramatic appearance and psychological reality resides in the difficulty pleasure, as expression of the fulfillment of a natural desire, has in extricating itself from the strictures that accompany a classical conception of good and evil, which are defining features of Christian culture. In his concluding commentary, which possesses a distinctive Baudelairian flavor, the narrator explains:

Mais, au-delà de l'apparence, dans le coeur de Mlle Vinteuil, le mal, au début du moins, ne fut sans doute pas sans mélange. Une sadique comme elle est l'artiste du mal, ce qu'une créature entièrement mauvaise ne pourrait être car le mal ne lui serait pas extérieur, il lui semblerait tout naturel, ne se distinguerait même pas d'elle; et la vertu, la mémoire des morts, la tendresse filiale, comme elle n'en aurait pas le culte, elle ne trouverait pas un plaisir sacrilège à les profaner. Les sadiques de l'espèce de Mlle Vinteuil sont des êtres si purement sentimentaux, si naturellement vertueux que même le plaisir sensuel leur paraît quelque chose de mauvais, le privilège des méchants. (*R* I, 162)

But beyond appearances, even in Mlle Vinteuil's heart, the evil, in the beginning at least, was probably not unmixed. A sadist of her sort is an artist of evil, something that an entirely bad creature could not be, for then evil would not be exterior to her, it would seem to her quite natural, would not even be distinguishable from her; and as for virtue, memory of the dead and filial tenderness, since she would not be devoutly attached to them she would take no sacrilegious pleasure in profaning them. Sadists of Mlle Vinteuil's sort are beings so purely sentimental, so naturally virtuous that even sensual pleasure seems to them something bad, the privilege of the wicked. (*S* 1, 164–65)

In its initial presentation within the pages of the *Recherche,* homosexual love is depicted as a theatrical, that is, cultural, phenomenon. It develops through mediation, indirection, ritualized language and gestures, at a distance from nature and the natural satisfaction of the senses in physical pleasure. Proust will develop his ideas on the topic of homosexuality at much greater length later in the novel, but the highly mediated quality of homosexual relations will remain a constant in the narrator's reflections and in the actions of the characters, both male and female, who are or who are revealed to be homosexual as the novel progresses. In the imaginary universe of the *Recherche,* the idea of a utopian natural space that would have existed prior to the irruption or interruption of culture in the specific domain of sexual relations is subjected to skeptical scrutiny. For Proust, homosexuality is part of, coextensive with, cultural modes of expression. The homosexual lover, like the creator of the *Recherche,* is an artist in search of a language to express the calculated modalities of his or her desire.

UN AMOUR DE SWANN [*A LOVE OF SWANN'S*]

The second section of *Du Côté de chez Swann* is a 200-page novella whose form differs quite noticeably from the remainder of the novel, but whose thematic content prefigures the major aesthetic and ethical concerns that occupy center stage throughout the *Recherche.* Unlike the rest of the text, *Un Amour de Swann* is told in the third person by an omniscient narrator, the same narrator who relates his own thoughts and experiences in the first person elsewhere in the work. The tightly constructed narrative establishes the base-line for the rest of the novel in three crucial thematic areas: the Proustian theory of love as it manifests itself in the jealous possessiveness of the lover and the elusive and mendacious object of his affections; the importance of art (in this case, both pictorial art and music) as domain of aesthetic transcendence; the role played by social setting or context in its relation to both the evolution of love and the revelations of art.

The social setting of the novella is that of the bourgeois *salon* in which men of professional accomplishment are brought together with a limited number of women (only the female protagonist, Odette de Crécy, is subject to lengthy description and psychological analysis) in their common love of the fine arts, cuisine, convivial excursions into the outskirts of Paris, and what they presume to be witty conversation. This milieu stands in marked contrast to the aristocratic *salons* that form the backdrop of the narrator's own gradual and sometimes vexed social apprenticeship. Yet just as the smallest and least differentiated invertebrate shares characteristics to be found at much higher levels of the evolutionary chain, in the same way the laws that govern the *petit clan* (*R* I, 185) organized and jealously guarded by M. and Mme Verdurin can be seen to function in the sumptuous apartments and châteaux of dukes and duchesses.

The first and fundamental law governing the *petit clan* is that of unconditional adhesion to the group. Those members and potential members of the group are continually put to the test by Mme Verdurin, otherwise known as the "boss" or "manager" (*la Patronne*), who will not tolerate a lack of "fidelity" to the "little set" or "little circle" (*S* 1, 191) she has taken great pains to put together. Proust adds a humorous flavor to his analysis of the Verdurin circle by comparing it, metaphorically, to the army (new members are "recruits") and to the church (they are "faithful" (*fidèles*) in the ecclesiastical sense, worshipping at the same altar of values and of taste). Underneath the facile witticisms of some and the aesthetic pretensions of others, underneath the indirect forms of conduct and of language that constitute a complex hieroglyphics to be deciphered by each adherent to the group, lies one brutal alternative: as a putative member of the "clan," you are continually in danger of exclusion. You are in or you are out; there is no in-between.

The stark alternative of inclusion versus exclusion is the structural foundation of *Un Amour de Swann*, a story with the simplest of plots which Proust uses to express the most convoluted of emotions. Charles Swann, whom we met as an older man in *Combray* and who, at the beginning of the novel, stood in the way of the narrator's obtaining his mother's good-night kiss, enters the Verdurin "clan" through the intercession of one of its "faithful," Odette de Crécy. Although he is not physically attracted to her at first, he falls in love with Odette, and because he loves her, becomes enamored of the Verdurins and converts to their social and aesthetic faith, blinding himself voluntarily yet only temporarily to their ridiculous mode of behavior and lamentable artistic taste. Halfway through the story, after he has consummated his love for Odette and after their relationship has become habitual, ritualized, the narrator introduces a new character named Forcheville, who becomes Swann's rival for Odette's affections. Forcheville eventually displaces and deposes the protagonist, who, having fallen from Odette's graces, is also expelled from the "clan" through the active intervention of Mme Verdurin.

Swann eventually recovers his social and aesthetic insight, realizes that he has been associating with vulgar and mean-spirited individuals, and enters into a period of depression and disillusionment. On a particular evening, Vinteuil's Sonata for Piano and Violin not only opens up for him the transcendent spaces of art, but also, in reawakening memories of his past happiness with Odette, serves to reveal that the feelings he once had for her are now a thing of the past. Shortly thereafter he discovers details about Odette's past liaisons, heterosexual and homosexual, which contribute to his suspicion that he had never truly known her, never understood the emotional abyss of her affective life. The novella ends with a comical, pseudo-Freudian dream and with Swann's disabused exclamation: "To think that I wasted years of my life, that I wanted to die, that I felt my deepest love, for a woman who did not appeal to me, who was not my type!" (*S* 1, 383).

The ironical tone of the narrative's last sentence, coupled with the moments of high comedy that characterize many of the descriptions of social events, in no way undermine the seriousness with which Proust, through his relation of Swann's adventures and misadventures, establishes a subtle, differentiated theory of love. This theory, which emerges in stepwise fashion as the text evolves, has as its foundational moment the initial presentation of love as a human relationship which is constructed and mediated rather than spontaneous and immediate in its effects. Whereas we are told, at the beginning of the story, that Swann's past liaisons had been with women whom he had found sensually appealing and who corresponded to a certain physical type, that part of the protagonist's existence is invisible to us readers. The only relationship we witness in *Un Amour de Swann* is one in which a woman who does not correspond to this physical type becomes gradually desirable through a psychological phenomenon which, throughout the text, is called an "association of ideas." Following is the narrator's first development of this topic:

> Autrefois on rêvait de posséder le cœur de la femme dont on était amoureux; plus tard sentir qu'on possède le cœur d'une femme peut suffire à vous en rendre amoureux. Ainsi, à l'âge où il semblerait, comme on cherche surtout dans l'amour un plaisir subjectif, que la part du goût pour la beauté d'une femme devait être la plus grande, l'amour peu naître, l'amour le plus physique, sans qu'il y ait eu, à sa base, un désir préalable. A cette époque de la vie, on a déjà été atteint plusieurs fois par l'amour; il n'évolue plus seul selon ses propres lois inconnues et fatales, devant notre coeur étonné et passif. Nous venons à son aide, nous le faussons par la mémoire, par la suggestion. En reconnaissant un de ses symptômes, nous nous

rappelons, nous faisons renaître les autres. Comme nous possédons sa chanson, gravée en nous tout entière, nous n'avons pas besoin qu'une femme nous en dise le début – rempli par l'admiration qu'inspire la beauté – pour en trouver la suite. (*R* I, 193–94; my emphasis)

At an earlier time one dreamed of possessing the heart of the woman with whom one was in love; later, to feel that one possesses a woman's heart may be enough to make one fall in love with her. And so, at an age when it would seem, since what one seeks most of all in love is subjective pleasure, that the enjoyment of a woman's beauty should play the largest part in it, love may come into being – love of the most physical kind – without there having been, underlying it, any previous desire. At this time of life, one has already been wounded many times by love; it no longer evolves solely in accordance with its own unknown and inevitable laws, before our astonished and passive heart. We come to its aid, we distort it with memory, with suggestion. Recognizing one of its symptoms, we recall and revive the others. Since we know its song, engraved in us in its entirety, we do not need a woman to repeat the beginning of it – filled with the admiration that beauty inspires – in order to find out what comes after. (*S* 1, 199–200; my emphasis)

Although there are certain isolated moments, in the first two volumes of the *Recherche*, in which the narrator is subject to spontaneous feelings of infatuation and incipient sexual desire, for the most part Proust concerns himself with the phenomenon of love as a "song" which is already "engraved in us in its entirety." As the narrator says here in a generalization that remains valid for the novel as a whole, "what one seeks most of all in love is subjective pleasure." The female figures in the *Recherche* – not only Odette here, but Gilberte, the Duchess of Guermantes, and Albertine later on – are not so much desirable in themselves as they are empty vessels into which the narrator projects his own desires and which he surrounds with an aesthetic aura of his own construction. Swann falls in love with Odette because he associates her with works of art – with the "little phrase" of Vinteuil's Sonata for Piano and Violin, and with Botticelli's painting of Jethro's daughter and Moses' wife, Zipporah, as it appears on the ceiling of the Sistine Chapel. Odette, who is a courtesan, a *demi-mondaine* of questionable reputation and highly questionable taste in the arts, gains prestige in Swann's mind as a result of these mental associations.

The passage we have just read, which theorizes love as a subjective construction, might give the impression that the experienced and somewhat "disillusioned" (*désabusé*) lover, because he knows all the words to love's "song," has control over that song, and thus over the love relationship itself. This is not always the case. In one of the most dramatic sequences of the novella, Swann, who has arrived late at the Verdurins' soirée and missed Odette, desperately pursues her in the shadows of nocturnal Paris, and, in the anxiety that grips him, recognizes that his intellectualized passion for her has now become a *need* (*besoin*):

De tous les modes de production de l'amour, de tous les agents de dissémination du mal sacré, il est bien l'un des plus efficaces, ce grand souffle d'agitation qui parfois passe sur nous. Alors l'être avec qui nous nous plaisons à ce moment-là, le sort en est jeté, c'est lui que nous aimerons. Il n'est même pas besoin qu'il nous plût jusque-là plus ou même autant que d'autres. Ce qu'il fallait, c'est que notre goût pour lui devînt exclusif. Et cette condition-là est réalisée quand – à ce moment où il nous fait défaut – à la recherche des plaisirs que son agrément nous donnait, s'est brusquement substitué en nous *un besoin anxieux, qui a pour objet cet être même*, un besoin absurde, que les lois de ce monde rendent impossible à satisfaire et difficile à guérir – le besoin insensé et douloureux de le posséder. (*R* I, 227; my emphasis)

Of all love's modes of production, of all the disseminating agents of the holy evil, surely one of the most efficacious is this great breath of agitation which sometimes blows down on us. Then the die is cast, and the person whose company we enjoy at the time is the one we will love. It is not even necessary for us to have liked him better than anyone else up to then, or even as much. What is necessary is that our predilection for him should become exclusive. And that condition is fulfilled when – at a moment like this, when we do not have him with us – the quest for the pleasures that his charm gave us is suddenly replaced in us by *an anxious need whose object is this person himself*, an absurd need which the laws of this world make impossible to satisfy and difficult to cure – the senseless and painful need to possess him. (*S* 1, 233–34; my emphasis)

The gradual and regular narrative progression of Swann's love for Odette – from an initial intellectual construction by association of ideas to a final vicious circle of lies informed by an unquenched jealousy – has the inexorable quality of classical tragedy (the large role played by jealousy in the novella reminds one of *Phèdre*, the play by Jean Racine [1639–99] which Proust admired precisely for its depiction of the heroine's jealous rage, and which the narrator quotes on multiple occasions in the *Recherche*). Yet the tragic tonality that accompanies the theme of love is counterbalanced by the feelings of joy and atemporal ecstasy experienced by the narrator when he makes the discovery of Vinteuil's music. In an important sense, the entirety of *Un Amour de Swann* can be understood as a combat between the disillusionment resulting from social and amorous experiences on the one hand, and the intimations of a higher, unworldly happiness, on the other.

From the beginning of the novella, Swann had associated the "little phrase" of Vinteuil's Sonata for Piano and Violin with Odette, and the sonata itself had become the emblem, or "national anthem" (*S* 1, 221) of their love. Yet whereas the sonata had appeared only briefly and fragmentarily in the earlier sections of the narrative development, it makes what one might call a major theatrical "entrance" at a crucial point during the soirée organized by the Marquise de Saint-Euverte (*R* I, 316–47; *S* 1, 324–55). After being expelled from the *petit clan*, thinking that he may never see Odette again, Swann hears the "little phrase" emerging from the background of the music performed at the soirée. Through its association with Odette, the musical phrase reawakens his past love for her, in a way that reminds the reader of the *petite madeleine* scene:

Mais tout à coup ce fut comme si elle [Odette] était entrée, et cette apparition lui fut une si déchirante souffrance qu'il dut porter la main à son cœur ... Et avant que Swann eût eu le temps de comprendre, et de se dire: "C'est la petite phrase de la sonate de Vinteuil, n'écoutons pas!" tous ses souvenirs du temps où Odette était éprise de lui, et qu'il avait réussi jusqu'à ce jour à maintenir invisibles dans les profondeurs de son être, trompés par ce brusque rayon du temps d'amour qu'ils crurent revenu, s'étaient réveillées et, à tire-d'aile, étaient remontés lui chanter éperdument, sans pitié pour son infortune présente, les refrains oubliées du bonheur. (*R* I, 339)

But suddenly it was as though she [Odette] had appeared in the room, and this apparition caused him such harrowing pain that he had to put his hand on his heart ... And before Swann had time to understand, and say to himself: "It's the little phrase from the sonata by Vinteuil; don't listen!" all his memories of the time when Odette was in love with him, which he had managed until now to keep out of sight in the deepest part of himself, deceived by this sudden beam of light from the time of love which they believed had returned, had awoken and flown swiftly back up to sing madly to him, with no pity for his present misfortune, the forgotten refrains of happiness. (*S* 1, 347)

In the same way that an involuntary act of remembrance, through the chance encounter of present and past taste sensations, opened the doors to the narrator's past in the scene of the *petite madeleine*, here the fortuitous appearance of the "little phrase" at a moment in which it was least expected has the capacity to reawaken Swann's love for Odette. Just as the pivotal scene in *Combray* was based, philosophically, on a clear conceptual opposition between involuntary versus voluntary memory, where the former is valued positively and the latter negatively, in the same way here, the narrator provides us with a clear distinction – between the "abstract" (which corresponds to the "voluntary") and the "essential" (which corresponds to the "involuntary"):

Au lieu des *expressions abstraites* "temps où j'étais heureux," "temps où j'étais aimé," qu'il avait souvent prononcées jusque-là et sans trop souffrir, car son intelligence n'y avait enfermé du passé que de prétendus extraits qui n'en conservaient rien, il retrouva tout ce qui de ce bonheur perdu avait fixé à jamais *la spécifique et volatile essence.* (*R* I, 339–40; my emphasis)

In place of the *abstract expressions* "the time when I was happy," "the time when I was loved," which he had often used before now without suffering too much, for his mind had enclosed within them only spurious extracts of the past that preserved nothing of it, he now recovered everything which had fixed for ever *the specific, volatile essence* of that lost happiness. (*S* I, 347–48; my emphasis)

It is important for the reader of the *Recherche* to understand, from the earliest phase of the novel, that Proust situates the fine arts – music, painting, theater, and creative writing – in the domain of "essences." What art, in the large sense of that term, reveals to us is something that precedes or exceeds the contingencies of everyday existence, of the habitual actions in which our lives are enmeshed. Yet it is very difficult to disengage art from existence. In Proust's imaginary universe, art does not exist detached from worldly concerns, but embedded in them, which is why, in its initial manifestation, Vinteuil's "little phrase" is bound up with Swann's love for Odette by an association of ideas. In the final pages of his description of the soirée at Mme de Saint-Euverte's, however, the narrator turns from his examination of the ways in which the musical phrase evokes the essence of Swann's love toward an evocation of that other world (i.e., the world beyond that of our habitual existence) which is created by the musician. It is in his description of this particular universe that Proust writes some of his most beautiful sentences about art as transcendent realm which reveals to us what would otherwise be the dark and unexplored emptiness of our soul:

[Swann] savait que ... le champ ouvert au musicien n'est pas un clavier mesquin de sept notes, mais un clavier incommensurable, encore presque tout entier inconnu, où seulement çà et là, séparées par d'épaisses ténèbres inexplorées, quelques-unes des millions de touches de tendresse, de passion, de courage, de sérénité, qui le composent, chacune aussi différente des autres qu'un univers d'un autre univers, ont été découvertes par quelques grands artistes qui nous rendent le service, en éveillant en nous le correspondant du thème qu'ils ont trouvé, de nous montrer quelle richesse, quelle variété, cache à notre insu cette grande nuit impénétrée et décourageante de notre âme que nous prenons pour du vide et pour du néant. Vinteuil avait été l'un de ces musiciens. (*R* I, 343–44)

[Swann] knew that ... the field open to the musician is not a miserable keyboard of seven notes, but an immeasurable keyboard still almost entirely unknown on which, here and there only, separated by shadows thick and unexplored, a few of the millions of keys of tenderness, of passion, of courage, of serenity which compose it, each as different from the others as one universe from another universe, have been found by a few great artists who do us the service, by awakening in us something corresponding to the theme they have discovered, of showing us what richness, what variety, is hidden unbeknownst to us within that great unpenetrated and disheartening darkness of our soul which we take for emptiness and nothingness. Vinteuil had been one of those musicians. (*S* I, 351–52)

As a repository for many of the grand themes of Proust's seven-volume novel, the microcosm of *Un Amour de Swann* puts into play the three large elements that jostle for supremacy throughout the text: society and its laws of inclusion and exclusion; love in its links to anxiety, jealousy, and mendacity; and the arts in their promise of aesthetic awakening and spiritual enrichment. As an inheritor of the tradition of nineteenth-century realism, as avid reader of Honoré de Balzac (1799–1850) and Gustave Flaubert (1821–80), Proust refused to espouse the conception of *l'art pour l'art*, or art for art's sake, firmly situating his characters and his story in a finely differentiated social space against which the psychodrama of their passions could be played out. At the same time, the author of the *Recherche* posited the existence of a separate world of art possessed of its own laws which communicates somehow with the largely unexplored inner treasury of our souls. Although art does not exist in our world, it cannot exist without that world. What art does is to open up areas of human potentiality by creating a language of its own, a language whose specificity and particularity it is the reader/interpreter's task to understand.

NOMS DE PAYS: LE NOM [*PLACE-NAMES: THE NAME*]

At a slim forty-five pages, the third and final section of *Du Côté de chez Swann* seems strangely detached from *Combray* and *Un Amour de Swann*, even to modern-day readers: it had to have been quite puzzling, both structurally and thematically, in 1913. This short episode is itself divided into three apparently disjointed parts, which the Pléiade editors provide with the following useful subtitles: "Rêverie sur des noms de pays" ("Day-dreaming about some place-names"); "Aux Champs-Elysées" ("On the Champs-Elysées"); and "Mme Swann au Bois" ("Mme Swann in the Bois" [i.e., the Bois de Boulogne, a forested area immediately to the west of Paris proper]). Structurally, it is impossible for the reader to understand "Rêverie sur des noms de pays" without having read *Noms de pays: le pays*, the second large section of *A l'Ombre des jeunes filles en fleurs*, situated some 250 pages later in the text. "Aux Champs-Elysées," which presents the young narrator's infatuation with Gilberte, the daughter of Charles Swann and Odette de Crécy (in a typical Proustian plot twist, the woman who was not his "type" eventually, and without narrative explanation, became Swann's wife), is a very short introduction to the much more developed first part of *A l'Ombre des jeunes filles en fleurs*. "Mme Swann au Bois" is one of the most beautiful passages of the novel, in form and in expression quite close to prose poetry, but whose major function might seem to be more purely aesthetic than thematically meaningful. As is often the case in the *Recherche*, Proust presupposes a second reading of his novel for its structural coherence to emerge in the mind of his reader.

This said, a closer inspection of the episode as a whole reveals that each of the three sub-sections is a variation on the same theme: namely, the difference, or distance, between an object as desired by the human consciousness and that object's concrete reality. Psychologically, this translates into the narrator's sense of deception or disillusionment. Beginning with a naïve belief in the possibility of attaining or possessing the dreamed place or person conjured up in his youthful imagination, the narrator eventually discovers that this place or person does not correspond to his mental projections. In the case of the place-names Balbec (an imaginary town in Normandy), Venice, and Florence, which the narrator, using the evocative potential of their sounds, transforms into fanciful and colorful images, we are provided with the following cautionary narrative anticipation:[10]

Mais si ces noms absorbèrent à tout jamais l'image que j'avais de ces villes, ce ne fut qu'en la transformant, qu'en soumettant sa réapparition en moi à leurs lois propres; ils eurent pour conséquence de la rendre plus belle, mais aussi plus différente de ce que les villes de Normandie ou de Toscane pouvaient être en réalité, et, *en accroissant les joies arbitraires de mon imagination, d'aggraver la déception future de mes voyages.* (*R* I, 380; my emphasis)

But if these names absorbed for ever the image I had of these towns, it was only by transforming that image, by subjecting its reappearance in me to their own laws; in consequence of this they made it more beautiful, but also more different from what the towns in Normandy or Tuscany could be in reality, and, *by increasing the arbitrary joys of my imagination, aggravated the future disappointment of my travels.* (*S* 1, 391; my emphasis)

Remarkably, the same pattern, which consists of the demystification of an original desire or belief, obtains for the love situation as for the act of day-dreaming about place-names. Not all writers equate, at the psychological or structural level, such apparently divergent mental activities as a highly aestheticized day-dreaming on places and the emotionally charged, rather more concrete, first infatuations of an adolescent. Such is, however, the case in Proust's world. The similarity, for Proust, lies in the fundamental importance of *images* for both activities – both their creative and evocative qualities, and their evanescence, that is, their ultimate capacity to disappoint when juxtaposed with reality. In the case of Gilberte, the narrator writes:

Tout le temps que j'étais loin de Gilberte, j'avais besoin de la voir, parce que cherchant sans cesse à me représenter son image, je finissais par ne plus y réussir, et par ne plus savoir exactement à quoi correspondait mon amour … Mais quand j'arrivais aux Champs-Elysées ... dès que j'étais en présence de cette Gilberte Swann sur la vue de laquelle j'avais compté pour rafraîchir les images que ma mémoire fatiguée ne retrouvait plus ... aussitôt tout se passait comme si elle et le fillette qui était l'objet de mes rêves avaient été deux êtres différents. (*R* I, 392–94)

All the time I was away from Gilberte, I needed to see her because, constantly trying to form a picture of her for myself, in the end I could not do it, and no longer knew precisely what the thing was to which my love corresponded ... But when I reached the Champs-Elysées ... as soon as I was in the presence of that Gilberte Swann on the sight of whom I had counted to refresh the images that my tired memory could no longer recapture ... immediately it was as if she and the little girl who was the object of my dreams had been two different creatures. (*S* I, 403–04)

In the final sub-section of *Noms de pays: le nom*, Proust creates a complex meditation on the passing of Time which serves as a general thematic recapitulation for *Du Côté de chez Swann* and as an anticipation of one of the major stumbling-blocks to be encountered by the narrator on his path toward discovering his vocation as writer. In one's search for "lost Time" – the layers and patterns of meaning underlying the past experiences that involuntary memory saves from oblivion – one inevitably runs up against a formidable obstacle which can best be described as the difference or distance between remembered and actual reality, or, as the narrator expresses it more poetically, as "la contradiction que c'est de chercher dans la réalité les tableaux de la mémoire" (*R* I, 419) ["what a contradiction it is to search in reality for memory's pictures" (*S* I, 430)]. Having set out to appreciate what he calls the "composite aggregation" (*S* I, 425) of the Bois de Boulogne as pure aesthetic construction, the narrator gradually comes to the realization that the Bois as particular place is traversed through and through by Time.

Looking in his memory for images of Odette Swann in her elegant horse-drawn carriage, the narrator is confronted with the disenchanted reality of "automobiles driven by moustached mechanics with tall footmen by their sides" (*S* I, 427). Destroyed in this juxtaposition of present to past is his *belief* (*croyance*): "And I no longer had any belief to infuse into all these new elements of the spectacle, to give them substance, unity, life" (*S* I, 428). The destruction of belief, which is another way of expressing the disillusionment stemming from the shattering of one's dreams or desires, occurs within a temporal setting. Within the dimension of time, difference or distance can be called the *fleeting* quality of existence, the fact that, all too often, one's memory cannot catch up with the continually renewed reality of human experience in its concrete actuality. In the final sentences of *Du Côté de chez Swann* the narrator gives voice to the power of the fleeting, *le fugitif* – a power against which the magic of involuntary memory must inevitably struggle and against which this intuitive and creative form of memory cannot easily be victorious:

Les lieux que nous avons connus n'appartiennent pas qu'au monde de l'espace où nous les situons pour plus de facilité. Ils n'étaient qu'une mince tranche au milieu d'impressions contiguës qui formaient notre vie d'alors; le souvenir d'une certaine image n'est que le regret d'un certain instant; et les maisons, les routes, les avenues, sont fugitives, hélas, comme les années. (*R* I, 420)

The places we have known do not belong solely to the world of space in which we situate them for our greater convenience. They were only a thin slice among contiguous impressions that formed our life at that time; the memory of a certain image is only regret for a certain moment; and houses, roads, avenues are as fleeting, alas, as the years. (*S* 1, 430)

CHAPTER 2

A l'Ombre des jeunes filles en fleurs [In the Shadow of Young Girls in Flower]

A l'Ombre des jeunes filles en fleurs, the second volume of *A la recherche du temps perdu*, appeared in 1919, six years after *Du Côté de chez Swann*. Deemed physically unfit for military service, Proust was able to spend the trying years of World War I writing his ever-expanding novel. Once it became possible for Paris publishing houses to resume operations, Proust was in contact with his editor at Gallimard, and began the arduous process of correcting proofs for what would be one of the most beautiful sections of his work. Although *A l'Ombre des jeunes filles en fleurs* initially received mixed reviews, a few short months later, in December 1919, it was awarded the *Prix Goncourt*, the most coveted of France's literary prizes.

The fact that Proust's poetically evocative work received more votes from the Goncourt jury than Roland Dorgelès's *Les Croix de bois*, a patriotic and sentimental novel glorifying the sacrifices of simple men during the war, added an element of controversy to the award, perhaps boosting the sales of a volume that, until that time, enjoyed the esteem of literary connoisseurs more than popular appeal. From 1919 until his death on November 18, 1922, Proust's notoriety as a writer was to increase steadily. During the final years of his life, which were spent in unremitting artistic labor, the appearance of successive volumes of the *Recherche* prompted considerable interest, not only in the French press, but throughout the literary centers of Europe. Whereas the novelty of *Du Côté de chez Swann* had caused at least as much shock as appreciation among its readers, the publication of *A l'Ombre des jeunes filles en fleurs* served to substantiate Proust's reputation as a novelist possessing a coherent aesthetic philosophy, psychological acuity, and a masterful prose style.

The second volume of the *Recherche* is divided into two large narrative blocks. The first is entitled *Autour de Mme Swann* [*At Mme Swann's*]; it takes place in Paris during the early adolescence of the narrator, who, initially pursuing Gilberte as the object of his incipient infatuation,

3 Grand-Hôtel de Cabourg, Normandy

eventually turns his attention to Gilberte's mother, formerly known to the reader as Odette de Crécy, now the wife of Charles Swann. The second section is entitled *Noms de pays: le pays* [*Place-names: The Place*]; it takes place in the fictitious Norman seaside resort called Balbec two years after the narrator has fallen out of love with Gilberte, and constitutes a symmetrical echo or "response" to the final episode of *Du Côté de chez Swann*, *Noms de pays: le nom* [*Place-names: The Name*]. Because of their geographical and chronological separation, the two sections might appear, at first, to be self-enclosed units; in fact, the second part builds upon the first and develops a number of its major themes. In this chapter, I shall be concerned with tracing some of the continuities that link the two parts, as well as with underlining the ways in which, beginning with *A l'Ombre*, Proust places his novel under the aegis of the *Bildungsroman* (novel of education or development, following in the wake of Goethe's *Wilhelm Meisters Lehrjahre* [1795–96] and Flaubert's *L'Education sentimentale* [1869]).

The education or development of the protagonist occurs not only through life experience (his progressive initiation into aristocratic society, his adventures and misadventures in love, the obstacles he encounters in the path of his self-realization or self-actualization), but also in the domain of the arts (theater, music, painting, writing). As Gérard Genette stated it in his technical study of narrative, or "narratology," if all works of literature can be considered amplifications of grammatical structures, then it might be possible (perhaps with a small dose of humor) to say that the entirety of the *Recherche* is a vastly magnified development of the sentence: *Marcel devient écrivain* ["Marcel," the narrator, becomes a writer].[1] Although the concrete decision to write does not occur until the concluding pages of the novel's final volume, the narrator's elective affinities with the arts become increasingly apparent with each successive volume, and are subject to substantial development in *A l'Ombre*. It is in this volume that his admiration for the actress La Berma opens up the world of the theater to him; it is here that he reads and encounters the celebrated writer Bergotte; and it is in this section of the novel that he visits the atelier of the contemporary artist Elstir, who initiates him into the laws of painterly composition whereby reality is transmuted into its aesthetic equivalent or analogon. The novel's second volume depicts the opening of the narrator's eyes onto the world of appearances, of phenomena as they initially detach themselves from their surroundings, offering themselves to the narrator's intellectual curiosity and aesthetic appreciation. It is also the story of the confrontation of idealized expectations with a disenchanted reality, a story that is told in parallel in the three large areas that dominate the *Recherche*: society, love, and art. I shall be attentive to each of these areas as I turn now to an examination of the volume's two sections.

AUTOUR DE MME SWANN [*AT MME SWANN'S*]

Society

The story of the narrator's infatuation with Gilberte, which in many ways prefigures his later, more developed love for Albertine, is inseparable from the gradual progress he makes in gaining admittance to the social milieu in which M. and Mme Swann gravitate. The fashionable apartment in which they live, which is initially presented as a charmed and inaccessible domain, eventually opens itself up to the narrator, allowing him to penetrate its secrets. In his description of the slow process whereby the forbidden becomes the familiar, Proust returns to the grand theme of exclusion versus inclusion that had been the basis for the social setting in *Un Amour de Swann*. Once admitted to the previously prohibited space, the narrator experiences feelings of euphoria and triumph. These are accompanied by a comical inversion of the role played by the guardian of that coveted space, the "implacable concierge" who, formerly viewed as a vengeful Fury poised to exercise his wrath upon the foolishly intrepid young man, now, like one of the Eumenides in the *Oresteia* of Aeschylus (525–456 BC), has been transformed into a benevolent deity presiding over the opening of the house to the young suitor for whom it holds no more secrets (*S* 2, 78). This reversal in amorous fortunes is conveyed, symbolically, by the narrator's change of position with respect to the windows of the Swanns' apartment: no longer facing them from the street as supplicant, he is now behind them, looking down upon arriving guests, who can easily mistake him for a relative of their hosts:

> Les fenêtres qui du dehors interposaient entre moi et les trésors qui ne m'étaient pas destinés un regard brillant, distant et superficiel qui me semblait le regard même des Swann, il m'arriva, quand à la belle saison j'avais passé tout un après-midi avec Gilberte dans sa chambre, de les ouvrir moi-même pour laisser entrer un peu d'air et même de m'y pencher à côté d'elle, si c'était le jour de réception de sa mère, pour voir arriver les visites qui souvent, levant la tête en descendant de voiture, me faisaient bonjour de la main, me prenant pour quelque neveu de la maîtresse de maison. (*R* I, 494)
>
> Soon, when I had spent a whole summer afternoon in Gilberte's room, it fell to me to open the very windows which, from the outside, had once interposed between me and treasures not meant for me a gleaming, haughty and superficial glance, which had seemed like the gaze of the Swanns themselves; yet now I was the one to let some fresh air in or even, if it was her mother's at-home day, to lean out alongside Gilberte and see the ladies as they arrived, stepping out of a carriage and sometimes glancing up to wave to me, as though thinking I was a nephew of their hostess. (*S* 2, 78)

This particular moment in the first section of *A l'Ombre des jeunes filles en fleurs* is emblematic of those rare but emotionally charged epiphanies which recur with some frequency throughout the novel, in which the narrator, fleetingly, believes he has overcome the obstacles interposed between his desires and their fulfillment. Much as in Balzac's *Le Père Goriot* [*Old Goriot*] (1835), doors (or, in this case, windows) that had been closed to a naïve but enterprising young protagonist eventually open magically, as if a charm had been broken, in a repetition of the "Open Sesame" motif from the *Arabian Nights*.[2] In reality, however, these moments are few and far between in each of the three broad thematic areas of the *Recherche* – society, art, and love. The narrator's temporary position in Gilberte's room, behind the windows looking down upon Mme Swann's guests, resembles the experience of the *petite madeleine* both in its tone of euphoria and in its evanescence. Not many pages later, the narrator's gradual disenchantment with Gilberte will begin, and he will find himself, like the unhappy protagonist of *Un Amour de*

Swann, expelled from the small and intimate circle in which he thought he would find happiness.

The narrator's mistake, in the social context, is to think that the environment he has temporarily penetrated is stable, that its *dramatis personae* are known quantities. In fact, according to the narrator's theoretical ruminations on the laws governing social groups, not only is each person in a group subject to dramatic shifts in status, but the groups themselves as larger structures form incessantly changing "figures" according to external political and social factors, thus subjecting individuals to a dizzying, "kaleidoscopic" series of wrenching upheavals. The narrator first broaches this general topic in his explanation of the reasons that underlie Mme Swann's acceptance in "official" society, while "fashionable ladies" refuse to frequent her *salon* (*S* 2, 91):

Les personnes [de la société conservatrice] … s'imaginaient que l'impossibilité de jamais inviter un "opportuniste," à plus forte raison un affreux "radical," était une chose qui durerait toujours, comme les lampes à huile et les omnibus à chevaux. *Mais pareille aux kaléidoscopes qui tournent de temps en temps, la société place successivement de façon différente des éléments qu'on avait crus immuables et compose une autre figure.* Je n'avais pas encore fait ma première communion, que des dames bien pensantes avaient la stupéfaction de rencontrer en visite une Juive élégante. Ces dispositions nouvelles du kaléidoscope sont produites par ce qu'on philosophe appellerait un changement de critère. Dreyfus en amena un nouveau, à une époque un peu postérieure à celle où je commençais à aller chez Mme Swann, et le kaléidoscope renversa une fois de plus ses petits losanges colorés. (*R* I, 507–08; my emphasis)

Those [from conservative society] … were convinced that the impossibility of ever inviting an Opportunist, let alone an unspeakable Radical, was something which would last for ever, like oil-lamps and horse-trams. *But after the manner of kaleidoscopes which are turned from time to time, society composes new designs by jumbling the order of elements which once seemed immutable.* By the time I had taken my first communion, prim and proper ladies were being confronted, to their astonishment, with elegant Jewesses in some of the houses they frequented. These new designs in the kaleidoscope are made by what a philosopher would call a change of criterion. Another of these was to come with the Dreyfus Affair, at a time which was slightly later than my first entry into the world of Mme Swann, and again the kaleidoscope shuffled its little tinted shapes. (*S* 2, 91–92; my emphasis)

The changes in the social "kaleidoscope" are a leitmotif in Proust's novel. Adumbrated in this passage is the notion that, every decade or so, the mysterious, indefinable "criteria" by which admission to a social circle is granted shift, allowing new access to certain groups, while others fade from view. The first era alluded to is the earliest stage of the Third Republic, shortly after Proust's birth. The "Opportunists" referred to in the quoted passage were led by Léon Gambetta (1838–82), and included both Charles Louis de Saulces de Freycinet (1828–1923) and Jules Ferry (1832–93). As advocates of a gradual integration of all classes of society into the newly formed Republic, they would be called pragmatists today. The strategy of opportunism lasted roughly from 1879 until 1885, but could not withstand the polarization of the French citizenry and an increased stretching of the political spectrum from far right to far left. The Dreyfus Affair, with its current of anti-Semitism, occupied the social scene and caused Parisian *salons* to change in character, from 1894 until 1906. Proust integrated the Affair and the multifaceted and cruel manifestations of anti-Semitism into the middle sections of the *Recherche*. A social generation later the effects of World War I impinged upon a decadent aristocracy; Proust inserted a development on these changes into the first section of *Le Temps retrouvé* [*Finding Time Again*], toward the end of the text.

In a general sense, the *Recherche* chronicles the rise of the bourgeoisie set against the twilight of the dying aristocracy (the vulgar social *arriviste*, Mme Verdurin, is "reincarnated" as the Princesse de Guermantes after World War I, at the conclusion of the novel), while it simultaneously describes the ways in which Jewish high society was at times parallel to but separate from society at large, at other times integrated into its fabric. The general Proustian law that accounts for social change is based not on logic, the effects of causality, or continuity, but on upheaval, disjunction, inexplicable reversals, and changes in "criteria" that are both dazzling and blinding to the observer.

Art

In the domain of the fine arts, *A l'Ombre des jeunes filles en fleurs* provides a practical testing ground for the aesthetic day-dreaming on place-names with which Proust had concluded *Du Côté de chez Swann*. In conjuring up idealized images of Florence, Venice, and Balbec, the young narrator had imagined each of these places as unified blocks of significance sculpted monochromatically, according to the associative resonance their phonetic composition evoked in his impressionable mind. Each city possessed its own distinct "color"; each city, much like a person, possessed what one could call an individuality or personality. But if places are like people, people are also like places in the imaginary universe of the *Recherche*. Characters appear initially as cut from one cloth, as having certain essential qualities that are invariable and that distinguish them with absolute clarity from others. This is true not only for the striving bourgeois and self-satisfied aristocrats we meet in the social sphere, but also (or perhaps, especially) for those artists who act as mentors and as intercessors for the narrator as he undertakes his long aesthetic apprenticeship. Two such figures who play important roles in the first part of *A l'Ombre* are the actress La Berma and the writer Bergotte.

In the same way that the apparent unitary significance of the placename "Balbec" will be tested in the second half of the volume, in its first half the narrator is forced to confront his idealized and simplified imaginings of the "essential" actress and writer with their actual physical beings, and with their respective artistic talents as they manifest themselves in the world – that is, not in abstraction, but in real space and in human time. What had seemed to be unified in the aesthetic realm turns out to be just as "kaleidoscopic" as the social world. La Berma and Bergotte as fictional figures are composed of disparate constitutive personality traits; the nature of their artistry is, at first glance, opaque to the narrator. In his encounters with them, the narrator is compelled to "read" La Berma and Bergotte in a progressive series of attempts and to compose his assessment of them from fragmented and mutually contradictory viewings or auditions. As he begins to form his own personal judgment of these artists, the narrator gradually disengages himself from the opinions of others and from received opinion. On the one hand, his discovery of the complexity of La Berma and Bergotte produces an initial disappointment; on the other hand, a close perspective on the specific achievements of each artist leads to theoretical meditations on the creative process as it occurs in real time. These meditations on aesthetic innovation provide an interesting counterpoint to the large theme of deception or disillusionment.

In the case of La Berma, the evolution of the narrator's sentiments – from idealization to initial deception to a modified form of appreciation – occurs in a series of clearly delineated steps. First, the narrator postulates the "indivisible" talent of La Berma, the specific location of this talent in time and space. Just as he can only imagine viewing a work by Carpaccio (*c.* 1460–*c.* 1525/26) in Venice, where it was painted, and not transplanted from its place of origin to the Louvre, in the same way La Berma is so tightly associated in his mind with the universe of Racine's *Phèdre* that he cannot imagine her acting in the drama of any other playwright (*R* I, 432–33; *S* 2, 14–15). Second, according to the narrator's belief system, the world in which works of art are created and appreciated possesses a greater reality than the everyday world in which we live. What he expects from the theatrical matinée in which La Berma appears is, in his words, nothing less than "access to truths which dwelt in a realer world than I did, truths which, once glimpsed, could never be taken from me by any of the nugatory incidents making up my futile existence" (*S* 2, 16). Third, however, in a typically Proustian devaluation of suspense, we learn, even before the narrator takes his seat in the theater, that the matinée "was, alas, a great disappointment" (*S* 2, 18). Whereas he had assumed that the physical medium in which Racine's play was to be represented would be transparent and that the female protagonist would be the talented vessel through which aesthetic truths would be revealed, in reality the mode of declamation adopted by La Berma interferes with the narrator's understanding of the author's carefully crafted verses. Both the specificity of La Berma's artistic talent and the significance of Racine's verse become obscured within the spatial and temporal constraints of the play's staging (*R* I, 440–41; *S* 2, 22–23). In a fourth and final stage which emphasizes both the young narrator's disillusionment and his naïveté, he confesses that he only begins to appreciate La Berma's art upon hearing the applause of the audience. Lacking self-confidence in his own aesthetic judgment, he is convinced by the sounds of enthusiastic clapping that what he has just witnessed must have been a memorable performance (*R* I, 441–42; *S* 2, 23).

The narrator's initial reaction to meeting Bergotte is quite similar, in its tone of humorous disillusionment, to his witnessing of La Berma in *Phèdre*. Returning to the theme of names as developed in *Noms de pays: le nom* [*Place-names: The Name*], the narrator describes the comical contortions he is forced to conjure up in order to make the newly discovered physical reality of Bergotte fit into the sanctuary of poetic associations he had constructed around the imagined identity of the man he had always characterized as "my soft-voiced bard with the white hair" (*S* 2, 123). Upon being introduced to the celebrated writer, the narrator undergoes an immediate sensation of shock:

Ce nom de Bergotte me fit tressauter comme le bruit d'un revolver qu'on aurait déchargé sur moi, mais instinctivement pour faire bonne contenance je saluai; devant moi, comme ces prestidigitateurs qu'on aperçoit intacts et en redingote dans la poussière d'un coup de feu d'où s'envole une colombe, mon salut m'était rendu par un homme jeune, rude, petit, râblé et myope, à nez rouge en forme de coquille de colimaçon et à barbiche noire. J'étais mortellement triste, car ce qui venait d'être réduit en poudre, ce n'était pas seulement le langoureux vieillard dont il ne restait plus rien, c'était aussi la beauté d'une œuvre immense que j'avais pu loger dans l'organisme défaillant et sacré que j'avais, comme un temple, construit expressément pour elle. (*R* I, 537–38)

The name "Bergotte" startled me as though it was a shot fired from a gun; but I was already bowing, going through the motions of polite behaviour. There in front of me, bowing back at me, like the conjuror in his tails emerging unscathed, while a dove flies up, from the smoke and dust of a detonation, I saw a stocky, coarse, thick-set, short-sighted man, quite young, with a red bottle-nose and a black goatee. I was heartbroken: it was not only that my gentle old man had just crumbled to dust and disappeared, it was also that for those things of beauty, his wonderful works, which I had once contrived to fit into that infirm and sacred frame, that dwelling I had lovingly constructed like a temple expressly designed to hold them, there was now no room. (*S* 2, 123)

Unlike the episode devoted to La Berma, however, the scene of the narrator's first meeting with Bergotte evolves from a comical to a much more serious tone. In a detailed and subtle analysis of the qualities of Bergotte's conversation, the narrator is led to meditate on what constitutes the writer's originality – i.e., the specificity of his style, which unlocks a fictional universe unlike any other. In this passage, the narrator distinguishes between those epigones of Bergotte who simply imitate the master's style without making it their own and Bergotte himself, who, with each sentence he crafts, inaugurates a new way of seeing the world:

... toute nouveauté ayant pour condition l'élimination préalable du poncif auquel nous étions habitués et qui nous semblait la réalité même, toute conversation neuve, aussi bien que toute peinture, toute musique originales, paraîtra toujours alambiquée et fatigante. Elle repose sur des figures auxquelles nous ne sommes pas accoutumés, le causeur nous paraît ne parler que par métaphores, ce qui lasse et donne l'impression d'un manque de vérité. (Au fond, les anciennes formes de langage avaient été elles aussi autrefois des images difficiles à suivre quand l'auditeur ne connaissait pas encore l'univers qu'elles peignaient. Mais depuis longtemps on se figure que c'était l'univers réel, on se repose sur lui.) (*R* I, 541–42)

... as anything new must first do away with the stereotype we are so used to that we have come to see it as reality itself, any new style of conversation, just like any originality in painting or music, will always seem convoluted and wearisome. We find its structuring figures so unwonted that the talker seems to be nothing more than a metaphor-monger, which fatigues the ear and hints at a lack of truthfulness. (Of course, the earlier speech-forms themselves were once images, which a listener unfamiliar with the world they described had difficulty in grasping. But they have long since come to be taken as the real world, the reliable world.) (*S* 2, 126–28)

With remarkable concision the narrator traces here a narrative of the evolution of the arts, which he relates using physical, psychological, and linguistic references. Physically, when the reader or spectator is confronted with a work that is truly new, he or she experiences fatigue, whereas the repetition of older forms produces a sense of tranquility, or repose. Psychologically, an innovative work of art, in upsetting our world of habit and of routine aesthetic assumptions, causes us to question its truthfulness: we feel that if something is unfamiliar, it must be untrue, which allows us to dismiss the new work without facing its challenges. Linguistically, the narrator compares the history of aesthetic reception, as well as the chronological evolution of art forms through history, to the progression of a poetic figure from its initial shocking and innovative charge through its universal acceptance to its stabilization and "death" in cliché or stereotype.[3]

What Proust is describing here, through the reflections of his narrator, is a law of artistic production and reception which would appear to have a certain regularity and universal validity. Each individual artist, in creating his or her own universe, is subject to this law. In order to innovate, the artist must first forge a language that is new from pre-existing materials, and must attempt to create works that do not succumb to repetition and self-parody. The danger for all artists, which is inherent in all forms of artistic creation, is that the productive metaphors which opened up a new world, through recurrent use, can degenerate into the commonplace idiom that reassures, but does not enlighten, its readers. In creating his own world of metaphorical equivalences, which he both theorizes and puts into practice in the second half of *A l'Ombre*, Proust sets as a challenge for himself the task of a continually renewed linguistic experimentation that would not fall prey to this omnipresent danger.

Love

Long sections of *A la recherche du temps perdu* are devoted to a minute, painstaking analysis of those human desires, projections, and idealizations we group under the one category of "love." If Proust continues to be read, translated, and studied a century after he began the first sketches of his novelistic project, it is in part because his work offers a coherent, if sometimes strange and idiosyncratic theory of love. This theory, which had been presented succinctly in the classical form of a third-person novella in *Un Amour de Swann*, is further developed in the story of the narrator's love for Gilberte, which occupies a substantial portion of *Autour de Mme Swann*. The foundation for the theory, as we have already seen in the case of Charles Swann's obsessive preoccupations with Odette de Crécy, is the subjective nature of love. Put bluntly, we can say that for Proust the object of one's love does not possess qualities that are, in and of themselves, lovable; rather, it is the lover who projects onto his or her beloved an aura of fantasy which is gradually woven into a web of anxiety, need, and jealousy.

Although the physical realm of love – sexuality in its quite diverse manifestations – is by no means absent from the *Recherche*, although sex is described with a directness and honesty not to be found in many of Proust's contemporaries, it must be said that love, including its sexual dimension, is (to quote Proust quoting Leonardo da Vinci) largely a thing of the mind, *cosa mentale*.[4] The presence of the other person is helpful in the obtaining of one's own physical pleasure, but perhaps not absolutely necessary if pleasure as such is in the mind of the desiring subject. This is evident in the one explicitly sexual scene between the narrator and Gilberte, when, as young adolescents beginning to discover the needs of their bodies, they "tussle" in one of the small parks adjoining the Champs-Elysées. In the narrator's words:

… nous luttions, arcboutés … et, au milieu de la gymnastique que je faisais … je répandis, comme quelques gouttes de sueur arrachées par l'effort, mon plaisir auquel je ne pus pas même m'attarder le temps d'en connaître le goût … Peut-être avait-elle obscurément senti que mon jeu avait un autre objet que celui que j'avais avoué, mais n'avait-elle pas su remarquer que je l'avais atteint. Et moi qui craignais qu'elle s'en fût aperçue … j'acceptai de lutter encore, de peur qu'elle pût croire que je ne m'étais pas proposé d'autre but que celui après quoi je n'avais plus envie que de rester tranquille auprès d'elle. (*R* I, 485)

… in that strained posture, we tussled with each other … and, in the middle of all my exertions … like a few drops of sweat produced by the effort, I shed my pleasure, before I even had time to be aware of the nature of it … Perhaps she had obscurely sensed that my antics had an ulterior motive, though she may have been unable to notice that my aim was now fulfilled. However, fearing that she might have detected it … I agreed to wrestle with her again, in case she might think my only purpose, now achieved, had been the pleasure which left me feeling no desire other than to sit quietly beside her. (*S* 2, 68–69)

The final section of *Autour de Mme Swann* is largely a thematic preparation and foreshadowing of the stages of love as they appear in Proust's fictional world: initial infatuation; physical consummation; the gradual transition from passion to habit; jealousy; the combat between obsessive desire and progressive indifference; the resolution to break off relations; ultimate forgetfulness. These stages appear, greatly amplified, in the fifth and sixth volumes of the novel, *La Prisonnière* [*The Prisoner*] and *Albertine disparue* [*The Fugitive*], Albertine having replaced Gilberte in the narrator's affections. In the Gilberte episode the reader discovers for the first time the narrator's intellectualization of love, which expresses itself in complex hesitation, irresolution, and hypothetical musing on what actions might or might not be taken at a particular moment in the evolution of a relationship. Whereas most classical depictions of love show an expectant lover who, facing obstacles, counts the minutes until he can next see his beloved, in Proust's world the lover can be seen extending the time until he next sees the object of his affections, prolonging it in a kind of mental game, much as a scientist might decide, for purely intellectual reasons, to change the conditions of the experiment he is performing. What follows is an interesting, but certainly rather curious, rumination on the advantages of the beloved's *absence* as it relates to general considerations on the "superposed" or "overlaid" levels of motivation in the lover's decision either to break up or to continue his liaison. In this passage we get a first glimpse at Proust's law of "intermittence" in love, which will be developed at much greater length during the narrator's stays at Balbec:

D'ailleurs, si je m'arrangeais toujours, avant d'aller chez Mme Swann, à être certain de l'absence de sa fille, cela tenait peut-être autant qu'à ma résolution d'être brouillé avec elle, à cet espoir de réconciliation qui se superposait à ma volonté de renoncement (bien peu sont absolus, au moins d'une façon continue, dans cette âme humaine dont une des lois, fortifiée par les afflux inopinés de souvenirs différents, est l'intermittence) ... Si je m'étais trouvé face à face avec elle chez sa mère nous aurions peut-être échangé des paroles irréparables qui eussent rendu définitive notre brouille, tué mon espérance et d'autre part en créant une anxiété nouvelle, réveillé mon amour et rendu plus difficile ma résignation. (*R* I, 581)

In always making sure, before I went to Mme Swann's, that Gilberte would be away, I may have been responding not just to my determination to have fallen out with her, but as much to that hope for a reconciliation which overlaid my wish to forgo happiness (few of such wishes are absolute, at least not continuously so, one of the laws of human make-up being intermittence) ... If I had happened to see her while visiting her mother, we might have said something irreparable, which would have made our estrangement definitive and annihilated all hope, while setting off new anguish in me, reawakening my love and making my resignation harder to bear. (*S* 2, 167)

In the hypothetical scenario evoked here, what is avoided is the presence of the beloved in the same space as the lover, or what the narrator, in the last sentence of the quoted passage, calls the absolute and unmediated *face à face* of two subjectivities. The Proustian account of love possesses a melancholy flavor because it postulates the emptiness of the beloved. But this postulation of emptiness may be a convenience for a lover who, being wary or perhaps afraid of a personality independent of his own, simply prefers to live in a universe in which his desires, even when directed outward, inevitably return to their place of origin, not enriched by an encounter with the other, but merely enhanced by the projective powers of his own imagination. The following brief statement, worthy in its pithiness and appeal to generality of the classical *moralistes*, can serve to conclude this brief incursion into the vast domain of Proustian love:

Quand on aime l'amour est trop grand pour pouvoir être contenu tout entier en nous; il irradie vers la personne aimée, rencontre en elle une surface qui l'arrête, le force à revenir vers son point de départ, et c'est ce choc en retour de notre propre tendresse que nous appelons les sentiments de l'autre et qui nous charme plus qu'à l'aller, parce que nous ne reconnaissons pas qu'elle vient de nous. (*R* I, 598)

When we are in love, our love is too vast to be wholly contained within ourselves; it radiates outwards, reaches the resistant surface of the loved one, which reflects it back to its starting-point; and this return of our own tenderness is what we see as the other's feelings, working their new, enhanced charm on us, because we do not recognize them as having originated in ourselves. (*S* 2, 185)

NOMS DE PAYS: LE PAYS [*PLACE-NAMES: THE PLACE*]

The second section of *A l'Ombre des jeunes filles en fleurs* begins with deceptive simplicity: "By the time my grandmother and I left for Balbec, two years later, I had reached a state of almost complete indifference towards Gilberte" (*S* 2, 221). Like the empty temporal spaces, or *blancs*, which Proust admired in Flaubert's novels,[5] the insertion of a two-year hiatus between the Parisian episode centered on Gilberte and Mme Swann and the dramatic shift to the Norman seaside resort of Balbec, in creating some breathing room in the narrative, allows for the presentation and evolution of a more mature narrator-protagonist in the ensuing pages. Whereas the narrator's relationship with Gilberte, with the one exception of the "tussling" scene, was largely confined to platonic day-dreaming, rather innocent conversation, and desultory letter-writing, his involvement with the "young girls in flower" incorporates the urgency of desire and the anxieties of the first-time suitor attempting to interpret the wishes of the young woman, or women, with whom he is falling in love for the first time.

In this part of the story, there is a broadening of the emotional spectrum. The narrator's relationship with his grandmother is developed far beyond the simple outline we observed in *Du Côté de chez Swann*. Added to the now amplified theme of love is the related theme of friendship, which emerges with the introduction of a new character into the novel, Robert de Saint-Loup. Other characters that had been mere caricatures or background figures, Bloch and the Baron de Charlus, become the objects of sustained psychological analysis. The "kaleidoscope" of society turns once again, with the introduction of two new figures – Mme de Villeparisis and the Princesse de Luxembourg – women of the Parisian aristocracy who re-create, in the holiday environment of the Grand-Hôtel de Balbec, a network of encounters and events (excursions, tea parties, dinners, parlor games) that guarantee the preservation of polite social norms in an initially unfamiliar place. The narrator's aesthetic education continues when he meets the painter Elstir and learns new lessons about the intimate but complex connections between material reality and the laws of artistic representation. This section of the novel introduces so many new elements and provides such new depth to previously enunciated themes that the reader's first impression might well be that of an overabundant richness, a treasure house of sensations and experience that defies categorization or classification.

At the same time, however, it is possible to read the entirety of *Noms de pays: le pays* as an intricate series of variations on one common theme: that of habit (or custom – in French, *habitude*). This motif, which Proust first discovered in the fourth chapter of John Ruskin's *Modern Painters II* (1846),[6] is the psychological nodal point around which the second section of *A l'Ombre* organizes itself. In the first two paragraphs of the episode, the narrator theorizes about the multiplicity of "selves" that composes a human being, the different incarnations of the "I" or *moi* which can appear, in defiance of linear chronology, according to the vagaries of the irregular and temporally disseminated passion we call love. The random memory of a particular impression related to Gilberte can cause the narrator, for a fleeting instant, to recover his former self, the self that loved Gilberte but that has now been consigned to forgetfulness (*oubli*). The painful and unpredictable dialectic of memory and forgetfulness is itself related to the larger territory of habit, as the narrator asserts with a quasi scientific air of certainty:

> Or, les souvenirs d'amour ne font pas exception aux lois générales de la mémoire, elles-mêmes régies par les lois plus générales de l'habitude. Comme celle-ci affaiblit tout, ce qui nous rappelle le mieux un être, c'est justement ce que nous avions oublié (parce que c'était insignifiant et que nous lui avions ainsi laissé toute sa force). C'est pourquoi la meilleure part de notre mémoire est hors de nous, dans un souffle pluvieux, dans l'odeur de renfermé d'une chambre ou dans l'odeur d'une première flambée, partout où nous retrouvons de nous-même ce que notre intelligence, n'en ayant pas l'emploi, avait dédaigné, la dernière réserve du passé ... C'est grâce à cet oubli seul que nous pouvons de temps à autre retrouver l'être que nous fûmes, nous placer vis-à-vis des choses comme cet être l'était, souffrir à nouveau, parce que nous ne sommes plus nous, mais lui, et qu'il aimait ce qui nous est maintenant indifférent. (*R* II, 4)
>
> Memories of love are, in fact, no exception to the general laws of remembering, which are themselves subject to the more general laws of habit. Habit weakens all things; but the things which are best at reminding us of a person are those

which, because they were insignificant, we have forgotten and which have therefore lost none of their power. Which is why the greater part of our memory exists outside us, in a dampish breeze, in the musty air of a bedroom or the smell of autumn's first fires, things through which we can retrieve any part of us that the reasoning mind, having no use for it, disdained, the last vestige of the past ... It is only because we have forgotten that we can now and then return to the person we once were, envisage things as that person did, be hurt again, because we are not ourselves any more, but someone else who once loved something that we no longer care about. (*S* 2, 222)

In this passage the narrator is refining and amplifying what he had asserted in the scene of the *petite madeleine*: namely, that the intelligence (translated here as "the reasoning mind"), as instrument of voluntary memory, is unable to connect with the essential experience of our earlier life. The reasoning mind has discarded into forgetfulness those primordial sensations which, in being rediscovered later by chance outside of ourselves, open up previously unimagined passageways to the defining moments of our past. This thread which the involuntary memory uncovers between past and present is tenuous and only occasionally visible. For it to become once more available to consciousness in its essential form, it must first subside and vanish; the "weakening" of habit is the necessary precondition for the reawakened strength of human experience as preserved in memory. At the same time, it is against the inertia of habit that the human being must struggle if he or she is to face that which is new and become capable of moving forward and encountering the problems and obstacles that inhabit the future. Much is at stake, philosophically and psychologically, when the narrator, initially accompanied by his grandmother, gets on a train at Saint-Lazare station and departs on his first voyage – to Balbec. The paragraph immediately preceding the description of the station and the first stages of the voyage constitutes a grand thematic statement which is expressed in a rather percussive allegorizing of habit:

A Paris j'étais devenu de plus en plus indifférent à Gilberte, grâce à l'Habitude. Le changement d'habitude, c'est-à-dire la cessation momentanée de l'Habitude, paracheva l'œuvre de l'Habitude quand je partis pour Balbec. Elle affaiblit mais stabilise, elle amène la désagrégation mais la fait durer indéfiniment. Chaque jour depuis des années je calquais tant bien que mal mon état d'âme sur celui de la veille. A Balbec un lit nouveau à côté duquel on m'apportait le matin un petit déjeuner différent de celui de Paris, ne devait plus soutenir les pensées dont s'était nourri mon amour pour Gilberte: il y a des cas (assez rares, il est vrai) où, la sédentarité immobilisant les jours, le meilleur moyen de gagner du temps, c'est de changer de place. Mon voyage à Balbec fut comme la première sortie d'un convalescent qui n'attendait plus qu'elle pour s'apercevoir qu'il est guéri. (*R* II, 4–5)

In Paris, it was because of Habit that I had become more and more indifferent to Gilberte. The change in my habits, that is the momentary suspension of Habit, put its finishing touch to that process when I set off for Balbec. Habit may weaken all things, but it also stabilizes them; it brings about a dislocation, but then makes it last indefinitely. For years past, I had been roughly modelling my state of mind each day on my state of mind of the day before. At Balbec, breakfast in bed – a different bed, a different breakfast – was to be incapable of nourishing the ideas on which my love for Gilberte had fed in Paris. There are instances, albeit infrequent, in which, the passing days having been immobilized by a sedentary way of life, the best way to gain time is to change place. My journey to Balbec was like the first outing of a convalescent who has not noticed until that moment that he is completely cured. (*S* 2, 222–23)

Balbec

From the moment of his arrival at the Grand-Hôtel de Balbec, when the ceiling of his bedroom must be "lowered" by his mind so that he can fall asleep (*R* II, 26–28; *S* 2, 244–46), to his encounters with Albertine and the other young girls in flower, to the lessons on art which he learns from Elstir, the narrator's sense of comfort, derived from his habitual mode of existence, is continually upset, his preconceived notions of the laws governing society, love, and art, put to the test on a daily basis. Although Proust's novel is by no means to be confused with the realist tradition (he has no intention of attempting to restitute, in his work, an aesthetic equivalent of "things as they are"), perhaps one reason the second half of *A l'Ombre des jeunes filles en fleurs* has been particularly popular with readers is that this painful confrontation with newness in every facet of life rings true as a depiction of adolescence, a short but intense period in which awkwardness, enthusiasm, elation, and disappointment share the same cluttered stage. As is often the case in real-life adolescence, some of those experiences that seem initially most striking, most powerful in their dramatic effects, are those of disappointment, or deception. One such experience occurs during the first section of *Noms de pays: le pays*. Here, the narrator is presented as a reader of signs who is faced with the difficulty of formulating a coherent interpretation of the physical and cultural geography into which he has entered; this landscape appears as a disjointed, fragmented assemblage.[7]

In the episode in question (*R* II, 19–21; *S* 2, 237–39) the narrator discovers that the town of Balbec, which he had imagined as a monumental unit encompassing both its church and the windswept Norman cliffs, is in fact two separate places: Balbec-le-Vieux, or Balbec-en-Terre, the landlocked site of the church with which he had been fascinated as a young boy; and Balbec-Plage, the seaside resort located some fifteen miles away. In the language of semiotics, we would say that the sign of Balbec, Balbec as sign, is split: the signifier, the acoustic image that had evoked, in the mind of the young narrator, one imagined space, is now revealed to designate two separate referents, two places in the world which have nothing in common except the first part of their names. This initial deception is followed by a second one. Whereas the narrator had imagined the church's famous statue, La Vierge du porche [The Virgin of the Porch], as inaccessible to the "vicissitudes" of reality and as possessing a "universal value" (*S* 2, 238), he now discovers it anchored in its context, ensconced in triviality:

Mon esprit … s'étonnait de voir la statue qu'il avait mille fois sculptée, réduite maintenant à sa propre apparence de pierre, occupant par rapport à la portée de mon bras une place où elle avait pour rivales une affiche électorale et la pointe de ma canne, enchaînée à la Place, inséparable du débouché de la grand-rue … soumise à la tyrannie du Particulier … c'était elle enfin l'œuvre d'art immortelle et si longtemps désirée, que je trouvais, métamorphosée ainsi que l'église elle-même, en une petite vieille de pierre dont je pouvais mesurer la hauteur et compter les rides. (*R* II, 20–21)[8]

My mind … was now amazed to see that the statue it had so often sculpted was reduced to nothing but its own shape in stone, cheek by jowl with an election notice, no less reachable than it, no less touchable with the tip of my cane, rooted to the square, inseparable from the junction with the high street … subjected … to the tyranny of the Particular … I now found [her – i.e., the Virgin of the Porch] transformed from the immortal work of art that I had longed to see into a little old woman in stone, whose height I could measure and whose wrinkles I could count. (*S* 238–39)

In the final sentence describing his disillusioning encounter with Balbec-en-Terre, the narrator shows that the name "Balbec," which in his youthful imagination had contained and enclosed a panoply of related images in one narrow sheath, now opens itself up and releases its contents to the outside. The narrator's voyage of discovery, which culminates in the imprudent intrusion into a taboo space, repeats the gesture of Pandora and signals an end to the linguistic illusions and beliefs of childhood:

Mais pour Balbec, dès que j'y étais entré, ç'avait été comme si j'avais entr'ouvert un nom qu'il eût fallu tenir hermétiquement clos et où, profitant de l'issue que je leur avais imprudemment offerte en chassant toutes les images qui y vivaient jusque-là, un tramway, un café, les gens qui passaient sur la place, la succursale du Comptoir d'Escompte, irrésistiblement poussées par une pression externe et une force pneumatique, s'étaient engouffrés à l'intérieur des syllabes qui, refermées sur eux, les laissaient maintenant encadrer le porche de l'église persane et ne cesseraient plus de les contenir. (*R* II, 21)

But with Balbec it felt as though, by going there, I had broken open a name which should have been kept hermetically sealed, and into which, through the breach which I had been ill-advised enough to make, replacing all the images I had allowed to escape from it, a horse-tram, a café, people crossing the square, a branch of the Savings Bank, under the irresistible forces of external pressure and air suction, had rushed into the vacuum left in the syllables, which had now closed upon them, turning them into a frame for the porch of my Persian church, and would never again be rid of them. (*S* 2, 239)

In the Balbec-en-Terre episode, the narrator's childhood imaginings come up against a deromanticized reality, and the cultural object he had valued so much – Balbec church – is wrenched from its idealized abstraction and placed into the trivial context of everydayness. The section concludes with the depiction of a disenchanted world, a place where the linguistic sign splits into opposed meanings. The statue which was thought to possess a pure and unified beauty becomes transformed (*métamorphosée*) into a caricature, a grotesque. Yet it is against this background of disappointment and failure that one of the most important episodes of *A l'Ombre des jeunes filles en fleurs*, the narrator's visit to Elstir's studio, takes place (*R* II, 190–99; *S* 2, 413–22). What happens during these pages constitutes a positive reversal in the narrator's fortunes as would-be apprentice in the arts, and turns on a reversal in the aesthetic value of the very notion of metamorphosis.

Elstir

Located in a middle-class suburban area distant from the center of Balbec in a house which, in its exterior appearance, is completely without distinction, Elstir's studio is a place of wonder and enchantment. Immediately upon entering the dark and cool enclosure of the artist's private space, the narrator experiences a powerful sense of happiness as he discovers the coming into being of a newly created world:

Je me sentis parfaitement heureux, car par toutes les études qui étaient autour de moi, je sentais la possibilité de m'élever à une connaissance poétique, féconde en joies, de maintes formes que je n'avais pas isolées jusque-là du spectacle total de la réalité. Et l'atelier d'Elstir m'apparut comme le laboratoire d'une sorte de nouvelle création du monde. (*R* II, 190)

I was perfectly happy among all the studies ranged about, for I glimpsed in them the possibility that I might rise to a poetic awareness, rich in fulfilling insights for me, of many forms which I had hitherto never distinguished in reality's composite spectacle. Elstir's studio seemed like a laboratory out of which would come a kind of new creation of the world. (*S* 2, 414)

Typical of all the moments of aesthetic revelation in the *Recherche* is the feeling of joy that accompanies the discovery of new truths about the world, as well as the intuition that what one habitually sees in the domain of everyday experience is without organization, without form. What separates the artist from other people is his or her capacity to *create form*. In speaking of "the possibility that I might rise to a poetic awareness," the narrator indicates that the observer or, in a general sense, reader, of artistic works can only understand the artifacts under consideration through a shared participation in the poetic process – poetry here being understood in its Greek etymological origin, as a making or creating. What Elstir offers the narrator is a series of new views onto the world, views which, taken together, constitute an original and irreplaceable reorientation of the eye toward "le spectacle total de la réalité."

In a first glance at the paintings, drawings, and sketches that are scattered around the studio, the narrator does not recognize those works of Elstir's that had become familiar to the public – mythological scenes and compositions betraying a Japanese influence – but finds himself surrounded by seascapes bearing the unmistakable imprint of the location in which they were composed, Balbec. Far from being mimetic or faithful imitations of their environment, however, the seascapes all consist of a transformation, or metamorphosis, of the real into an imaginative construct, which the narrator, borrowing from the linguistic domain, calls "metaphor":

Naturellement, ce qu'il avait dans son atelier, ce n'était guère que des marines prises ici, à Balbec. Mais j'y pouvais discerner que le charme de chacune consistait en une sorte de métamorphose des choses représentées, analogue à celle qu'en poésie on nomme métaphore et que si Dieu le Père avait créé les choses en les nommant, c'est en leur ôtant leur nom, ou en leur en donnant un autre qu'Elstir les recréait. Les noms qui désignent les choses répondent toujours à une notion de l'intelligence, étrangère à nos impressions véritables, et qui nous force à éliminer d'elles tout ce qui ne se rapporte pas à cette notion. (*R* II, 191)

Almost all of the works I could see about me in the studio were, of course, sea-scapes done recently here in Balbec. But I could see that their charm lay in a kind of metamorphosis of the things depicted, analogous to the poetical device known as metaphor, and that, if God the Father had created things by naming them, Elstir recreated them by removing their names, or by giving them another name. The names of things always express a view of the mind, which is foreign to our genuine impressions of them, and which forces us to eliminate from them whatever does not correspond to that view. (*S* 2, 415)

What the narrator describes here relates quite closely to the observations he had made in the *petite madeleine* scene, where he had asserted that the "intelligence," as servant of voluntary memory, was incapable of recovering the essence of the past. In the case of Elstir's imaginary universe, the "intelligence" is linked to the act of conventional naming and, being "foreign to our genuine impressions" of things, is similarly not up to the task of leading the artist or his public to a discovery of the essential relations among things. Authentic art, for Proust, is a recreation of the world, which is to say, a renaming of the world. This renaming is metaphorical in the sense that one term, in being substituted for another, causes a *transfer* or *transport* to take place from one territory to another, whereby conventional frontiers and limits are effaced or abolished (the Greek noun *metaphora* means, literally, a carrying from one place to another, and, metaphorically, a transferring to one word the sense of another). Innovative art is necessarily and inevitably shocking in that it forces its interpreter to see the world in its initial phenomenal presence before the delimitations of rational thought have imposed upon it a grid of commonplace significance. A case in point, in Elstir's seascapes, is the blurring of the boundaries which we establish, in our habitual mental representations, between the land and the sea:

Mais les rares moments où l'on voit la nature telle qu'elle est, poétiquement, c'était de ceux-là qu'était faite l'œuvre d'Elstir. Une de ses métaphores les plus fréquentes dans les marines qu'il avait près de lui en ce moment était justement celle qui comparant la terre à la mer, supprimait entre elles toute démarcation. C'était cette comparaison, tacitement et inlassablement répétée dans une même toile qui y introduisait cette multiforme et puissante unité, cause, parfois non clairement aperçue par eux, de l'enthousiasme qu'excitait chez certains amateurs la peinture d'Elstir. (*R* II, 192)

Those infrequent moments when we perceive nature as it is, poetically, were what Elstir's work was made of. One of the metaphors which recurred most often in the sea-pictures which surrounded him then was one which compares the land to the sea, blurring all distinction between them. And it was this comparison, tacitly, tirelessly repeated in a single canvas, imbuing it with its powerful and multifarious unity, which was the source of the enthusiasm felt, though sometimes they were not quite aware of this, by many lovers of Elstir's painting. (*S* 2, 415)

After giving a number of examples of paintings in which Elstir put into practice this theory of first impressions (which Proust derives from Ruskin's analyses of the technical innovations achieved in the art of J.M.W. Turner [1775–1851][9]), the narrator concludes the scene with the artist's masterful and rhetorically florid description of Balbec church,[10] an act of scholarly interpretation and of erudition which might seem surprising coming from a man whose creative efforts seemed focused on the undermining of the paradigms of rational thought. This apparent contradiction concerning a man who, in his creative activity, abnegates his "intelligence" while making ample use of it in his critical works, could easily serve as a self-portrait of Proust himself, who bases his novel on the theory of a metaphorical style quite similar to that of Elstir, while suffusing its pages with layers of historical, literary, and cultural references, worn lightly but enriching the work immeasurably. In the following statement, the reader can be excused for substituting "Proust" for "Elstir":

> L'effort qu'Elstir faisait pour se dépouiller en présence de la réalité de toutes les notions de son intelligence était d'autant plus admirable que cet homme qui, avant de peindre, se faisait ignorant, oubliait tout par probité, car ce qu'on sait n'est pas à soi, avait justement une intelligence exceptionnellement cultivée. (*R* II, 196)
>
> The effort made by Elstir, when seeing reality, to rid himself of all the ideas the mind contains, to make himself ignorant so as to paint, to forget everything for the sake of his own integrity (since the things one knows are not one's own), was especially admirable in a man whose own mind was exceptionally cultivated. (*S* 2, 419)

The large theme of the discrepancy between immediate or superficial appearances and the difficult search for a deeper reality that at first eludes the observer or reader is not confined to the arena of art, but emerges, as well, in the narrator's sometimes awkward attempts to understand the temperament and motivations of those characters who begin to play a major role in the text beginning with *A l'Ombre des jeunes filles en fleurs*. In the concluding pages of the current chapter, I shall turn my attention first to the Baron de Charlus, then to Albertine. I shall wait until the next chapter to discuss the importance of Robert de Saint-Loup. Each of these characters possesses personality traits that appear confusing or contradictory on a first reading; each of them is like an obscure text calling for patient elucidation. The progressive unfolding of this elucidation constitutes a large segment of the narrative's texture, in that these three central figures periodically reappear, in surprisingly varied metamorphoses, from the second until the final volume of the novel.

Charlus

The Baron de Charlus, who was to be seen only fleetingly in *Du Côté de chez Swann*, makes a grand appearance, or rather, series of contradictory appearances, in a passage occupying nearly twenty pages in the early development of *Noms de pays: le pays* (*R* II, 108–26; *S* 2, 329–48). Making use of a technique that Molière had used to great effect in his play *Tartuffe* (1664), in which the eponymous protagonist of the drama is first presented indirectly through the other characters' opinions of him before occupying center stage in the fullness of his hypocritical demeanor, the narrator at first provides his reader with tantalizing glimpses of Charlus, with a mini-portrait provided by his nephew, Saint-Loup. If we were to take this portrait at face value, we would conclude that the baron is a fanatic for physical exercise (Saint-Loup supposes that his uncle will be walking a long distance from the château he is temporarily occupying to Balbec, sleeping in farms along the way); that he circulates essentially among the highest and most exclusive members of the aristocracy, his pride and snobbery resulting quite often in acts of extraordinary insolence; that he is doubtless a Don Juan, at once hyper-masculine and homophobic, having once violently beaten a man who had the effrontery to proposition him; that he is highly cultivated and refined in his dress and his manners, but also compulsive and strange in his insistence on fulfilling his aesthetic desires, having summoned musicians to play string quartets by Ludwig van Beethoven (1770–1827) in his private apartments.[11]

With this background established by Saint-Loup, the text then presents the Baron de Charlus twice, in rapid succession. In the first sequence the narrator does not know who he is, and in the second he is formally introduced to the baron, whom he retroactively recognizes as being the same person he had seen initially. In a curious sense, the reader is being asked to resort to the same theory of "first impressions" that had been operative in the scene in Elstir's studio. In order to understand the complexity of the Baron de Charlus, it is best that we do not forget our first impressions of him, which are based upon a pure observation of his unconscious gestures and mannerisms, and which the later knowledge we gain through a formal social introduction tends to domesticate or normalize. Whereas in a mundane social situation the baron is polite and gracious in a highly conventional sense, when the narrator and the reader first catch sight of him, at a moment when the elegantly dressed aristocrat thinks he is unobserved, we have a far different picture. It is important to emphasize that the first time the narrator sees Charlus, he does not know the latter's identity:

> Je tournai la tête et j'aperçus un homme d'une quarantaine d'années, très grand et assez gros, avec des moustaches très noires, et qui, tout en frappant nerveusement son pantalon avec une badine, fixait sur moi des yeux dilatés par l'attention. Par moments, ils étaient percés en tous sens par des regards d'une extrême activité comme en ont seuls devant une personne qu'ils ne connaissent pas des hommes

à qui, pour un motif quelconque, elle inspire des pensées qui ne viendraient pas à tout autre – par exemple des fous ou des espions. Il lança sur moi une suprême œillade à la fois hardie, prudente, rapide et profonde, comme un dernier coup que l'on tire au moment de prendre la fuite. (*R* II, 110–11)

I glanced round and saw a very tall, rather stout man of about forty, with a jet black moustache, who stood there nervously flicking a cane against the leg of his trousers and staring at me with eyes dilated by the strain of attention. At times, they seemed shot through with intense darting glances of a sort which, when directed towards a total stranger, can only ever be seen from a man whose mind is visited by thoughts that would never occur to anyone else, a madman, say, or a spy. He flashed a final look at me, like the parting shot from one who turns to run, daring, cautious, swift and searching. (*S* 2, 332)

This strange person, the same person who belongs to the inner circle of the Jockey Club, the same person who will be so attentive to the narrator's grandmother in the following scene, is the Baron de Charlus. His importance among the host of characters in the *Recherche* can hardly be overemphasized. Patterned in part on the decadent poet and dandy Robert de Montesquiou, whose portrait by Whistler (see illustration 5) is perhaps more memorable than the former's own irritatingly precious verse, and in part on Balzac's fictional character Vautrin, Charlus is at the center of two thematic constellations in the novel. On the one hand, as the brother of the Duc de Guermantes, he plays a considerable role in the aristocratic *salons* which will be the setting for extensive sections of the text; on the other hand, precisely in the complicated play between appearances and reality, he is a crucial figure in Proust's portrayal of the psychodrama of human sexuality.

Although the true nature of the baron's sexual leanings does not emerge explicitly until the beginning of the novel's fourth volume, *Sodome et Gomorrhe*, it is rather difficult for the reader to be as naïve as the narrator-protagonist in his or her interpretation of certain physical manifestations which would seem to point toward the reasons for the character's apparently bizarre behavior. Not only is Charlus's gaze, insistently and repeatedly described throughout the episode, a fairly obvious manifestation of aggression toward the narrator, but there is also the matter of the baron's voice, which is evoked in an extraordinary description whose sexual implications the young narrator-protagonist does not understand as well as his reader might, or should:

M. de Charlus ne laissait pas seulement paraître une finesse de sentiment que montrent en effet rarement les hommes; sa voix elle-même, pareille à certaines voix de contralto en qui on n'a pas assez cultivé le médium et dont le chant semble le duo alterné d'un jeune homme et d'une femme, se posait au moment où il exprimait ces pensées si délicates, sur des notes hautes, prenait une douceur imprévue et semblait contenir des chœurs de fiancées, de sœurs, qui répandaient leur tendresse. (*R* II, 122–23).

M. de Charlus not only showed a delicacy of sentiment which is indeed rarely to be found in a man; but his very voice, like certain contralto voices in which the middle register has been insufficiently trained and which, in song, sounds rather like an antiphonal duet between a young man and a woman, rose as he expressed these subtle insights to higher notes, took on an unexpected gentleness and seemed to echo choirs of brides and loving sisters. (*S* 2, 344)

It may be useful to dwell for a moment on the mode of presentation chosen by Proust for his ample and innovative developments on the theme of human sexual identity. With the exception of one unusual passage which we shall discuss in due course, Proust's narrator does not address this issue in a rhetorically inflated, bombastic, or preachy way, and does not make of it the topic for a philosophical debate, as André Gide did in the Socratic dialogue format he adopted for his notorious pamphlet, *Corydon* (published in successive segments from 1911 to 1920, and as a complete signed text in 1924, two years after Proust's death). Rather, the question of sexual identity is always presented theatrically and narratively, as a sequence of obfuscations, surprises, unmaskings, and discoveries that develop within a temporal framework, unfolding over the entirety of the *Recherche*.

The remarks on the coexistence, within the same person, of a strong sadistic homophobia and a delicate feminine persona constitute the first step in what will be a lengthy development on male homosexuality as the "imprisonment" of a woman in a man's body. This development is not simply or essentially the expression of a theoretical position, however. Proust's theory of homosexuality, if there is such a thing, is more properly a narratively deployed semiotics in which the would-be partners in a homosexual encounter stage an elaborate choreography of moves and counter-moves which are always subject to erroneous as well as correct interpretation. In the case of the heterosexual narrator and the strange Baron de Charlus (whose strangeness is the convoluted sign pointing to his homosexual identity), Proust devised a series of meetings, of carefully staged scenes, in which the exterior manifestations of the baron's leanings could come progressively to light, in which the narrator's blindness to his interlocutor's devices and motivations would become progressively less plausible.

The first of these scenes (which is neatly and symmetrically counterbalanced by a passage in the next volume, *Le Côté de Guermantes*, which we shall be analyzing) occurs at the end of the episode we are now considering. Charlus knocks unexpectedly on the narrator's door at night and pays him a visit. Very little occurs, but much is to be gleaned from what is not said in an apparently innocuous conversation. Charlus empathizes with the narrator's anxiety at going to sleep, compliments him on his close relationship with his grandmother, and offers to lend him a book by Bergotte, but does not do so at that moment because Aimé, the *maître-d'hôtel*, is unavailable to ensure the delivery of the item. As the baron paces back and forth in the room, the narrator muses, with rather delicious naïveté: "I felt he had something he wanted to say to me but that he could not find the right words" (*S* 2, 346). On the following morning, as the narrator prepares for a swim in the ocean, Charlus takes him aside:

> ... comme M. de Charlus s'était approché de moi pour m'avertir que ma grand-mère m'attendait aussitôt que je serais sorti de l'eau, je fus bien étonné de l'entendre me dire, en me pinçant le cou, avec une familiarité et un rire vulgaires: "Mais on s'en fiche bien de sa vieille grand-mère, hein? petite fripouille?" – "Comment monsieur, je l'adore! ..." (*R* II, 125–26)
>
> ... he [M. de Charlus] came down to tell me my grandmother would like to see me as soon as I came out of the water, and, as he spoke, he pinched me on the neck, with a most vulgar laugh and an air of familiarity:
>
> "Who's the naughty little rascal, then, who couldn't care less about what his old granny wants?"
>
> "I adore her, Monsieur!" (*S* 2, 347)

A few days later, in a sign of apparent regret at his indecorous outburst, Charlus sends the narrator the promised book by Bergotte, "morocco-bound and with a panel of incised leather on its front cover showing a sprig of forget-me-not in half-relief" (*S* 2, 348). As we shall see, this gift with the symbolic flower will become the point of departure of the symmetrical scene in *Le Côté de Guermantes* in which the baron's behavior becomes even more extreme in its histrionic excesses. For the moment, limiting ourselves to this one expository scene, we can observe two distinct points: first, the unpredictable alternation between the offering and the retraction of gestures signaling friendship or more than friendship, which leaves the narrator in an interpretative quandary; second, the capacity of Charlus to destroy the equanimity of the narrator, and, by making him angry, remove him from the zone of aesthetic distance and descriptive neutrality that he generally occupies in the text.

Most fascinating in Charlus's sly suggestion that the narrator "couldn't care less" about his grandmother is the fact that he may be correct in his intuition, and that the narrator's protestation, "I adore her, Monsieur!" may be another instance of Freudian–Proustian denial or *Verneinung.* The reader is left to pursue an intriguing but disturbing analogy. Could it be that just as Charlus's hyper-masculinity hides "choirs of brides and loving sisters," the narrator's overt adoration of his grandmother conceals a profound indifference to her fate? We shall need to return to this hypothesis, improbable as it might seem, in our analysis of the narrator's relationship with his grandmother, as it develops in the next volume of the novel. As we leave Charlus momentarily for Albertine, as we turn from the eccentricities of a middle-aged aristocrat to the playful and enigmatic charm of a young girl, we remain nevertheless within the same essential thematic register – of masks and disguised motivations, surprising revelations of character and temperament, and the seductive power of misleading signs.

Albertine

The narrator's fascination with Albertine, which eventually becomes a fully-fledged obsession occupying hundreds of pages in the later volumes of the novel, emerges quite slowly in the second half of *A l'Ombre des jeunes filles en fleurs*. At first Albertine is of no more interest to the narrator than some of the other members of *la petite bande* – Rosemonde, Gisèle, or especially Andrée, who, at various moments, plays the role of Albertine's rival for the young man's affections. Often described in metaphorical terms – either as a frieze sculpted against the background of the ocean or as a cloudy mist (*une nébuleuse*) – the group of young girls is initially an undifferentiated mass rather than a series of distinct individuals. The narrator's desires hesitate or alternate between and among each particular figure; and it is this hesitation, this difficulty for the person in love to decide exactly where he should focus his attention, that forms the basis for a theoretical meditation on what occurs during the earliest moments in the development of a love relation:

> L'état caractérisé par l'ensemble de signes auxquels nous reconnaissons d'habitude que nous sommes amoureux … était aussi différent de ce que nous appelons amour que diffère de la vie humaine celle des zoophytes où l'existence, l'individualité, si l'on peut dire, est répartie entre différents organismes … Tel pour moi cet état amoureux divisé simultanément entre plusieurs jeunes filles. Divisé ou plutôt indivis, car le plus souvent ce qui m'était délicieux, différent du reste du monde, ce qui commençait à me devenir cher au point que l'espoir de le retrouver le lendemain était la meilleure joie de ma vie, c'était plutôt tout le groupe de ces jeunes filles, pris dans l'ensemble de ces après-midi sur la falaise. (*R* II, 268–69)
>
> No doubt my state of mind, marked by the presence of symptoms which we usually interpret as meaning we are in love … was as different from what we call love as human life differs from the life of zoophytes, in which existence or

individuality, so to speak, is divided among different organisms … And for me that was the loving state, simultaneously divided among several young girls, in which I lived. Divided, or rather undivided, for more often than not what I found delightful and different from everything else in the world, what had begun to endear itself to me so intensely that the sweetest joy in life was the hope of being with them again the next day, was really the whole group of girls, taken together, inseparable from those breezy afternoon hours up on the cliffs. (*S* 2, 492)

As the novel's second volume evolves toward its conclusion, however, Albertine begins to separate herself from the group and to acquire distinctive characteristics in the mind of the narrator, who judges, in a moment of willful decisiveness, that he must visit her in her room at the Grand-Hôtel one evening and discover what he calls "the precious substance of her pink body" (*S* 2, 508). Confident in his success, the narrator imagines that the hotel, and the evening itself, were no longer "empty," but that, in his words, they "were the repository of my happiness." As the passage develops, images of fullness and of swelling begin to flood the text, and there is a striking inversion, within the narrator's imagination, of the relative importance of his own self and of the world around him:

La vue du cou nu d'Albertine, de ces joues trop roses, m'avait jeté dans une telle ivresse … que cette vue avait rompu l'équilibre entre la vie immense, indestructible qui roulait dans mon être, et la vie de l'univers, si chétive en comparaison … Je me penchai vers Albertine pour l'embrasser. La mort eût dû me frapper en ce moment que cela m'eût paru indifférent ou plutôt impossible, car la vie n'était pas hors de moi, elle était en moi … Comment le monde eût-il pu durer plus que moi, puisque je n'étais pas perdu en lui, puisque c'était lui qui était enclos en moi. (*R* II, 285–86)

The sight of her [Albertine's] naked throat and her excessively pink cheeks had so intoxicated me … as to have upset the balance between the tumultuous and indestructible immensity of the life surging through me and the paltry life of the universe … I leaned over to kiss Albertine. Had death chosen that instant to strike me down, it would have been a matter of indifference to me, or rather it would have seemed impossible, for life did not reside somewhere outside me: all of life was contained within me. (*S* 2, 509–10)

The rhetorical manipulations of container (*contenant*) and contained (*contenu*) in this passage are uncannily similar to those we observed in the *petite madeleine* scene. In the same way that the evanescent taste of the cake dipped in tea was thought capable of supporting "the immense edifice of memory" (*S* 1, 50), the narrator describes the immeasurable strength of "the tumultuous and indestructible immensity of the life surging through me" in contradistinction to "the paltry life of the universe." In both scenes, the narrator's sense of being filled with power or with a precious essence not only causes an inversion in the natural order of magnitude between the exterior world and the self, but leads toward the counterintuitive hypothesis that death itself has become less probable. Corresponding to the assertion we have just read in the scene at the Grand-Hôtel ("Had death chosen that instant to strike me down, it would have been a matter of indifference to me, or rather it would have seemed impossible, for life did not reside somewhere outside me: all of life was contained within me"), we have the following proposition in the *petite madeleine* episode, which, with its explicit allusion to the operation or action of love, seems to foreshadow the later passage with Albertine:

> Un plaisir délicieux m'avait envahi, isolé, sans la notion de sa cause. Il m'avait aussitôt rendu les vicissitudes la vie indifférentes, ses désastres inoffensifs, sa brièveté illusoire, *de la même façon qu'opère l'amour*, en me remplissant d'une essence précieuse: ou plutôt cette essence n'était pas en moi, elle était moi. J'avais cessé de me sentir médiocre, contingent, mortel. (*R* I, 44; my emphasis)
>
> A delicious pleasure had invaded me, isolated me, without my having any notion as to its cause. It had immediately made the vicissitudes of life unimportant to me, its disasters innocuous, its brevity illusory, *acting in the same way that love acts*, by filling me with a precious essence: or rather, this essence was not in me, it was me. I had ceased to feel I was mediocre, contingent, mortal. (*S* 1, 47; my emphasis)

The narrative consequences of the two scenes could not be more different, however. Whereas the revelatory experience of involuntary memory causes Combray to emerge from oblivion, becoming the initial site of the narrator's search for lost Time, the reversals in the order of things in the second passage prove to be the signs of a young man's delusions of grandeur and of the lack of congruence between his fantasies and reality. At the end of the scene, Albertine's curt and dramatic refusal to grant the desired kiss and her ringing of the bell next to her bed in an appeal for help signal an abrupt and disillusioning conclusion to the narrator's amorous pursuit; he was unable to read the signs she was exhibiting in her facial expression, her gestures, and her comportment, and had merely assumed that his will to power could encounter no obstacle in his would-be partner. Although both passages are suffused with the same rhetorical manipulations and exhibit, up until the end, the same dramatic structure, the success of the *petite madeleine* scene and the failure of the encounter between the narrator and Albertine need to be taken seriously *as* contrastive experiences. The reader is left to ponder whether the earlier episode succeeds because everything takes place within one individual whose mind is, in the narrator's words, both the seeker and "also the obscure country where it must seek" (*S* 1, 48), while in the second passage we have two separate subjectivities, one of which remains a *terra incognita* for the other. The preference for self-reflection over dialogue with another human being, for solitary contemplation over the exchange of ideas and emotions in a friendship, finds a powerful echo in the theatrically staged impossibility of the love situation, which, in the Proustian universe, would seem to require more knowledge of the other than the self can possess.

CHAPTER 3

Le Côté de Guermantes [The Guermantes Way]

Occupying some 600 pages, the third volume of *A la recherche du temps perdu* is the longest of the series. Opting to avoid what might have been a volume of unwieldy bulk, Proust decided to publish it in two nearly equal parts – *Le Côté de Guermantes I,* which appeared in 1920, and *Le Côté de Guermantes II,* which appeared in 1921. The practically motivated two-part division is not lacking in thematic and narrative symmetries, however. Each volume contains one very large social scene around which the remainder of the story gravitates: in *Guermantes I,* one day of action (*R* II, 451–594; *S 3,* 149–294) centers on the *salon* of Mme de Villeparisis, who had made her first appearance in Balbec in the previous volume; and in *Guermantes II,* more than 120 pages are devoted to a single dinner party hosted by the Duc and Duchesse de Guermantes (*R* II, 709–834; *S 3,* 414–546). In narrative terms, the principal effect of these scenes is to slow things down considerably, creating in the reader the impression that time has been frozen. Whereas in the compact novella *Un Amour de Swann* a number of years were compressed into 200 pages, here a single scene expands to more than half of that length.

It is perhaps for this reason that a natural reaction of many of Proust's readers has been to experience some discouragement at this juncture in the novel. The author has subjected his fiction to such an uncommonly high degree of deceleration that the reader can lose track of the forward movement with which one generally associates novels of education or development. The other obstacle which the reading public of the twenty-first century encounters in these meticulously described social gatherings is the thematic material on which the episodes are based – much of it topical, grounded in the political and social events of the period. Although the extensive footnotes in the Pléiade edition and the more concise references included by Penguin are of considerable help, it must be said that these are the moments in Proust's novel which are most distant from our reality and which require the greatest degree of

4 Marcel Proust at the time of his voluntary service

editorial mediation for the contemporary Anglophone (and possibly also Francophone) reader.

At the same time, however, these long stretches of narrative "desert" that we all must traverse are thematically necessary, in that they constitute, precisely through their length and in the calculated immobility they produce, a practical textual illustration of the major argument underlying the entirety of *Le Côté de Guermantes*: namely, the inanity and superficiality of social discourse, and the perverse capacity of this discourse to impede the narrator from attaining the object of his search, or *recherche*. Although the narrator is still unaware, in the middle sections of the novel, that the sum of his experiences might constitute the material for a novel-to-come, along the way he has undergone isolated moments of revelation that seemed to point beyond the world of the habitual toward a territory that promises a tantalizing form of redemption (the *petite madeleine* scene being the most obvious but not the only example of this aesthetically grounded promise).

Le Côté de Guermantes, from start to finish, constitutes an extended pause in the narrator's aesthetic education, while at the same time adding an important dimension to the large theme of disillusionment that had been developed in *A l'Ombre des jeunes filles en fleurs*. In the same way that the magic of place-names dissolved in the confrontation between the dreamed Balbec and its disenchanted and split reality, the third volume of the *Recherche* will put to the test the narrator's naïve belief in the magic surrounding the one prestigious name of "Guermantes." In an important sense, then, *Le Côté de Guermantes* is rigorously parallel to *A l'Ombre des jeunes filles en fleurs*, and merely carries out, at the level of people, what the previous volume had illustrated at the level of places. Those early readers who became ensconced or paralyzed in the myriad political and social details of the third volume were unable to see this strong parallel at the highest thematic level: with so many trees, the forest could indeed remain hidden. Yet Proust provided strong opening and closing statements that highlight the motif of the initial aura and its subsequent dissolving as the name "Guermantes" and the names of other aristocratic families come up against the petty reality of the people they designate.

Wishing to penetrate what he initially believes to be the nearly inaccessible and arcane world of the highest Parisian society, the Faubourg Saint-Germain, the narrator, thinking like a latter-day Eugène de Rastignac,[1] imagines that a strategically obtained invitation to the home of the Duc and Duchesse de Guermantes will open up to him the previously hidden objective reality of their fabled existence:

> Mais comme le voyageur, déçu par le premier aspect d'une ville, se dit qu'il en pénétrera peut-être le charme en en visitant les musées, en liant connaissance avec le peuple, en travaillant dans les bibliothèques, je me disais que si j'avais été reçu chez Mme de Guermantes, si j'étais de ses amis, si je pénétrais dans son existence, je connaîtrais ce que sous son enveloppe orangée et brillante son nom enfermait réellement, objectivement, pour les autres, puisque enfin l'ami de mon père avait dit que le milieu des Guermantes était quelque chose d'à part dans le faubourg Saint-Germain. (*R* II, 329–30)

But like a traveller who is disappointed by his first impression of a city and who tells himself that he might perhaps penetrate its charm by visiting its museums, getting to know its inhabitants and working in its libraries, I assured myself that, had I been a regular visitor to Mme de Guermantes's house, were I one of her circle, were I to enter into her life, I should then know what was really enclosed within the brilliant orange-colored envelope of her name, know it objectively, through the eyes of others, since, after all, my father's friend had said that the Guermantes were an exclusive set in the Faubourg Saint-Germain. (*S* 3, 27)

Although the narrator's family, wishing to provide his ailing grandmother with "cleaner air" (*S* 3, 8) than apparently had been available at their previous Paris dwelling, had moved to within quite close proximity to the Duc and Duchesse de Guermantes – in fact, to apartments adjoining the Hôtel de Guermantes – the moral or symbolic distance between the two places could not be greater. To emphasize this distance, the narrator speaks of the Guermantes' door-mat as a threshold, as a liminary location beyond which he imagines a higher or "ideal" social reality to exist. The figure of the door-mat as threshold appears near the beginning and near the end of *Le Côté de Guermantes*; its repetition creates the same symmetrical effect as book-ends that enclose and limit the volumes (and the diverse stories within these volumes) that they contain. At the entryway to the third volume, we have:

Il est vrai que mon esprit était embarrassé par certaines difficultés, et la présence du corps de Jésus-Christ dans l'hostie ne me semblait pas un mystère plus obscur que ce premier salon du Faubourg situé sur la rive droite et dont je pouvais de ma chambre entendre battre les meubles le matin. Mais la ligne de démarcation qui me séparait du faubourg Saint-Germain, pour être seulement idéale, ne m'en semblait que plus réelle; je sentais bien que c'était déjà le faubourg Saint-Germain, le paillasson des Guermantes, étendu de l'autre côté de cet Equateur. (*R* II, 330)

It is true that my mind was hampered by certain difficulties, and the presence of Jesus Christ in the sacrament seemed to me no more obscure a mystery than this leading salon of the Faubourg Saint-Germain being situated on the right bank and the fact that, every morning, from my bedroom, I could hear its carpets being beaten. But the line of demarcation that separated me from the Faubourg Saint-Germain seemed to me all the more real because it was purely ideal; I had a strong sense of it already being the Faubourg when I saw, spread out on the other side of this Equator, the Guermantes door-mat. (*S* 3, 28)

At the beginning of the long episode that centers on the Guermantes family and that depicts the narrator as an apprentice gradually learning from various mentor figures the laws governing high society, the lowly door-mat, which his mother finds to be "in a dreadful state" (*S* 3, 28) and beyond whose reality she is incapable of seeing, possesses, for the ambitious young man, an iconic value and has the capacity of conflating the real and the ideal. Yet more than 500 pages later, having experienced the silliness, the conceit, and the emptiness of the Faubourg, the narrator returns to the same image in order to illustrate the depths of his disillusionment. Accompanying the roll-call of names of the nobility attending the Guermantes' dinner party is a sense of deflation very much akin to the "pneumatic" escape of the magical attributes that had initially adhered to the name of Balbec, as the linguistic Pandora's box was opened in *Noms de pays: le pays.* Here, in the social context, we have:

Les noms cités avaient pour effet, de désincarner les invités de la Duchesse, lesquels avaient beau s'appeler le Prince d'Agrigente ou de Cystria, que leur masque de chair et d'inintelligence ou d'intelligence communes, avait changé en hommes quelconques, si bien qu'en somme j'avais atterri au paillasson du vestibule, non pas comme au seuil, ainsi que je l'avais cru, mais au terme du monde enchanté des noms. (*R* II, 831)

The names I had heard uttered had a disembodying effect on the Duchesse's guests – in spite of the fact that they might be called the Prince d'Agrigente or the Prince de Cystria – whose masks of flesh and absent or vulgar intelligence had transformed them into rather ordinary specimens, to the point that I ended up feeling that I had landed on the Guermantes door-mat not as upon the supposed threshold but at the terminus of the magic world of names. (*S* 3, 542)

Before the reader reaches this disenchanted "terminus," however, he or she is obliged to witness and, it must be said, to endure minutely crafted conversations between members of the European nobility whose subject-matter is largely dissolved by the precious verbal jousting and attention to form that characterizes aristocratic discourse. Unlike the ambitious bourgeois who bases his identity and self-image on what he has accomplished or created during his lifetime, the aristocrat, whose name and fortune depend upon the efforts of distant ancestors, has nothing to show in present time but his wit – in French, his *esprit.* In an important section of *Le Côté de Guermantes II*, the narrator notes that, however superficial this form of rarified discourse might appear, "the sparkle of conversation at the Guermantes' did have something real about it, even tenuously so" (*S* 3, 458). He goes on to explain that this form of sophisticated wit has as its precondition, as the "soil" on which it flourishes, defeated intellectual ambitions and unrealized efforts in the world. What he calls "la plus rare floraison de mondanité" (*R* II, 751) ["the rarest flowering of society sophistication" – *S* 3, 458] springs from desires and projects that have been abandoned and buried. The aristocrats described by Proust in the third volume of his novel do not possess intelligence in the strict sense, but rather wit, or *esprit*, which is to be understood as "cette forme supérieure, plus exquise de l'intelligence élevée jusqu'à une variété de talent verbal" (*R* II, 752) ["this superior and more exquisite form of intelligence, elevated to a type of verbal talent" (my translation)].

But what form does this "elevated" type of intelligence take, concretely? One senses that Proust is having fun with his reader as he provides a pseudo-philosophical definition of *esprit* while illustrating this definition with myriad trivial examples. One such example of the *esprit de Guermantes*, which, we are told, remained memorable in Parisian society long after its utterance, had as its origin the Baron de Charlus's purported wish to give to his sister the beautiful château de Brézé – a magnificent edifice surrounded by some of the most spectacular forests in France, but which his sister did not appreciate and did not wish to accept. The Duc de Guermantes, Charlus's brother, went on to say: "Well, someone told my wife all about it and said that if my brother was giving this house to our sister it wasn't so much to please her as to tease her [*ce n'était pas pour lui faire plaisir, mais pour la taquiner*]. What this person actually said was that Charlus was such a tease" (*S* 3, 462; *R* II, 756). Having heard all this, playing on the proximity in sound between *taquin* ("teaser") and Tarquin, and alluding to the seventh king of Rome, Lucius Tarquinius Superbus (535–510 BC), the Duchesse then uttered the famous phrase, descriptive of Charlus's fabled arrogance (in Latin: *superbia*) and considered by her audience to be the summit of wit: "Taquin le Superbe" (which the Penguin translator does a remarkable job of transposing, while keeping the Roman context, as "Teaser Augustus" – *R* II, 756). This, then, is the *esprit de Guermantes*, the "elevated" form of intelligence possessed by the happy few of the French nobility and distilled into its purest form by the Duchesse.

Clearly, we cannot accuse Proust of believing that this play on words constitutes something elevated, nor can we assume that he wishes his readers to espouse such a belief. Rather, what Proust does throughout *Le Côté de Guermantes* is to envelop and diffuse all manner of topics – from the least significant to the weightiest – in this kind of verbal banter, to such an extent that it is sometimes difficult to pierce the witty envelope and find beneath it a subject-matter which might be worthy of our scrutiny. Although there are many instances, in this volume, of the disparity between what is being discussed and how it is being discussed, perhaps the most notable one, both politically and socially, is that of the Dreyfus Affair, which emerges most often cloaked in comedy, or even absurdity. Appearing from time to time in off-hand remarks and allusions, the Dreyfus Affair is given its most extensive treatment in a humorous dialogue (or non-dialogue) between the narrator's Jewish friend, and aspiring writer, Bloch, and the distinguished practitioner of the diplomatic art of verbal evasiveness, M. de Norpois (*R* II, 530–45; *S* 3, 229–45). In this intricately constructed fifteen-page scene, the two interlocutors speak with, or rather, at each other, while the other guests of Mme de Villeparisis intervene with opinions of their own, on Dreyfus's guilt or innocence, on the role of the government in the revealing and suppressing of evidence in the case, and on the question of whether Jews should be admitted within the ranks of high society during a period of raging anti-Semitism.

A comic tone pervades the entirety of the scene, but the initial problem for the inquisitive Bloch – is M. de Norpois a *dreyfusard* or an *anti-dreyfusard*, a partisan of the Jewish officer's innocence or a believer in his guilt – becomes gradually displaced by a second motif, one with which we are by now familiar: namely, the matter of social inclusion or exclusion. The first half of the episode bears the distinct imprint of Molière, France's premier comic playwright. Just as in Molière's plays there are scenes based upon the mechanical repetition of a character's hesitations concerning the truth of what he or she is witnessing (often of the type: "Yes, I know she loves me, there can be no doubt," followed almost immediately by "No, she can't possibly love me, I see that with my eyes only too clearly"), in this case, within the space of a few lines, Bloch thinks to himself "So, he's a Dreyfusard, beyond a shadow of a doubt," followed by "No, he's definitely an anti-Dreyfusard" (*S* 3, 237). Throughout the scene, Proust amuses himself and his reader with an excellent pastiche of the language of diplomacy taken to its furthest limit, which is that of a complete opaqueness in the speaker's (non-) expression of his political position. In the end, one senses that M. de Norpois may be the scariest of reactionaries, as he slips from considerations of the government's final disposition of the case to a direct confrontation with Bloch as young citizen on the subject of the latter's patriotism:

> Mais une fois l'action gouvernementale mise en mouvement, le gouvernement saurez-vous l'écouter? Quand il vous conviera à remplir votre devoir civique, saurez-vous l'écouter, vous rangerez-vous autour de lui? A son patriotique appel saurez-vous ne pas rester sourds et répondre: "Présent!"? (*R* II, 542)
>
> But once the machinery of government has been set in motion, will you actually listen to what the government has to say? When it calls upon you to perform your duty as a citizen, will you rally to it? When it makes its patriotic appeal, instead of turning a deaf ear, will you be able to answer: "Present!"? (*S* 3, 242)

What becomes evident as the scene progresses is that we are not observing a political debate between two characters who, despite possibly differing opinions, occupy the same shared space of discourse and values.

Rather, we are witnessing a conversation between a man who, however unintelligible his views might be, nevertheless proceeds from the firm conviction that he speaks for and in the name of France, and a marginal figure unaware of his marginality who, because he is a Jew at the turn of the century, cannot lay claim to the unquestioned values of the country he inhabits. The more Bloch doggedly pursues M. de Norpois and the other guests about the positions they espouse in the Affair, the more the reader senses that, in a certain sense, Bloch has no right to speak in this group: in French, *il n'a pas droit à la parole.* Long before M. de Norpois questioned Bloch on the latter's patriotism, the Duchesse had said to her gentile friends, with disarming but chilling simplicity:

"Je vous trouve tous aussi assommants les uns que les autres avec cette affaire," dit la Duchesse de Guermantes qui, au point de vue mondain, tenait toujours à montrer qu'elle ne se laissait mener par personne. "Elle ne peut pas avoir de conséquence pour moi au point de vue des Juifs pour la bonne raison que je n'en ai pas dans mes relations et compte toujours rester dans cette bienheureuse ignorance." (*R* II, 535)

"I find you all as deadly boring as each other about the entire thing," said the Duchesse de Guermantes, who, in social terms, was always anxious to demonstrate that she did not allow herself to be led by anyone. "The case can't make any difference to me so far as the Jews are concerned, for the very good reason that I don't know any and I intend to remain in that state of blissful ignorance." (*S* 3, 234–35)

At the microcosmic level of the small social group, the episode of the conversation between M. de Norpois and Bloch is a repetition of what happened to Dreyfus at the macrocosmic level of the French nation. At the conclusion of the scene, in much the same way that Swann was excluded from the "little clan" of the Verdurins, Bloch is "executed" and driven away from the home of Mme de Villeparisis, who decides, in observing the dynamic of the conversation, that the young man is no longer admissible to the society of her friends. Dreyfus is made to suffer the ignominy of the highly inhospitable Devil's Island; Bloch is driven from the social Eden he had sought to inhabit, exiled in outer darkness. What complicates things considerably for the reader who might tend to empathize with Bloch's plight, however, is the fact that Bloch is portrayed as a highly disagreeable, fatuous figure whose overblown Homeric phraseology, coupled with his unpleasant mannerisms and physical appearance, make of him nothing more or less than a caricature.

The Jew as caricature is not exactly an unproblematic literary phenomenon, especially in the light of the cruel depictions and distortions of Jewish "racial" traits as practiced by the Nazis slightly more than a decade after Proust's death – depictions and distortions which Proust could not have foreseen, but which we as contemporary readers cannot possibly bracket from our minds as we read the *Recherche* today. As we reach the midpoint of the novel, two of its characters – Bloch and the Baron de Charlus – begin to exceed the bounds of traditional realist verisimilitude and become figures of excess, of *démesure*, depicted with the broadest of brush-strokes. Of inevitable interest, of course, is the fact that the two features or facets of Proust's own identity that set him apart from the majority of his countrymen – his maternal Jewish origins and his homosexuality – become the object of a fictional transposition that would seem to tend toward masochism and abjection. In banishing from himself and from his Christian and heterosexual narrator "the Jew and the homosexual within," was Proust performing a kind of self-purification which is, in fact, a self-mutilation? Even if the reader is justifiably wary of psychological reductionism and of establishing excessively simple parallels between a writer's life and the characters inhabiting his work, it is difficult not to be both intrigued and unsettled by the reduction to caricature of both Bloch and Charlus (to whom we shall return very shortly).

Despite the sheer length of the social scenes contained in *Le Côté de Guermantes*, and despite the principal effect they produce within the narrative – that of creating an overlay of superficiality that tends to block or mute the serious issues that occasionally emerge from underneath the ebb and flow of convoluted conversations – the third volume of the *Recherche* is also the place in which three themes of fundamental importance to the novel are developed in detail and with considerable subtlety: the theory and practice of friendship; sexual identity and seduction; illness and death. I shall consider each of these in succession.

FRIENDSHIP

It has often been speculated that the narrator's best friend, Robert de Saint-Loup, was patterned after Proust's own brother, also named Robert. According to this hypothesis, the close and continued affectionate relationship between Proust and his brother finds an evident and obvious outlet for expression in the intricately described bond between the narrator and Saint-Loup, which begins in Balbec and continues for the length of the novel. What the narrator has to say about friendship, however, is far from transparent. Not only does he make it clear to the reader, from the earliest days of his encounters with Saint-Loup, that he is essentially using Robert's influence to get to know the latter's aunt, the Duchesse de Guermantes, and the society in which she circulates, but the concrete relations between the two young men are often used in an illustrative or paradigmatic manner, as examples of the complexities and pitfalls of friendship.

Proust not only states that friendship is a multi-layered phenomenon, like a difficult text requiring an adept interpreter, but, over the course of the *Recherche*, he elaborates what amounts to a coherent theory of friendship, which is itself based upon the principles underlying the earliest version of his novel, the text we call *Contre Sainte-Beuve*. It is from the basis of the early distinction between an artist's *moi superficiel* (the outwardly-directed self that is exhibited in social settings) and his or her *moi profond* (the self that must be discovered in an act of introspection and that creates works of art) that the narrator of the finished novel elaborates his views on friendship. Because these views are expressed with such clarity, one might say dogmatism, it has been tempting for readers of Proust, and even for some of Proust's best critics, to oversimplify the question, and to conclude that friendship in the novel is fully defined or encapsulated by the narrator's theory of friendship. In fact, the theory is clear and it is important for an understanding of the *Recherche*, but there is also a practice of friendship which exhibits rougher edges than the theory, and which is worthy of scrutiny. Let us begin with the theory, which is initially enunciated just after the narrator has met Robert de Saint-Loup at Balbec, in the second half of *A l'Ombre des jeunes filles en fleurs*. In *Le Côté de Guermantes* the narrator returns explicitly to this theory, and expects the reader to have remembered its essential elements. In *A l'Ombre*, evoking his excuses not to see Saint-Loup, the narrator describes friendship as "a form of self-abdication" (*S* 2, 483), and criticizes conversation as the vapid "mode of expression" of friendship:

La conversation même qui est le mode d'expression de l'amitié est une divagation superficielle, qui ne nous donne rien à acquérir. Nous pouvons causer pendant toute une vie sans rien dire que répéter indéfiniment le vide d'une minute, tandis que la marche de la pensée dans le travail solitaire de la création artistique se fait dans le sens de la profondeur, la seule direction qui ne nous soit pas fermée, où nous puissions progresser, avec plus de peine il est vrai, pour un résultat de vérité. (*R* II, 260)

Even conversation, which is friendship's mode of expression, is a superficial digression, through which we can make no acquisition. We may converse our whole life away, without speaking anything other than the interminable repetitions that fill the vacant minute; but the steps of thought which we take during the lonely work of artistic creation all lead us downwards, deeper into ourselves, the only direction which is not closed to us, the only direction in which we can advance, albeit with much greater travail, towards an outcome of truth. (*S* 2, 483–84)

What the narrator has to say about friendship in *Le Côté de Guermantes* differs little from this statement, and is merely a metaphorically amplified version of the same essential thought, in which the insubstantial and unrealized self, dependent upon the external support of friendship, finds a suspect form of protection in the "hospitalization" afforded it by the other person:

> J'en étais arrivé à Balbec, à trouver le plaisir de jouer avec des jeunes files moins funeste à la vie spirituelle, à laquelle du moins il reste étranger, que l'amitié dont tout l'effort est de nous faire sacrifier la partie seule réelle et incommunicable (autrement que par le moyen de l'art) de nous-même, à un moi superficiel, qui ne trouve pas comme l'autre de joie en lui-même, mais trouve un attendrissement confus à se sentir soutenu sur des étais extérieurs, hospitalisé dans une individualité étrangère. (*R* II, 689)
>
> I had reached the point in Balbec, of thinking that the pleasure of playing with a group of girls has a less pernicious effect on the life of the mind, to which at least it remains foreign, than friendship, which is totally bent on making us sacrifice the only part of ourselves that is real and incommunicable (except through art) to a superficial self which, unlike the other, finds no joy on its own; what it finds instead is a vague, sentimental satisfaction at being cherished by external support, hospitalized in the individuality of another person. (*S* 3, 393)

It should be of no small interest to the reader of Proust that the same narrator who propounds this disabused theory describes the practice of friendship with a greater degree of nuance. Two substantial sections of *Le Côté de Guermantes* center on this theme (*R* II, 369–440, *S* 3, 67–139; *R* II, 688–708, *S* 3, 392–411). The first, near the beginning of *Le Côté de Guermantes I,* takes place in the garrison town of Doncières, where Saint-Loup is doing his military service and where the narrator visits him and gets to know his fellow officers. The second, from *Le Côté de Guermantes II,* takes place, like most of the action of the third volume, in Paris, while Saint-Loup is off-duty.

The entirety of the Doncières episode is certainly one of the happiest of the novel, one of those very few moments when the narrator appears to be completely content and devoid of any trace of the anxiety, jealousy, and insatiable curiosity that characterize most of his relations with the other characters. In this section of the text Robert tends to the narrator's every need, ensures that his quarters are suitable for comfort and undisturbed sleep, and organizes dinners for the military men of his acquaintance at which the narrator is the featured and honored guest. One particularly beautiful paragraph describes a hotel near the barracks which, in the warm glow of the evening light, resembles a Flemish painting. It is in the center of this highly aestheticized tableau that Robert, explicitly called "my friend," waits for the narrator. The painting alluded to here, *Le Dénombrement devant Bethléem* (*Census of the People at Bethlehem*), is by Pieter Bruegel and was completed in 1566. Like many of Bruegel's works, which depicted everyday life in the simplest of environments and circumstances, this picture is not situated in biblical territory (contemporary Jordan), but in a Flemish village under the snow. Proust associates friendship with the glow of the hotel's fires on which a rich bounty of chickens, pigs, and lobsters are being cooked, which contrasts with the brisk weather outside:

Et précisément à l'hôtel où j'avais rendez-vous avec Saint-Loup et ses amis et où les fêtes qui commençaient attiraient beaucoup de gens du voisinage et d'étrangers, c'était … une affluence (digne de quelque "Dénombrement devant Bethléem," comme en peignaient les vieux maîtres flamands), d'arrivants qui s'assemblaient par groupes … Et dans la grande salle à manger que je traversai le premier jour, avant d'atteindre la petite pièce où m'attendait mon ami, c'était aussi à un repas de l'évangile figuré avec la naïveté du vieux temps et l'exagération des Flandres que faisait penser le nombre des poissons, des bécasses, des pigeons, apportés tout décorés et fumants par des garçons hors d'haleine. (*R* II, 397)

And indeed at the hotel where I was to meet Saint-Loup and his friends the beginning of the festive season was attracting a great many people from near and far … I discovered an influx of new arrivals (worthy of some *Census of the People at Bethlehem* such as the Old Flemish Masters painted) gathering there in groups … Similarly, in the big dining-room, which I had passed through on my first day here on my way to the small room where my friend awaited me, one was again reminded of some Biblical feast, portrayed with the naïvety of former times and with Flemish exaggeration, because of the quantity of fish, chickens, grouse, woodcock, pigeons, brought in garnished and piping hot by breathless waiters. (*S* 3, 95)

The second section on friendship, a twenty-page episode from *Le Côté de Guermantes II*, is not so much based on the creation of an aesthetic atmosphere as it is constructed on a subtle argument that moves forward in a series of carefully articulated gradations. The passage begins with a definition of friendship which I have already quoted – as the sacrifice of the deep self to the superficial self and as the pleasure of "hospitalization" felt by the superficial self as it surrounds itself in the suspect cocoon of easy gratification provided by the other person. Yet at the end of the very paragraph in which this definition is enunciated, the narrator pauses to qualify the dogmatism of his tone:

Mais quelle que fût mon opinion de l'amitié, même pour ne parler que du plaisir qu'elle me procurait, d'une qualité si médiocre qu'elle ressemblait à quelque chose d'intermédiaire entre la fatigue et l'ennui, il n'est breuvage si funeste qui ne puisse à certaines heures devenir précieux et réconfortant en nous apportant le coup de fouet qui nous était nécessaire, la chaleur que nous ne pouvons pas trouver en nous-même. (*R* II, 689)

But whatever my view of friendship, to mention only the pleasure it procured me, so mediocre in quality that it seemed to fall half-way between fatigue and boredom, there is no potion so deadly that it cannot in certain circumstances become precious and restorative by providing us with just the boost we needed and the warmth we are unable to muster of our own accord. (*S* 3, 393)

As the passage develops, the narrator wonders whether Saint-Loup's friendship for him derives more from personal elective affinities or from the latter's good breeding. Yet as the episode reaches its conclusion, the narrator includes a striking descriptive paragraph, one of those moments of the *Recherche* that has been memorable for most readers and which is often cited for the virtuosity with which Proust couples physical movement with an ethically based pantomime. In this scene, thinking that his friend might be catching cold, Saint-Loup quite acrobatically darts between and over restaurant tables in order to deliver a "big vicuna cloak" to the narrator. In a sense, what his gestures portray, without the use of words (or of grand theoretical position-taking) *is* friendship. What the narrator calls Saint-Loup's "steeplechase" *performs* the ethical reality of friendship. At the end of the paragraph, we have:

[E]t quand Saint-Loup ayant à passer derrière ses amis grimpa sur le rebord du dossier et s'y avança en équilibre, des applaudissements discrets éclatèrent dans le fond de la salle. Enfin arrivé à ma hauteur, il arrêta net son élan avec la précision d'un chef devant la tribune d'un souverain, et s'inclinant, me tendit avec un air de courtoisie et de soumission le manteau de vigogne, qu'aussitôt après, s'étant assis à côté de moi, sans que j'eusse eu un mouvement à faire, il arrangea, en châle léger et chaud, sur mes épaules. (*R* II, 705)

[A]nd when Saint-Loup, who needed to pass behind his friends, climbed on to the back of their bench and moved along it in a balancing act, muffled applause broke out from the body of the room. When he reached my seat he brought himself to a halt with the precision of a chieftain paying tribute before the throne of a sovereign and, stooping down, he courteously and submissively handed me the vicuna cloak, which, a moment later, when he had sat down beside me, he arranged around my shoulders as a light, warm shawl, without my having to lift a finger. (*S* 3, 410)

Although at first the narrator is tempted to believe that Saint-Loup's gracious and graceful movements might have derived more from "something he had inherited, by birth and upbringing, from his race" (*S* 3, 411) than from his own personal feelings, at the very end of the episode, in an artful pirouette of dialectical argumentation, there is a synthesis of the personal and the atavistic made possible by the exercise of a "supreme liberty" in which, we are told, is to be found the realization of true friendship. Upon reading this passage, it is difficult to take at face value and as definitive statements what the narrator has to say elsewhere, under the influence of his *Contre Saint-Beuve* philosophical stance, about the spiritually impoverishing effects of friendship:

Et je savais bien aussi que ce n'était pas qu'une oeuvre d'art que j'admirais en ce jeune cavalier [Saint-Loup] déroulant le long du mur la frise de sa course … [L'] assurance, l'agilité, la courtoisie avec lesquelles il venait déposer autour de mon corps frileux le manteau de vigogne, tout cela n'était-ce pas comme des amis plus anciens que moi … et qu'il me sacrifiait au contraire par un choix que l'on ne peut faire que dans les hauteurs de l'intelligence, avec cette liberté souveraine dont les mouvements de Robert étaient l'image et dans laquelle se réalise la parfaite amitié. (*R* II, 708)

And I was more than aware, too, that it was not merely a work of art I was admiring in this young horseman [Saint-Loup] unfolding along the wall the frieze of his cantering path … [T]he assurance, agility and courtesy with which he had wrapped the warm vicuna cloak around my shivering body – were not all these things like friends of longer standing in his life … whom he was none the less sacrificing to me out of choice, the sort of choice that can be made only by a lofty mind, with that supreme liberty reflected in Robert's impulses and in which perfect friendship thrives? (*S* 3, 413)

MYSTERIOUS SEXUALITY AND THE LANGUAGE OF SEDUCTION

The two forms of human intimacy examined at great length in the *Recherche* are friendship and love, which are subjected to both theoretical analysis and narrative development. We learn of friendship through the narrator's relationship with Saint-Loup, and, to a lesser extent, Bloch; we experience the emotional exhilaration and psychological abysses of love through Swann's affair with Odette and the narrator's far more extended relationship with Albertine (a relationship which is largely "on hold" in *Le Côté de Guermantes,* but which nearly devours the penultimate volumes of the novel, *La Prisonnière* and *Albertine disparue*). But there is a third sort of relationship, confined to an all-male sphere, which had been theorized and personally espoused by Gide in *Corydon* – that of a "Socratic" intellectual and physical intimacy between an older man and his younger disciple/lover – the possibility of which Proust stages in a strange scene in *Le Côté de Guermantes II,* only to discard. This highly theatrical fifteen-page episode (*R* II, 840–54; *S* 3, 551–65) occurs immediately following the Guermantes dinner party, in the early hours of the morning. The narrator is responding to the Baron de Charlus's invitation to see him, but, because of the unusual hour, is initially hesitant to do so.

In a nocturnal visit which is an obvious symmetrical *réplique*, or response, to the short scene in which Charlus called upon the narrator in the Grand-Hôtel de Balbec and presented him with a book by Bergotte, "morocco-bound and with a panel of incised leather on its front cover showing a sprig of forget-me-not in half-relief" (*S* 2, 348), now the narrator arrives on a return visit, to encounter the older man on the latter's own terrain, in a sumptuous but alienating environment. The entirety of the passage centers on the difficulty the narrator has in deciphering Charlus's elaborate coded language – a language whose key becomes available, in explicit form, only in the subsequent volume, *Sodome et Gomorrhe*. Yet here, as was the case in Balbec, it is difficult for the reader to be as naïve as the narrator appears to be, difficult for him or her not to see the meaning toward which the signs of the baron's convoluted and often contradictory discourse points.

Much of the serious subtext as well as the comical tone of the episode depends on the difficulty the two interlocutors have in establishing any form of reciprocity in their conversation: what we witness here is the kind of skewed communication the French designate as a dialogue of the deaf, *un dialogue de sourds*. At the very beginning of the scene, while the narrator is still in his carriage on the way from the Guermantes' party, he imagines that his visit to the baron will consist essentially of his own descriptions of the past few hours, his own recent discoveries of aristocratic mores, with which he is far less familiar than his host. Given the rather extraordinary turn of events that characterizes the latter stages of the scene, it is important to keep in mind that it begins with the narrator's own narcissistic self-absorption, with an interior monologue which he thinks (erroneously) he can simply turn into a narrative that will necessarily amuse and fascinate Charlus:

> [J]e sonnai à la porte de M. de Charlus, et ce fut en longs monologues avec moi-même, où je me répétais tout ce que j'allais lui narrer et ne pensais plus guère à ce qu'il pouvait avoir à me dire, que je passai tout le temps que je restai dans un salon où un valet de pied me fit entrer, et que j'étais trop agité pour regarder. (*R* II, 840)
>
> [I] rang at M. de Charlus's door, and it was in a long monologues with myself, in which I rehearsed everything I was going to tell him with scarcely a thought of what he might have to say to me, that I spent the whole of the time awaiting him in a drawing-room into which I had been shown by a footman, and which I was too wound up to take in. (*S* 3, 551–52)

The scene as a whole constitutes a reversal of this naïve supposition. The narrator never has a chance to say anything to Charlus about the Guermantes' dinner, for the simple reason that the baron takes over a "conversation" which is, in fact, a monologic and maniacal exercise in accusation, diatribe, and insult. The two major accusations brought against the narrator by his host are: that he is incapable of reading, and that he is guilty of calumny. On the first point, Charlus ironizes at some length on the narrator's incapacity to recognize the symbolism of the morocco-bound volume of Bergotte (the forget-me-not embossed upon the cover should have signified quite clearly to the young man the desire of the donor not to be forgotten, and thus should have caused the former to acknowledge the gift, to respond appropriately). The second point, far more obscure and never in any way justified or substantiated by the accuser, is that the narrator has supposedly slandered Charlus in some outrageous but ill-defined way.

Throughout the scene, the narrator is, quite literally, at a loss for words: there is nothing he can say to rectify retroactively his weakness as a reader of symbols of affection; and there is nothing he can do to stanch the flow of vituperation issuing from the baron's serpent-like mouth. Just as the narrator's words of protestation in Balbec – that he "adored" his grandmother, in response to the baron's accusation that he "couldn't care less about what his old granny wants" (*S* 2, 347) – were inept (and perhaps even unconvincing, as we shall see shortly), in the same way, when the narrator, in response to the accusations of calumny, says "Believe me, Monsieur, I have said nothing that could offend you" (*S* 3, 557), his denial, in its very blandness, stands in sharp contrast to the vituperative hyperbole unleashed immediately thereafter by an incensed Charlus. The following passage, which I am excerpting from a much longer stream of abuse, stands as one of the more remarkable moments of verbal pyrotechnics in the novel:

"Et qui vous dit que j'en suis offensé?" s'écria-t-il avec fureur en se redressant violemment sur la chaise longue où il était resté jusque-là immobile, cependant que, tandis que se crispaient les blêmes serpents écumeux de sa face, sa voix devenait tour à tour aiguë et grave comme une tempête assourdissante et déchaînée … "Pensez-vous qu'il soit à votre portée de m'offenser? Croyez-vous que la salive envenimée de cinq cents petits bonshommes de vos amis juchés les uns sur les autres arriverait à baver seulement jusqu'à mes augustes orteils?" (*R* II, 846)

"And who says that I'm offended?" he broke out furiously, starting up with a jerk on the sofa on which he had so far been reclining motionless, while, as the pallid, frothing snakes in his face stiffened tensely, his voice became alternately shrill or deep like the deafening uproar unleashed by a storm … "Do you imagine you have the power to offend me? Have you no idea to whom you are speaking? Do you imagine that the poisonous spittle of five hundred little men of your sort, hoisted on to each other's shoulders, could even drool on to the tips of my august toes?" (*S* 3, 557–58)

As outrageous as Charlus's discourse and demeanor may be, the point he makes through his comparison of the Lilliputian narrator and his friends to his own "august" Brobdingnagian person is a serious one: everything in the scene hinges on the power differential between the would-be Socratic mentor and his disarmed disciple. In a very real sense, the narrator does not have the power to offend Charlus. The only thing he can do is to flail about in a comical way, directing his anger at what we should call a stage prop in this highly theatrical episode – a top hat that had been placed, somewhat incongruously, on the floor next to the baron's sofa:

> D'un mouvement impulsif je voulus frapper quelque chose, et un reste de discernement me faisant respecter un homme tellement plus âgé que moi ... je me précipitai sur le chapeau haut de forme neuf du Baron, je le jetai par terre, je le piétinai, je m'acharnai à le disloquer entièrement, j'arrachai la coiffe, déchirai en deux la couronne, sans écouter les vociférations de M. de Charlus. (*R* II, 847)
>
> I was seized with a compulsion to hit something, and, with the little discernment I had left, not wanting to show bodily disrespect to a man so much older than myself ... I grabbed hold of the Baron's new top hat, threw it to the ground, trampled on it, and, bent on pulling it to pieces, I ripped out the lining, tore the crown in two, heedless of the continuing vociferations of M. de Charlus. (*S* 3, 558)

There is an uncanny similarity between this episode and the scene of sadism at Montjouvain as depicted in *Combray*, in which Mlle Vinteuil and her companion translate the confused anger and frustration of their emotions into an act of ritualized violence – spitting on the photographic image of the deceased M. de Vinteuil. There is a similar indirection of translated action here as well, with the top hat playing the role of objective correlative to Charlus himself. Yet there is also a fundamental difference in the staging of the scenes, having to do, precisely, with the question of power. In the Montjouvain passage, the narrator sits comfortably outside the illumined window which frames the strange spectacle of ritualized cruelty, much as a spectator is separated, by a proscenium, from the action taking place on the stage of a theater. In that case, the narrator is in a position of power because, like all voyeurs, he sees without being seen. In Charlus's apartment, however, the narrator is the object of the scrutiny of others (not only the baron, who dwarfs him and defeats him in verbal jousting, but his footmen, who may have witnessed the scene in its entirety and only pretend to be passing by). The episode is an important one because of its very incongruity, its strangeness – a strangeness that is due not just, or not essentially, to the baron's erratic behavior, but to the highly unusual defensive posture in which the narrator, *as* object of the scrutiny of others, finds himself.

The fact that this is one of the very few moments in the novel in which the narrator succumbs to uncontrollable anger must be seen in the light of the subject-matter of the scene: namely, the question of homosexual seduction. The narrator, unlike Proust, is heterosexual. But could it be that he is heterosexual because he is a bad reader of signs? Could it be that the best possible defense mechanism against the power of homosexual seduction, for this narrator, is ignorance, a certain form of literal-mindedness (forgetting that *myosotis* means forget-me-not, forgetting that fact quite strategically, when remembering it might help to configure what Charlus has in mind in his giving of gifts)? Throughout the scene, Charlus speaks of "propositions" and "declarations," and at the conclusion of the early morning rendezvous he even suggests, first, that the narrator might consider spending the night in one of the rooms of his spooky, "greenish" (*S* 3, 552, 561) home,[2] or second, that he accompany the baron on a moonlight carriage ride into the Bois de Boulogne, a place that was and continues to be notorious as a dark and convenient place for assignations.

All of these signs remain unread, and this for a strategic narrative reason. Proust is waiting until the beginning of the subsequent volume, *Sodome et Gomorrhe*, to reveal to the reader, in a passage of extraordinary figural density, the emergence of homosexuality as explicit grand theme. To do so, he needs his narrator to be the unobtrusive observer and to regain the aesthetic distance he had enjoyed at Montjouvain. The nocturnal scene with the Baron de Charlus represents a path not taken in the novel, a monologue of linguistic excess and misdirected behavior, and a seduction misunderstood by the narrator. If it is a succumbing to seduction, a "Happy Fall," that made possible the redemptive power of Christianity, it is a "Happy Ignorance," an imperviousness to seduction, that saves the narrator from homosexual otherness and that makes possible the emergence of homosexuality, as a magnificently complex but finally decipherable code, in the second half of the *Recherche*.

ILLNESS AND DEATH

As the narrator moves beyond adolescence and into adulthood, part of his evolution as a protagonist (part of his "education" in the sense of *Bildung*) involves an initiation into the horizon of mortality that defines the human condition. The reader will remember that the death of Aunt Léonie, the mediating background figure for the *petite madeleine* scene in *Combray*, occurred in a remarkably foreshortened parenthetical statement (*R* I, 156; *S 1*, 153–54). In *Le Côté de Guermantes*, however, two of the major characters

(Bergotte and Swann) suffer from serious illnesses which are described in some detail, and another, the narrator's grandmother, after a prolonged period of physical agony and emotional distress, dies. Once he had made the strategic editorial decision to divide the third and longest volume of his novel into two parts, Proust placed the initial phases of the grandmother's illness at the end of *Guermantes I* (some fifteen pages) and the stages leading up to her death at the beginning of *Guermantes II* (some thirty-five pages), thus ensuring that a strong thematic continuity would unite the separately published volumes, and that the reader, having witnessed the early developments of her suffering, would wish to discover, in the next, separately published section, whether she would recover or succumb.

The combined, two-part episode is not a complete compositional success. It is stitched together from a series of fragments that Proust had written over more than a decade, some dating from the early drafts of the novel. It is only too clear, at certain narrative junctures, that somewhat awkward inserts are being made into a text that slips into asides and substantial digressions.[3] This said, there are specific passages within the whole which are worthy of close study, and which stand out as some of the most memorable moments in the novel. Especially notable is the double perspective with which the narrator treats the phenomenon of mortal illness: from within (sickness as aggressive infection, as an inner attack of alien forces upon the body), and from without (the individual's march toward death as social event, as pretext for self-satisfied group commiseration, and for the expression of various forms of empathy, authentic and inauthentic). Added to this shifting focus is an extended satire on medicine which draws heavily from the comedies of Molière and which defines medical science as "a compendium of the successive and contradictory mistakes of doctors" (*S* 3, 295). The primary tension underlying the entirety of the episode is the disparity between the physical agony of the grandmother, which is an inner process, an ebb and flow of acute suffering and occasional respite fundamentally invisible to others, and the objectification of the elderly woman, both by medicine and by the socially organized individuals who observe her gradual and inevitable demise.

The most obvious comical element in the passage is the sheer multiplication of doctors who attend to the grandmother at one point or another in the evolution of her illness. First it is Cottard, known to us as one of the regulars in the *petit clan* of Mme Verdurin, and who returns here as faithful family doctor (*R* II, 594–96; *S* 3, 294–96); next it is Dr. du Boulbon, who attempts to convince his patient that her illness has no somatic ground, but is a figment of her very active "nervous" imagination (*R* II,

597–602; *S* 3, 297–303);[4] third, it is "the famous Professor E***," whom the narrator meets quite fortuitously and persuades to see his grandmother for a few precious minutes, while the doctor is thinking primarily of the dinner party he is about to attend (*R* II, 609–14; *S* 3, 311–16); fourth, it is the fleeting "specialist X" (*R* II, 620–21; *S* 3, 322), who appears and disappears in the space of one paragraph and who, rather uncannily like Freud's occasional disciple Wilhelm Fliess (1858–1928),[5] was convinced that all ailments, physical or mental, originate in the nose; and fifth but certainly not least, the flamboyant Docteur Dieulafoy, quite possibly patterned on the real Georges Dieulafoy (1839–1911), a noted French doctor who directed the Hôtel-Dieu clinic in 1896, but whose name sounds like a hybrid creation drawn directly from Molière's *Le Malade imaginaire* [*The Imaginary Invalid*] (1673) (*R* II, 637–40; *S* 3, 340–43).[6]

Ironically, it is the pressed-for-time Professor E***, more obviously interested in the status of the formal attire he is about to put on than in the physical state of his transient patient, who is the most honest of the lot, and who tells the narrator: "There is no hope for your grandmother" (*S* 3, 315). Alone among the five practitioners, Professor E*** expresses a medical truth leading to a sober reflection of the narrator's – a reflection that quite possibly encapsulates the fifty-page episode in its totality. While the professor berates a domestic for not having punched the buttonhole of his jacket to exhibit his decorations, the narrator is left to ponder: "The Professor raged away as I stood on the landing gazing at my grandmother, for whom there was no hope left. Each of us is very much alone" (*S* 3, 316).

The scene of the grandmother's illness and death, despite its complexity and its digressive character, is built upon a series of defensive strategies by which the quite diverse group of people who come into contact with the dying woman during her final days, attempt to deny the fundamental fact of their own irremediable solitude. This is not only the case for Bergotte, who visits the grandmother on a regular basis but has become far too dependent upon the public's reception of his work to continue to draw inspiration from his own creative sources, and who has become, in a certain sense, a stranger to himself. Nor is this strategy limited to the Duc de Guermantes and Saint-Loup, who pay social visits to their ailing acquaintance but are too concerned with their own elevated social status to attend to her needs or to be reminded, through her, of their own mortality.

Perhaps the most striking scene of the entire episode, a short passage that concludes *Le Côté de Guermantes I*, captures most forcefully the essential characteristic of each social group to surround the individuals that compose it in a protective cocoon, and in so doing, to exclude from envelopment in this protective layer all other individuals who, for the most arbitrary and arcane of reasons, do not fit the mold that has been shaped by the group in question. This scene occurs in public lavatories located near the Champs-Elysées, the physical location in which the narrator's grandmother suffers a mild stroke, thereby beginning her descent toward death. It is of no small ironical importance that, in a volume whose action takes place nearly exclusively at the highest levels of the Parisian aristocracy, Proust chooses to generalize his reflections on the laws governing *all* social groups not among the arbiters of taste, but in the lowliest and most distasteful of places.

As is often the case in the *Recherche*, the narrative frame of the episode is as important as the framed material. Dr. du Boulbon has managed to convince both the narrator and his mother that the grandmother's illness has no physical basis, and that she needs fresh air more than anything; this is the origin of the ill-fated excursion to the Champs-Elysées on a warm day when the grandmother should have stayed in bed. Of special importance is the fact that this brief respite from the sickroom suits the narrator's plans perfectly. Had he remained at home caring for his grandmother, he would have missed the opportunity to be with friends, whom he plans to meet on the Champs-Elysées and with whom he plans to dine later that same evening in the outskirts of Paris. It is therefore with his own pleasure in mind that the narrator begins the excursion. This egotism, and the "indifference" which is referred to in the passage below, should make us reflect upon whether the Baron de Charlus was completely wrong when, in Balbec, he said that the narrator "couldn't care less about what his old granny wants" (*S* 2, 347):

> Ayant refusé obstinément que maman restât avec elle, elle [ma grand-mère] mit, toute seule, un temps infini à sa toilette et maintenant que je savais qu'elle était bien portante, *et avec cette étrange indifférence que nous avons pour nos parents tant qu'ils vivent*, qui fait que nous les faisons passer après tout le monde, je la trouvais bien égoïste, d'être si longue, de risquer de me mettre en retard quand elle savait que j'avais rendez-vous avec des amis et devais dîner à Ville-d'Avray. (*R* II, 604; my emphasis)
>
> After obstinately refusing to let Mama stay and help her, left on her own she [my grandmother] took an endless time to dress, and now that I knew she was not ill, *with that strange indifference we show towards our family during their lifetime*, which makes them the last people to be taken into consideration, I thought it very selfish of her to take so long and to risk making me late when she knew that I had to meet with friends and was going off to dinner in Ville-d'Avray. (*S* 3, 304–05; my emphasis)

The entire passage requires translation. The phrase "now that I knew she was not ill" means "now that Dr. du Boulbon has allowed me to become indifferent toward my grandmother"; and the "selfishness" of the grandmother is the fictitious and willful mirror image of the true selfishness of the narrator. It is a matter of exquisite irony, therefore, that the grandmother, abandoned by her family to an unacknowledged physical suffering, finds relief, literally and metaphorically, in public toilets, in a *lieu d'aisance*, toward which she flees immediately upon arriving at the Champs-Elysées. There, a grotesquely made-up woman who had appeared briefly in *A l'Ombre des jeunes filles en fleurs* when the narrator and Gilberte had played on the Champs-Elysées,[7] occupies center stage as the person who allows or denies entrance to those who need to use the facilities that she supervises. Designated playfully as the "Marquise" by the narrator, this woman acts very much like Parisian society matrons, in that she controls access to a place she considers to be exclusive. Whereas she shows considerable kindness to the grandmother, who stays for a long time in the small cabin that has been allocated to her, the "Marquise" denies entrance to another woman who seems to be in great need, falsely alleging that there are no vacant stalls "with a snobbish bite in her voice," and saying to the park-keeper with whom she has been engaged in conversation: "She looked like a bad payer to me" (*S* 3, 307). It is the grandmother, who, upon emerging, weak and disheveled, from her cubicle, has the appropriate last word for the episode, which also anticipates the very last words of *Le Côté de Guermantes*, to which we shall turn shortly:

> "J'ai entendu toute la conversation entre la 'Marquise' et le garde," me dit-elle. "C'était on ne peut plus Guermantes et le petit noyau Verdurin. Dieu! qu'en termes galants ces choses-là étaient mises." Et elle ajouta encore, avec application, ceci de sa Marquise à elle, Mme de Sévigné: "En les écoutant je pensais qu'ils me préparaient les délices d'un adieu." (*R* II, 607–08)[8]
>
> "I heard the whole of that conversation between the 'Marquise' and the park-keeper," she said. "She couldn't have been more like the Guermantes or that little Verdurin clan if she tried. What a genteel way of putting such things!" And she went on to add an apposite remark from her own special Marquise, Mme de Sévigné: "As I listened to them I thought they were preparing to bid me a delightful farewell." (*S* 3, 308)

It should come as no surprise to the reader that, in a volume devoted to social satire in which matters of the utmost seriousness are enveloped in wit or deflated by irony, the narrator, making use of a symmetrical echo effect, concludes *Le Côté de Guermantes II* on the same note as *Le Côté de Guermantes I*, with an emphatic contrast between the illness and imminent death of an individual, on the one hand, and the indifference of others to that person's fate, on the other. In *Guermantes I* the grandmother suffered her first stroke in solitude, separated from a grandson preoccupied with his own pleasures. In the final pages of *Guermantes II* Swann announces to the Duc and Duchesse de Guermantes that he will be unable to accompany them on a voyage to Italy ten months hence, since his doctors tell him he will die before that time. Like Professor E*** in his dealings with the grandmother, the Guermantes are in a hurry to attend a social event (in this case, a dinner hosted by the Marquise de Saint-Euverte) and have no patience for Swann's ills. Upon learning the dire news from her good friend, the Duchesse hesitates for an instant, wondering what she should do facing what is for her a rare moral dilemma:

Placée pour la première fois de sa vie entre deux devoirs aussi différents que monter dans sa voiture pour aller dîner en ville, et témoigner de la pitié à un homme qui va mourir, elle ne voyait rien dans le code des convenances qui lui indiquât la jurisprudence à suivre et ne sachant auquel donner la préférence, elle crut devoir faire semblant de ne pas croire que la second alternative eût à se poser, de façon à obéir à la première qui demandait en ce moment moins d'efforts, et pensa que la meilleure manière de résoudre le conflit était de le nier. (*R* II, 882)

Poised for the first time in her life between two duties as far removed from each other as getting into her carriage to go to a dinner-party and showing compassion for a man who was about to die, she could find no appropriate precedent to follow in the code of conventions and, not knowing which duty to honour, she felt she had no choice but to pretend to believe that the second alternative did not need to be raised, thus enabling her to comply with the first, which at that moment required less effort, and thought that the best way of settling the conflict would be to deny that there was one. (*S* 3, 595)

The remainder of the scene consists of the Duc and Duchesse reassuring Swann, and, like Dr. du Boulbon with the narrator's grandmother, insisting that his illness is a figment of his imagination. Upon discovering that his wife has put on black shoes with a red dress, the Duc de Guermantes sends her back to find a red pair, all the while complaining of his delicate stomach while lending a deaf ear to the very polite Swann. The passage concludes memorably, with the Duc's stentorian words of encouragement to Swann:

"Et puis vous, ne vous laissez pas frapper par ces bêtises des médecins, que diable! Vous vous portez comme le Pont Neuf. Vous nous enterrerez tous!" (*R* II, 884)

"Now mind you don't let all this damned doctors' nonsense get to you. They're fools. You're in strapping shape. You'll live to see us all in our graves!" (*S* 3, 597).

A fitting ending to a volume that, more than any other in the *Recherche*, remains firmly tethered to the amoral cruelty of social convention and to the exclusionary violence of so-called polite society. This victory of dinner parties over substance, of frivolity over the final seriousness of human existence considered against the background of mortality, is only temporary, and constitutes a disappointingly empty and momentary pause along the path of the narrator's apprenticeship. As we now move to the second half of the novel, as the aesthetic and ethical stakes become higher, the power and the appeal of the social sphere as desired and idealized world for the narrator become attenuated. In the end, the Guermantes Way, for all of its external brilliance, will have constituted nothing more or less than a magnificent but disenchanted detour, an extended desert whose aridity the narrator had to experience, before plunging into new and stranger territories than those he had sought, with mixed success, to map.

CHAPTER 4

Sodome et Gomorrhe [Sodom and Gomorrah]

Nearly as lengthy as *Le Côté de Guermantes,* its successor volume, *Sodome et Gomorrhe,* was published in two parts, the first in 1921, the second in 1922 just a few months before Proust's death. This fourth volume of the novel was the last one that Proust was able to complete, and it bears all the signs of a careful and symmetrical composition. Divided into four chapters, each of which is preceded by short references to the broad outline of the plot's development, *Sodome et Gomorrhe* exhibits a clear structural design and was obviously intended by its author to be as reader-friendly as possible in its formal presentation, especially because the content of the volume was bound to shock and disconcert many of its readers in 1922.

The two long chapters of *Sodome et Gomorrhe,* chapters 2 and 3, are framed by two much shorter chapters, each of which explores the complexity of human sexual relations in ways that were to revolutionize European literature in the twentieth century. In chapter 1, in an elaborate, rhetorically complex and highly theatrical scene, Proust paints a picture of male homosexual relations centered on the Baron de Charlus, whose proclivities now reveal themselves with utmost clarity to the narrator. Significant sections in chapters 2 and 3 are devoted to an analysis of Charlus's often contradictory and outrageous behavior, seen now in the light of his homosexual identity. At the same time, these central chapters contain a series of hints and clues directed toward the narrator's gradual awareness that the young woman he loves, Albertine, has doubtless had physical liaisons with other women. When, at the end of chapter 4 in a desperate moment of decision-making, the narrator decides to move from Balbec to Paris with the idea of eventually marrying Albertine, it is with the knowledge that the object of his desires, having lived with and loved women, is, to a significant degree, mysterious, unknowable, and impossible to possess.

Whereas in the first half of the *Recherche,* the theme of intimacy (friendship and love) occupied an important position among other

5 James McNeill Whistler, *Arrangement in Black and Gold: Comte Robert de Montesquiou-Fezensac*

themes – society and the laws of *mondanité*; the political realities of Third Republic France (via the character of Norpois and the inclusion, within the novel, of the Dreyfus Affair); aesthetic theory and practice (Vinteuil's music, Bergotte's writing, Elstir's painting); and the creative force of involuntary memory – as of the first chapter of *Sodome et Gomorrhe*, physical desire and love as obsessive need become the near-exclusive focus of the narrator's experiences and reflections. It would not be an exaggeration to assert that chapter 1 of *Sodome et Gomorrhe*, located exactly at the midpoint of the text, constitutes a second Overture, a new beginning for the *Recherche*. Whereas the work's initial pages, centered on a man caught between sleep and wakefulness, set forth concisely the thematic network of the novel-to-come in symphonic fashion, what I am calling the second Overture, the scene of the Baron de Charlus's fortuitous meeting with a younger man of his own orientation, Jupien, constitutes a resolute narrowing of perspective, a concerted focus on sexuality *per se* – one might even say, to use an infelicitous phrase, a sexualizing of the narrative. To play with words: an examination of human sexual orientation implies, in Proust's universe, a reorientation of the novel in its entirety. We as readers now see the world created by Proust through a different lens, one that illuminates the profoundly sexual nature of many, if not all, human actions.

As we make the jolting shift, via the characters of Charlus and Albertine, away from the presuppositions of a normative heterosexuality (presuppositions that remain embedded in the plot throughout the novel because of the narrator's own constant and unquestioned heterosexual identity), the actions of the fictional figures we encounter from here on begin to appear increasingly strange, bizarre, even grotesque. The scene of sadistic and ritualized violence at Montjouvain which seemed out of place in the peaceful and idyllic environment of Combray now becomes a point of reference for important episodes in *Sodome et Gomorrhe*, as we shall see shortly. As of the novel's fourth volume, the exception becomes the norm, the marginal and the eccentric begin to occupy the center of the text as it evolves toward territories that had never been explored with the painstaking lucidity, or the stylistic virtuosity, with which Proust illuminates them in the final years of his life.

The challenge faced by Proust as he altered the focus of his psychological analysis so radically, toward a large-scale examination of the indirect as well as overt ramifications of homosexual mores, was how to do so within the social and aesthetic parameters he had already established in the preceding 1,500 pages of his novel. If the first chapter of *Sodome et Gomorrhe* was to be a disruption of the previously existing order of things in his fictional universe, it could not be a destruction of this order, lest the *Recherche* as a whole fall into incoherence. Proust was able to establish a delicate equilibrium between his increased emphasis on sexuality and the overall thematic continuity of his text by inserting both the Charlus and the Albertine narrative strands within the general web of the novel of education, or *Bildungsroman*, in the specific social settings he had established in the previous three volumes: namely, the increasingly intersecting worlds of the Faubourg Saint-Germain and the *salons* of the ascending bourgeoisie.

The reader can continue to follow what is one of the longest and most visible threads of the narrative – that of the narrator's progressively successful social integration (in *Sodome et Gomorrhe*, he becomes the darling of the Guermantes family as well as a coy but sought-after recruit to the *petit clan* of the Verdurins) – while simultaneously observing the erratic behavioral and linguistic excesses of Charlus, who, already included in all the invitations to the social functions of the Faubourg, also manages, as Swann had done in the past, to ingratiate himself with Mme Verdurin. M. de Charlus is thus physically present for many of the luncheons, evenings, teas, and excursions in which the narrator finds himself involved, both in Paris and during the second stay in Balbec, which occupies the final two-thirds of the volume. While Albertine does not appear in Parisian high society, she is to be found in and around the Grand-Hôtel de Balbec, and is to be seen acting suspiciously and flirtatiously with the characters whom the narrator sees on a daily basis. Although presented as a dramatic interruption of the narrative flow, the abyss of homosexuality is not in itself a new place, but opens up within the familiarity of already existing social structures. Both Charlus and Albertine must be "read" against the horizon of the known; it is precisely the difficulty the narrator and the other characters have in integrating them into habitual forms of conduct and discourse that helps to establish their difference, their radical otherness.

As the narrator enters the early phase of adulthood, his capacity to observe the capricious absurdity of social practices is presented in tandem with his ability to discern the codes and covert conventions by which sexual desire is communicated. On the one hand, he is able, for the first time, to see Charlus for what he is; on the other hand, his increased lucidity extends to the analysis of the ways in which current political events and artistic fashion impinge upon the ascendance or decline of social groups, both in Paris and in Balbec. Throughout *Sodome et Gomorrhe* the Dreyfus Affair continues to infiltrate and upset the balance of previously cohesive *salons*, as the main characters in the novel take and change position in their view of the disgraced officer's guilt or innocence: Saint-Loup, initially a convinced *dreyfusard*, attenuates the level of his support and portrays himself as a staunch supporter of the army; the Prince and Princesse de Guermantes, as well as the Duc de Guermantes, declare themselves for Dreyfus and reorganize the hierarchy of their social acquaintances accordingly; Swann is so caught up in the pro-Dreyfus movement that he now considers all *dreyfusards* to be essentially and fundamentally intelligent;

while, on the other side of the spectrum, Odette has formed her own *salon* around the figure of Bergotte, but the popularity of her newly formed "clan" owes at least as much to her ardent *anti-dreyfusard* sentiments as it does to the intellectual aura of the acclaimed writer ostensibly at its center.

In a general sense, the Dreyfus Affair as portrayed in *Sodome et Gomorrhe* serves to develop the theme of society as a continually evolving "kaleidoscope" which we have already encountered in earlier sections of the text. The more the novel progresses, the more it becomes evident to the narrator that the laws which govern social practice are the laws of fashion, which are themselves predicated on relativity and instability. Proust's social comedy bases itself on the notion that nothing is stable in organized groups of human beings except instability: *plus ça change, plus c'est la même chose*. The prestige of people, like the initial mystery of places, is subject to the erosion of habit and to the demystification that inevitably accompanies the narrator's insight into the ephemeral and superficial reasons underlying the constant upheavals of the social landscape.

Set against this general law of disenchantment which resonates throughout the novel, the theme of homosexuality, or sexual *inversion*, to use the narrator's term, introduces an element of novelty and disruption into the scheme of things. The addition of Charlus to the Verdurin group at La Raspelière in the latter stages of the volume produces what could be called a counter-effect to the dulling process of habit – an effect which the narrator defines as *strangeness*, or *étrangeté*. Throughout this chapter, I shall be arguing that it is this concept of *étrangeté*, viewed as the introduction of something new and unsettling into the habitual mix, that can serve as the organizing principle for the entirety of *Sodome et Gomorrhe* – the volume of the *Recherche* that contains the most surprises, the most reversals of perspective, and the most challenges to the narrator's ability to comprehend the world and its inhabitants of any section of the novel. The narrator's concise overview of the revolution which takes place in the *petit clan* of the Verdurins because of Charlus's participation in its activities can serve as a point of departure for our reading of several specific emblematic passages in the text's fourth volume, all of which, in their various ways, serve as remarkably rich, subtle, and sometimes convoluted developments of the notion of *étrangeté*:

Mais bientôt ... les fidèles avaient réussi à dominer la gêne qu'ils avaient tous plus ou moins éprouvée au début, à se trouver à côté de M. de Charlus. Sans doute en sa présence ils gardaient sans cesse à l'esprit ... l'idée de l'étrangeté sexuelle qui était incluse en leur compagnon de voyage. Mais cette étrangeté même exerçait sur eux une espèce d'attrait … Dès le début, d'ailleurs, on s'était plu à reconnaître qu'il était intelligent. "Le génie peut être voisin de la folie," énonçait le docteur [Cottard] … A cette première période on avait donc fini par trouver M. de Charlus intelligent malgré son vice (ou ce que l'on nomme généralement ainsi). Maintenant c'était sans s'en rendre compte à cause de ce vice qu'on le trouvait plus intelligent que les autres. (*R* III, 428–29)

But soon … the faithful had succeeded in overcoming the awkwardness they had all more or less felt at the start, on finding themselves next to M. de Charlus. No doubt in his presence, they kept always before them … the idea of the sexual strangeness enclosed within their travelling companion. But this strangeness even held a sort of attraction for them … They had been pleased to acknowledge right from the start, moreover, that he was intelligent. "Genius may lie next to madness," announced the [Doctor Cottard] … In this first period, they had in the end therefore found M. de Charlus to be intelligent in spite of his vice (or what is generally so termed). Now it was, without their realizing it, because of that vice that they found him more intelligent than the others. (*S* 4, 434–35)

The introduction of Charlus into the Verdurin "clan" is much like the introduction of a catalyst into a heretofore stable mixture of chemicals: the catalyst causes a demonstrable chemical reaction, in this case enhancing and speeding up the ability of the "faithful" to recognize and appreciate sexual otherness, but is in itself not susceptible to change. As is the case in a chemistry experiment, the reactions of the substances – here, fictional entities whose defining personality traits are known to the reader – take place over time. There is a progression from an initial "awkwardness" at merely being in the same space as Charlus toward an increased recognition, on the part of the "faithful," of what the narrator calls the former's "intelligence," which derives from and is inseparable from his "sexual strangeness." It is perhaps not insignificant that Proust chooses to insert the parenthetical phrase "(or what is generally so termed)" immediately upon characterizing Charlus's homosexuality as a "vice." What the adherents to the Verdurins' social group are, in fact, *un*learning in their increased familiarity with the baron is the traditional, Old Testament association of homosexual practices with vice – a vice whose practitioners are subject to absolute destruction in the episode of the Cities of the Plain, Sodom and Gomorrah, to which the title of the *Recherche*'s fourth volume transparently alludes.[1] While dulling the moral valance of homosexuality, the narrator also sheds light on what he considers to be its cognitive and aesthetic dimensions. To live as a practicing and lucid homosexual is to gain an understanding of things that is quite possibly unavailable to the heterosexual majority.

In reading this crucial passage, it is important to recognize, simultaneously, two points: the first, as stated, is a decoupling of homosexual behavior from the moral strictures that have accompanied it for so long in the Judeo-Christian tradition; the second, however (by no means to be confused with a mere reversal of the first or with a radical moral neutralization of homosexuality), is that homosexual experience is "singular, refined and monstrous" (*S* 4, 435), whereby each of these terms needs to be taken, in the specific context of the Proustian universe, with utmost seriousness. Homosexual experience, which Proust has the intelligence and grace of not reducing to the blandness of a "lifestyle," is singular in that it cannot be generalized into one overarching modality of behavior or practice; it is refined because the homosexual, in order to communicate with his or her peers, must elaborate complex codes of gesture and discourse that remain outside the purview of heterosexual norms; it is monstrous in the sense that it expresses itself in the mode of excess, or *démesure*, taking on forms that can be so strange as to be indecipherable to the heterosexual. Although he is doubtless patterned on Balzac's Vautrin, an outsized character whose criminal past and homosexual leanings combine the diabolical with the romantic/sentimental,[2] Proust's Charlus surpasses his model in the sheer magnitude of his unfettered ego, in his preening and strutting and vainglorious rants. As I proceed now to an analysis of four separate passages in *Sodome et Gomorrhe*, all of which stand under the aegis of strangeness, or *étrangeté*, I shall begin with the justly celebrated explicit revelation of Charlus's sexual identity with which Proust opens the second half of *A la recherche du temps perdu*.

*"La scène de la conjonction," or Charlus and Jupien conjoined (*R *III, 3–33;* S *4, 5–36)*

Twenty pages before the conclusion of *Le Côté de Guermantes,* having just received an invitation from the Prince and Princesse de Guermantes but wondering if the invitation is in fact for him, the narrator decides to wait for the Duc and Duchesse de Guermantes on the stairway leading to their apartments in order to ascertain their judgment of the matter. Still unsure of his status in the Parisian social hierarchy, the narrator is in need of a second opinion, and thinks that his aristocratic neighbors can provide it for him. It is during this wait on the stairway that he is able to observe what he calls "a moral landscape" that is to revolutionize his view of the world (*R II,* 861; *S* 3, 573). For strategic compositional reasons, the narrator waits to relate this event until the beginning of the subsequent volume, thereby endowing it with considerable dramatic effect. As was the case for the scene of sadism at Montjouvain, the narrator finds himself perfectly situated to observe the strange actions of the Baron de Charlus; as in the earlier episode, he can see without being seen, and is thus in the position of a voyeur. The initial pages of *Sodome et Gomorrhe* contrast markedly with the scene of the narrator's nocturnal visit to Charlus in the previous volume, in that here, rather than being the object of the baron's deviated affections and unpleasant scrutiny, the narrator is at a safe distance from him and occupies a point of view whose fortuitous location would seem to sin against the laws of fictional verisimilitude.

Not only does the narrator face this issue of improbability or implausibility head-on (realizing that any reader of traditional realist fiction could easily object to the excessive ease with which the unobserved observer gains a panoramic view of the scene), but he creates a further dimension to this question by adding to the human drama of the "conjunction" of Charlus and the suddenly revealed object of his lust, the tailor Jupien,[3] a parallel natural drama – that of a possible second "conjunction," between an orchid in the courtyard below which he can see from his privileged perspective and a bumble-bee possibly on the way to pollinate it. From the very beginning of the episode, the theme of chance (in French, *hasard providentiel* – *R* III, 4) resonates as a veritable leitmotif and applies both to the human and the botanical spheres. It is by pure chance that Jupien happens to emerge from his shop precisely as the baron crosses the courtyard (at a time of the day in which the older man usually does not cross this courtyard); and it would be a matter of pure chance were the bumble-bee to succeed in pollinating an orchid which is personified, at various points in the scene, as a female figure "awaiting" this fecundation.

What is unusual, strange, and strangely beautiful about this scene is the continual overlap between the human and the botanical. On the one hand, in pursuing the hypothesis of the orchid's pollination, the narrator muses: "the flower-woman [*la fleur femme*] that was here would, should the insect come, arch her 'styles' coquettishly and, in order to be penetrated more fully by him, would imperceptibly, like a hypocritical but ardent young damsel, come to meet him half-way" (*S* 4, 6–7; *R* III, 4). Here, the flower behaves like a flirtatious young woman, and is so much a woman, so to speak, that she is designated as a *fleur femme*, in much the same way that the young girls at Balbec, according to an inversion of this figure, were "jeunes filles en fleurs," or girls metamorphosed into flowers. On the other hand, when Charlus makes his theatrical entrance, we have the following comparison, which blurs the borders of the zoological and botanical spheres and which complicates considerably the usual subordination of the object evoked for poetic effect in a simile (in this case, the bumble-bee) and the subject to which it is compared (Charlus):

Au même instant où M. de Charlus avait passé la porte en sifflant comme un gros bourdon, un autre, un vrai celui-là, entrait dans la cour. Qui sait si ce n'était pas celui attendu depuis si longtemps par l'orchidée, et qui venait lui apporter le pollen si rare sans lequel elle resterait vierge? (*R* III, 8)

At the selfsame instant that M. de Charlus passed through the gateway whistling like a fat bumble-bee, another one, a real one this time, entered the courtyard. Who knows whether it was not the one so long awaited by the orchid, that had come to bring her the rare pollen without which she would remain a virgin? (*S* 4, 10)

Throughout the passage Proust plays with the idea of a double coupling, or *conjonction*: one in which two human beings, providentially placed opposite each other on the stage of an inner Parisian courtyard, move toward each other with the aesthetic grace of a dance movement and with the inevitability of a shared destiny; and another one in which an insect is drawn, with similar beauty and by a parallel fate, to an awaiting orchid. The humor of the situation consists in the fact that Charlus, who is merely *like* a bumble-bee, is successful in his very real seduction of Jupien (the narrator is quite explicit in describing the orgasmic sounds he hears from the room adjoining the one in which the two new lovers have sought refuge – *R* III, 11; *S* 4, 13); whereas, at the very end of the scene, the narrator, having concentrated solely on the human drama of the two men, concludes with a conditional and perhaps fictitious wistfulness: "[I] was distressed at having, by attending to the Jupien–Charlus conjunction, perhaps missed the fertilization of the flower by the bumble-bee" (*S* 4, 36).

Of primary importance in the elaborate staging of the male couple's coming-together is the continual use of natural metaphors to describe their behavior, especially in the light of the classical prejudice by which the activity of homosexual men is termed "unnatural" – all the more "unnatural" since, unlike in heterosexual relations, fertilization (botanically expressed, pollination) cannot occur. The rhetorical bravura of the episode rests upon the sheer insistence with which the narrator multiplies his metaphors and transforms a human interaction into a mythical or fabulous one. As was the case in certain passages of *A l'Ombre des jeunes filles en fleurs*, we find ourselves in a universe of hybrid creatures, part plant, part insect, part human, which circulate freely across those boundaries that rational thought has erected in order to separate the human from the non-human, culture from nature.

A more detailed reading of the scene than is possible here would need to point out the complexity of the nature–culture dichotomy as it plays itself out from the beginning until the end of the episode. On the one hand, in the early paragraphs of the chapter, the narrator seems to establish a clear opposition between the unpleasant excessive behavior of the baron, his *étrangeté* viewed as a fictitious dissimulation, and his true nature, his inherent naïve goodness. In this scheme, Charlus's machismo is a cultural mask beneath which, on rare occasions such as the *conjonction* scene, one is able to glimpse his authentic and "natural" self. This authentic self lying under the inauthentic exterior is that of a woman hiding under a falsely constructed man. In the passage that follows, we have the concise expression of Proust's sexual theory: that homosexual men are *hommes-femmes*, that is to say, fabulous creatures exhibiting the distinguishing traits of both sexes but who are, in essence, women:

> Je regrettais pour lui [Charlus] qu'il adultérât habituellement de tant de violences, *d'étrangetés déplaisantes* ... la bonté qu'au moment où il sortait de chez Mme de Villeparisis, je voyais s'étaler si naïvement sur son visage. Clignant des yeux contre le soleil, il semblait presque sourire, je trouvai à sa figure vue ainsi au repos *et comme au naturel* quelque chose de si affectueux, de si désarmé, que je ne pus m'empêcher de penser combien M. de Charlus eût été fâché s'il avait pu se savoir regardé; car ce à quoi me faisait penser cet homme qui était si épris, qui se piquait si fort de virilité ... c'était à une femme! (*R* III, 5–6; my emphasis)
>
> I regretted for his [Charlus's] sake that he should habitually adulterate, by his many violences, *his disagreeable idiosyncrasies* ... the amenity and kindness I could see displayed so artlessly on his face at the moment when he emerged from Mme de Villeparisis's. Blinking against the sunlight, he seemed almost to be smiling, and in his face, seen thus in repose *and as it were in its natural state*, I found something so affectionate, so defenceless, that I could not help reflecting how angry M. de Charlus would have been had he known he was being watched; for what he put me in mind of, this man who was so enamoured of, who so prided himself on, his virility ... was a woman! (*S* 4, 7–8; my emphasis)

Only one page after this paragraph, however, the notions of strangeness and naturalness or naïveté are no longer opposed to each other as unpleasant culturally elaborated surface and ethically admirable depth, but are placed in parallel and treated essentially as equivalents. In his overview of the scene that is being deployed in front of his eyes, the narrator states, with a disarming directness: "Cette scène n'était, du reste, pas positivement comique, elle était empreinte d'une étrangeté, ou si l'on veut, d'un naturel, dont la beauté allait croissant" (*R* III, 7) ["This scene was not positively comical, however, it was imbued with a strangeness, or if you like a naturalness, the beauty of which continued to grow" (*S* 4, 9)].[4] Although it is necessarily a matter of conjecture for the reader to determine what Proust might be trying to do in shifting and upending the philosophical categories on which he is founding his discourse, it may be that this transfer of the concept of "strangeness" from the side of culture to that of nature rests upon a shift in point of view. Viewed from the perspective of heterosexual normativity, Charlus's behavior is strange and, in Proust's words, "positively comical." But viewed from Charlus's own perspective – that of a homosexual man trying to seduce another man who, he senses, shares his orientation – his actions are natural. And these very actions, if viewed by a spectator willing to share rather than reject his point of view, can appear beautiful. Underlying the rhetorical complexity of the scene is a fundamental problem in communication: how can a narrator who has adopted a heterosexual persona stage homosexual love in its phenomenal beauty to an audience or readership that is assumed to be otherwise orientated? Will the beauty of the phenomenon necessarily become translated as something strange, or even comical?

The balancing act that Proust had to perform in writing a semi-autobiographical novel in which the narrator is sometimes Proust and sometimes some other entity or voice is nowhere more apparent in its precarious difficulty than in this scene. A more thorough reading of the passage would show that it is divided into three large sections, the first and third of which center on the Charlus–Jupien conjunction and abide by fictional convention. The narrator, as exterior observer, relates what he sees of the unfolding drama and comments upon the significance of the explicit revelation of Charlus's sexuality for his own understanding of the world. The second section, however (*R* III, 16–28; *S* 4, 18–30), detaches itself from any semblance of adherence to the norms of narrative logic and becomes a rhetorically charged atemporal discourse, a cry of despair and a plea for understanding in which, quite simply, *a different voice speaks* – not the voice of the ostensibly heterosexual narrator who has been weaving his story of aesthetic and sentimental education, but the voice of someone who speaks from within homosexuality, and who has an allegory to relate on the sufferings and misfortunes of the homosexual *race*.

From the twelve-page passage to which I now refer, I am able to quote only one part of a much more developed whole in which, significantly, the historical destiny of homosexuals is continually compared to that of the Jews. It is as if, in this highly concentrated section of the *Recherche*, Proust shed all pretense at aesthetic distance and allowed both his maternal Jewish background and his homosexual identity to emerge into the light and to temporarily arrest the forward thrust of his narrative. For the limited purposes of my argument, I shall cite only the first long sentence of this elaborate disquisition:

Race sur qui pèse une malédiction et qui doit vivre dans le mensonge et le parjure, puisqu'elle sait tenu pour punissable et honteux, pour inavouable, son désir, ce qui fait pour toute créature la plus grande douceur de vivre; qui doit renier son Dieu, puisque même chrétiens, quand à la barre du tribunal ils comparaissent comme accusés, il leur faut, devant le Christ et en son nom, se défendre comme d'une calomnie de ce qui est leur vie même; fils sans mère, à laquelle ils sont obligés de mentir toute la vie et même à l'heure de lui fermer les yeux; amis sans amitiés, malgré toutes celles que leur charme fréquemment reconnu inspire et que leur cœur souvent bon ressentirait; mais peut-on appeler amitiés ces relations qui ne végètent qu'à la faveur d'un mensonge et d'où le premier élan de confiance et de sincérité qu'ils seraient tentés d'avoir les ferait rejeter avec dégoût, à moins qu'ils n'aient à faire à un esprit impartial, voire sympathique, mais qui alors, égaré à leur endroit par une psychologie de convention, fera découler du vice confessé l'affection même qui lui est la plus étrangère, de même que certains juges supposent et excusent plus facilement l'assassinat chez les invertis et la trahison chez les Juifs pour des raisons tirés du péché originel et de la fatalité de la race? (*R* III, 16–17)

A race on which a malediction weighs and which must live in falsehood and in perjury, because it knows that its desire, which, for every created being, is life's sweetest pleasure, is held to be punishable and shameful, to be inadmissible; which must deny its god, since, even if Christian, when they stand arraigned at the bar of the court, they must, before Christ and in his name, defend themselves, as if from a calumny, from what is their life itself; sons without a mother, to whom they are obliged to lie even in the hour when they close her eyes; friends without friendships, notwithstanding all those that their frequently acknowledged charm inspires and which their often kindly hearts would respond to; but can we give the name of friendship to relationships that vegetate only by virtue of a lie and from which the first impulse of trust and sincerity which they might be tempted to show would cause them to be rejected in disgust, unless their dealings are with an impartial, or even a sympathetic spirit, but who then, misled in their regard by a conventional psychology, will ascribe to the vice confessed the one affection that is the most alien to it, just as certain judges presume and excuse murder more readily among the inverts and betrayal among Jews for reasons deriving from original sin and the fatality of the race? (*S* 4, 18–19)

This is an arresting, disquieting, and haunting but not typical moment within the vast reaches of the *Recherche*. For the most part, the narrator keeps his distance – from the excesses and violence of the other characters, from the absurdity of the human comedy as it evolves in social settings, and even, through the use of irony and self-deprecation, from his own human failings. Here, however, one senses more strongly than anywhere else in the novel, Proust's own anguish, his own frustrations, and especially, his fundamental and heartfelt solitude. Despite the very different context, perhaps the final message conveyed in this unusually direct confession about the homosexual "race" is the same one we already saw in the narrator's cryptic comment on the discouraging words pronounced by the eminent Professor E*** upon recognizing the imminent death of his grandmother: "Each of us is very much alone" (*S* 3, 316).

Les Intermittences du coeur [The Intermittences of the Heart] *(*R *III, 148–78;* S *153–83)*

A third of the way into *Sodome et Gomorrhe* the narrator decides to leave Paris for a second stay in Balbec, which occupies the remainder of the volume. There appear to be two essential motivations underlying his wish for a change of location: an aesthetic one (certain "images" of the seascape that remain embedded in his memory call for a return visit – *R* III, 149; *S* 4, 154); and a more practical one (the strong desire to see the lady's-maid of Mme Putbus, a recurring figure occupying the narrator's erotic reveries but who is frustratingly evanescent and physically absent throughout the text – *R* III, 149–52; *S* 4, 155–57).[5] Yet as of the fifth paragraph of the new episode, the narrator informs us, in an explicit foreshadowing of things to come, that neither the novelty of new aesthetic sensations nor the "exaltation" of erotic projects will change the pattern of his life. The shift of place, by which he initially hopes to break out of the dulling patterns of habit, turns out to be illusory.[6]

Du moins à Balbec, où je n'étais pas allé depuis longtemps, j'aurais cet avantage … que le sentiment de la réalité n'y serait pas supprimé pour moi par l'habitude comme à Paris où, soit dans ma propre maison, soit dans une chambre connue, le plaisir auprès d'une femme ne pouvait pas me donner un instant l'illusion, au milieu des choses quotidiennes, qu'il m'ouvrait accès à une nouvelle vie … Or cette illusion, je l'aurais peut-être dans un pays nouveau où renaît la sensibilité, devant un rayon de soleil, et où justement achèverait de m'exalter la femme de chambre que je désirais: or on verra les circonstances faire non seulement que cette femme ne vint pas à Balbec, mais que je ne redoutai rien tant qu'elle y pût venir, de sorte que ce but principal de mon voyage ne fut ni atteint, ni même poursuivi. (*R* III, 151)

At least in Balbec, where I had not been for a long time, I should have the advantage … that my sense of reality would not be suppressed for me by habit as it was in Paris where, whether in my own house, or in some familiar bedroom, pleasure with a woman was unable to give me for a single moment the illusion, in the midst of everyday objects, that it was opening the way for me to a new life … But I would perhaps have this illusion in a new landscape, where, before a ray of sunlight, the sensibility is reborn, and where the lady's-maid whom I desired would indeed finally inflame me; but we shall see circumstances so decree not only that this woman should not come to Balbec, but that I dreaded nothing so much as that she might come, with the result that this principal object of my journey was neither attained nor even pursued (*S* 4, 156).

The naïveté of the narrator consists in his belief that novelty alone – in this case, the imagined direct influence of a new place on his sensibility – has the capacity to change his life. His thought process is future-driven, and can be summarized as a simple logical sequence: if I leave Paris for Balbec, the new landscape and my encounter with the desired woman will combine to open up for me new avenues of experience. Ironically, however, what the text produces, in the remarkable thirty-page prelude to the second Balbec sequence, is a renewal of the narrator's sensibility through a revisiting of the past. It is a return backward in time, a complex retracing of mental steps and second experiencing of initially unexamined events and emotions that opens up a strange new world to the narrator. Here, the *étrangeté* emerges not from the enactment of sexual rituals that call for interpretation, but from the uncanny cohabitation of life and death within a shared temporal expanse. This self-contained narrative block is entitled *Les Intermittences du coeur*, a phrase Proust had at one point considered as a possible title for his novel, before choosing *A la recherche du temps perdu*. It refers to the fickle quality of the human heart, or, less romantically, the human memory, which consists of its tendency not to grasp the significance of transformative events when they occur, but only later, when those events have long disappeared from consciousness.

Shortly after explaining that the "principal object" of his journey will not be attained, in an explicit redeploying of the theme of involuntary memory, the narrator recounts a dramatic event that disrupts his first night during his second stay in Balbec. While leaning over to remove his boots, he is suddenly compelled to relive the first night of his first stay in Balbec, a night in which his grandmother had come to his aid, taken off his boots, and comforted him as he faced the high ceilings of the new room in which he felt alienated and abandoned. What emerges from oblivion is not the abstract image of his grandmother, but rather, in the same way that the *petite madeleine* had opened up Combray in its essence, here it is the grandmother herself, the grandmother as paradoxically more real, more alive than in life, who comes back to occupy his room and awaken his emotions:

Bouleversement de toute ma personne. Dès la première nuit, comme je souffrais d'une crise de fatigue cardiaque, tâchant de dompter ma souffrance, je me baissai avec lenteur et prudence pour me déchausser. Mais à peine eus-je touché le premier bouton de ma bottine, ma poitrine s'enfla, remplie d'une présence inconnue, divine, des sanglots me secouèrent, des larmes ruisselèrent de mes yeux ... Je venais d'apercevoir, dans ma mémoire, penché sur ma fatigue, le visage tendre, préoccupé et déçu de ma grand-mère, telle qu'elle avait été ce premier soir d'arrivée, le visage de ma grand-mère, non pas de celle que je m'étais étonné et reproché de si peu regretter et qui n'avait d'elle que le nom, mais de ma grand-mère véritable dont, pour la première fois depuis les Champs-Elysées où elle avait eu son attaque, je retrouvais dans un souvenir involontaire et complet la réalité vivante. (*R* III, 152–53)

A convulsion of my entire being. On the very first night, as I was suffering from an attack of cardiac fatigue, trying to overcome the pain, I bent down slowly and cautiously to remove my boots. But hardly had I touched the first button of my bottine, before my chest swelled, filled with an unknown, divine presence, I was shaken by sobs, tears streamed from my eyes ... I had just glimpsed, in my memory, bent over my fatigue, the tender, concerned, disappointed face of my grandmother, such as she had been on that first evening of our arrival; the face of my grandmother, not that of the one whom I had been surprised and self-reproachful at having missed so little, who had nothing of her but her name, but of my true grandmother, the living reality of whom, for the first time since the Champs-Elysées, where she had suffered her stroke, I had rediscovered in a complete and involuntary memory. (*S* 4, 158)

The same young man who, in subsequent volumes of the *Recherche*, is to experience similar bouts of anxiety and jealousy to those that made Swann miserable in his early liaison with Odette, here provides his readers with a compelling description of love in its purest, most disinterested form – as that state which counteracts the "aridity of the soul" (*S* 4, 158) and recreates the very identity of that person (in this case, the narrator) who, without this love, would be utterly lost. Love as the restoration of the self to the self by the other: this is Proust's definition of the curative value of the emotion. At the same time, however, the return of the grandmother from death to a paradoxical and uncanny life causes a jumbling of chronological time and the substitution of the past for the present self within the narrator's consciousness. Upon reliving his grandmother's agony, he is reduced to the state of a being who *is* nothing but excruciating pain ("I was nothing more than the being who had sought refuge in his grandmother's arms" – *S* 4, 159), and who finds himself precipitated into a moment of the past which, because of the intensity of its affect, seems to have occurred just moments before. These initial reflections lead to a further meditation on what the narrator calls, in a memorable phrase, "cette contradiction si étrange de la survivance et du néant entrecroisés en moi" (*R* III, 156) ["this strange contradiction between survival and oblivion, intersecting within me" (*S* 4, 161)]. The grandmother, who has been dead for some time, lives again through "the intermittences of the heart." It is this ghostly return to life that enacts the "contradiction" constituted by the intertwined threads of her survival through involuntary memory and the finally understood reality of her death.[7]

If the grandmother's death has become real after the fact, it is because it has become interiorized by the narrator. If, on the one hand, the grandmother had the power to restore the narrator to himself, to make him whole, on the other hand, with the effective realization of her death, of the oblivion which is now her place, the narrator can assert that his grandmother has become part of himself; she has entered him, so that the past suffering he inflicted on her he now feels within himself:

Mais jamais je ne pourrais plus effacer cette contradiction de sa figure, et cette souffrance de son cœur ou plutôt du mien; car comme les morts n'existent plus qu'en nous, c'est nous-mêmes que nous frappons sans relâche, quand nous nous obstinons à nous souvenir des coups que nous leur avons assénés. Ces douleurs, si cruelles qu'elles fussent, je m'y attachais de toutes mes forces, car je sentais bien qu'elles étaient l'effet du souvenir que j'avais de ma grand-mère, la preuve que ce souvenir était bien présent en moi. (*R* III, 156)

But never would I be able to erase that contradiction from her face, or that suffering from her heart, or rather from my own; for since the dead exist only in us, it is ourselves that we strike unrelentingly when we persist in remembering the blows we have dealt them. I clung to these sorrows, however cruel they might be, with all my strength, for I felt indeed that they were the effect of my memory of my grandmother, the proof that this memory which I had was indeed present in me. (*S* 4, 161)

The theme of survival, or living on beyond death, is present not only in the first half of the episode, where the grandmother's survival is to be understood as her continued interiorized presence within the narrator's consciousness, but also in the second half of the *Intermittences* section, where, in a truly uncanny metamorphosis, the narrator's mother "becomes" the grandmother by beginning to resemble her physically, by adopting her mannerisms, her habits, and even her admiration for the *Letters* of Mme de Sévigné. For the remainder of the novel, the mother will replace the grandmother and will take over her role, acting as confidante and protector, providing an unconditional love that is not always reciprocated. It is the seamlessness of this substitution, the ease with which the character traits are passed on from mother to daughter, which allows for the narrator to overcome his grief, to accomplish the phases of the mourning process, and for the narrative to break out of its suspended state and to move forward. Whereas in the Charlus–Jupien conjunction scene the natural realm was interwoven with cultural elements and occluded by a fundamental strangeness, in the final paragraph of *Les Intermittences du coeur* Proust concludes the episode in a paean to nature, a celebration of the return and restoration of life after death has been resuscitated, then enveloped within the mourner's mind. Walking alone along a road his grandmother had once taken with Mme de Villeparisis, the narrator sees what first appear to be refined effects of art, but discovers, upon closer inspection, the pure expression of natural beauty:

Mais dès que je fus arrivé à la route ce fut un éblouissement. Là où je n'avais vu avec ma grand-mère au mois d'août que les feuilles et comme l'emplacement des pommiers, à perte de vue ils étaient en pleine floraison, d'un luxe inouï … Des mésanges bleues venaient se poser sur les branches et sautaient entre les fleurs, indulgentes, comme si c'eût été un amateur d'exotisme et de couleurs qui avait artificiellement créé cette beauté vivante. Mais elle touchait jusqu'aux larmes parce que, si loin qu'elle allât dans ses effets d'art raffiné, on sentait qu'elle était naturelle, que ces pommiers étaient là en pleine campagne comme des paysans, sur une grande route de France. (*R* III, 177–78)

But the moment I reached the road, what bedazzlement. There where, in August, with my grandmother, I had seen only the leaves and as it were the emplacement of the apple trees, they were in full flower for as far as the eye could see, unimaginably luxuriant … Blue tits were coming to settle on the branches and were leaping about among the indulgent flowers, as if it were some lover of exoticism and of colours who had artificially created this living beauty. But it moved one almost to tears because, however excessive these effects of a refined artifice, you felt that it was natural, that these apple trees were there, in the heart of the countryside, like peasants, on one of the highways of France. (*S* 4, 182–83)

*A conversation on the esplanade of the Grand-Hôtel and its effects (*R *III, 200–29;* S *4, 205–35)*

Despite the heavy emphasis on the sexual dimension of intimate human relationships in *Sodome et Gomorrhe,* there is one short, essentially comical scene in the volume in which it would seem that Proust wished to remind his readers that questions of aesthetic appreciation and artistic beauty were not to disappear entirely from the novel. The episode itself – a conversation which takes place on the esplanade in front of the Grand-Hôtel de Balbec – has as its participants the narrator, Albertine, an unnamed lawyer who collects the works of a technically accomplished artist of the second rank, Henri Le Sidaner (1862–1939), the society matron Mme de Cambremer, and her daughter-in-law, Mme de Cambremer, née Legrandin. The scene is important for its intrinsic content, which, for the most part, is centered on questions of artistic representation and on the evolution of contemporary painting and music; but it is also of interest because of the ways in which one of its less noticeable themes – that of lying – reflects the narrative frame that surrounds it.

The short passage on the esplanade appears, on the surface, to be a classical case of comic relief in which the reader is asked to forget momentarily the serious question that is raised immediately before and also after it: namely, that of Albertine's purported lesbian adventures and, therefore, the degree to which the narrator can expect to gain the exclusive love of an elusive woman whose tendency to dissemble and to assume the masks of a Protean identity render her opaque to his jealous scrutiny. At the same time, however, the narrator's own mendacious attitude within the episode furnishes a curious echo-effect for the passages surrounding it, to such a degree that the discussion on aesthetics becomes enveloped and submerged in an ethical quagmire. Adding to the complexity of the juxtaposition between the framed scene and its larger frame is the fact that the combat between nature and culture which underlies the entirety of *Sodome et Gomorrhe* is staged with particular thematic subtlety and stylistic brilliance in this thirty-page section.

Preceding the conversation on the esplanade, the narrator asks himself whether Albertine will end up resembling Odette de Crécy, and wonders whether the "accounts" (*récits*) he hears concerning Albertine's liaisons with young women might point toward his own future suffering:

> Ces récits contribuèrent à faire que dans l'avenir mon imagination faisait le jeu de supposer qu'Albertine aurait pu, au lieu d'être une jeune fille bonne, avoir la même immoralité, la même faculté de tromperie qu'une ancienne grue [i.e., Odette], et je pensais à toutes les souffrances qui m'auraient attendu dans ce cas si j'avais dû l'aimer. (*R* III, 200)
>
> These accounts helped to ensure that in future my imagination played the game of supposing that, instead of being a good girl, Albertine might have the same immorality, the same capacity for deception, as a former whore [i.e., Odette], and I thought of all the suffering that would have awaited me in that event had I ever had to love her. (*S* 4, 205)

At the conclusion of the scene, after Albertine has rewarded the narrator, for the first time apparently, with a "French kiss," thereby temporarily calming his anxieties, the narrator includes a paragraph of reflection on the evanescence of human happiness in which he asserts that the only way to preserve the momentary satisfaction he has been granted would be to leave Balbec, isolate himself, and live with the fragile resonance of what he calls "the tonality of happiness." At the end of the scene's outer frame, in a moment of profound disillusionment, the narrator theorizes: "all we can taste of happiness is that simulacrum which had been granted me at one of those unique moments when a woman's kindness, or her caprice, or chance, applies to our desires, in a perfect coincidence, the same words and the same actions as if we had truly been loved" (*S* 4, 235).

In an act of narrative anticipation, the reader is being warned that the calming influence of the kiss and Albertine's apparent affection for the narrator can only be temporary, and, in fact, participate in the realm of the lie. A careful reading of this short paragraph of warning puts the reader in a position not to be surprised when, at the very end of *Sodome et Gomorrhe*, in a scene we shall be examining next, with the revelation of Albertine's probable friendship with Mlle Vinteuil, the terrible image of Montjouvain completely blots out exterior reality and plunges the protagonist into despair. The narrator's decision, in the final sentence of the volume, to marry Albertine, is an act of compulsive desperation carried out despite and in the face of evidence – that Albertine is, in fact, like Odette, and that the *récits* concerning the latter will be repeated, in a series of cruel variations, in *La Prisonnière* and *Albertine disparue*, simply with different *dramatis personae*. The eerie or uncanny thing is the fact that the relationship between the narrator and Albertine could be a repetition of a previously told story, *un récit déjà raconté*.

Turning now to the smaller segment on the esplanade, we find a witty social conversation based upon the interrelated questions of art, culture, taste, and theory. What makes the passage quintessentially Proustian is not only its very particular comic tone, but the fact that one of its central themes – the chronological evolution of artistic modes of representation – is itself contained within textual time, being punctuated by the day's gradual yielding to night.[8] To mark concretely the passing of time within the text, the narrator mentions the relative position of a group of seagulls on the horizon three times in the first half, and once again in the second half of the scene:

(*S* 4, 208): "We gazed at the calm sea, where stray gulls floated like white petals."

(*S* 4, 211): "The sun just then getting lower, the seagulls were now yellow, like the water-lilies in another canvas of that same series by Monet."

(*S* 4, 215): "'Oh, they're flying away!'" exclaimed Albertine, pointing to the seagulls which, ridding themselves for a moment of their floral incognito, were rising as one towards the sun."

(*S* 4, 228) (The following reference occurs in the second part of the episode, in the larger frame narrative. Mme de Cambremer and her entourage have departed; the narrator is alone with Albertine in his room at the Grand-Hôtel): "I went as far as the windows; the gulls had settled again on the waves; but now they were pink."

In changing color from white to yellow to pink and in passing from a state of immobility to flight back to immobility, the seagulls infuse the text with a sense of fluctuating natural life. Yet it is clear, from the first description of the birds, that they are of interest to the narrator and to his interlocutors only insofar as they can be compared to something else – either flowers *per se* ("like white petals"), or flowers as represented in an Impressionist painting (the celebrated series of water lilies painted at Giverny by Claude Monet [1840–1926]). Nature becomes a pretext for cultural appropriation. Part of the humor of the scene derives from the participants' inability to see nature except as refracted through the lens of a culturally composed prism.

One senses that the scene on the esplanade in its totality was written as a set piece to illustrate Proust's theory concerning *conversation* as a debased form of communication, as a mode of flight from self-reflection and from the intellectual and moral depth that can be found in the serious work of art.[9] What is interesting in this episode, however (and what differentiates it from those moments of the novel in which the narrator engages, in a quite serious tone, in aesthetic philosophizing), is that the narrator himself indulges, in his conversational *badinage*, in the lowest kinds of inauthentic verbiage. From the very beginning of the passage, the aesthetic pronouncements of the participants, including those of the narrator, are suffused with a morally suspect light. Rather than speak for himself and transmit whatever ideas he might, in fact, possess about nature and art, the narrator adopts another voice, or the voice of another. Let me now quote once more the first seagull description, but in context:

Nous regardions la mer calme où des mouettes éparses flottaient comme des corolles blanches. A cause du niveau de simple "médium" où nous abaisse la conversation mondaine, et aussi notre désir de plaire non à l'aide de nos qualités ignorées de nous-mêmes, mais de ce que nous croyons devoir être prisé par ceux qui sont avec nous, je me mis instinctivement à parler à Mme de Cambremer, née Legrandin, de la façon qu'eût pu faire son frère. "Elles ont," dis-je, en parlant des mouettes, "une immobilité et une blancheur de nymphéas." (*R* III, 203)

We gazed at the calm sea, where stray gulls floated like white petals. Because of the level of simple "medium" to which worldly conversation reduces us, and also our desire to please with the help, not of qualities of which we are ourselves unaware, but of what we believe must be prized by those we are with, I began instinctively to talk to Mme de Cambremer, *née* Legrandin, in the manner in which her brother might have done. "They have," I said, referring to the gulls, "the whiteness and stillness of water-lilies." (*S* 4, 208–09)

Nowhere in the *Recherche* is the complex position or situation of the narrator more evident than in this comic scene. On the one hand, it is the narrator's voice that enunciates in a cool, disinterested tone an interesting view on the evolution of the arts (he speaks against the idea of a linear "progress" from Richard Wagner [1813–1883] to Claude Debussy [1862–1918], for example, and argues for a more subtle notion of the successor artist's intellectual and intertextual coming to terms with his predecessor, "for we use the weapons won in battle after all finally to liberate ourselves from him whom we have momentarily vanquished" [*S* 4, 215]). On the other hand, however, as participant in the conversation, the narrator enjoys "torturing" (see the words "torture" and "the rack" as they appear in *S* 4, 213–14) Mme de Cambremer, née Legrandin, each time she is guilty of enunciating an opinion which, in his view, is naïve – as when she indicates her disdain for artists who, in preceding the contemporary period, possess no value in her system of aesthetic judgment: Nicolas Poussin (1594–1665), who supposedly pales in comparison with J.M.W. Turner (1775–1851) and the Impressionists, and Frédéric Chopin (1810–49), whose works, we are told, have been relegated to the dust-bin of history by Debussy. When the narrator informs her that Edgar Degas (1834–1917) admires Poussin and that Debussy is a defender of Chopin, he enjoys watching his interlocutor squirm, as she decides that perhaps another look at Poussin might be worthwhile, and that, after all, there might be some content residing in the arabesques of Chopin's musical phrases.

Of primary interest to the reader of Proust is that the linkage between the framed scene on the esplanade and the larger frame section on the vexed relationship between the narrator and Albertine is provided in the figure of the narrator himself. The common strand that brings together the two narrative threads is the theme of questioning, but in the ancient and violent sense of the French phrase meaning to torture: *mettre à la question*. Just as the narrator "tortures" the young Mme de Cambremer by dismantling the fragile web of her aesthetic opinions, in the same way, in the second half of the episode, he uses manipulative questioning and a deceitful, fictitious narrative of a liaison he has supposedly had with Andrée, to pry open from Albertine the depths of her presumed lesbian identity:

> Aussitôt seuls et engagés dans le corridor, Albertine me dit: "Qu'est-ce que vous avez contre moi?" Ma dureté avec elle m'avait-elle été plus pénible à moi-même? N'était-elle de ma part qu'une ruse inconsciente se proposant d'amener vis-à-vis de moi mon amie à cette attitude de crainte et de prière qui me permettrait de l'interroger, et peut-être d'apprendre laquelle des deux hypothèses que je formais depuis longtemps sur elle était la vraie? [i.e., Albertine "bonne" et hétérosexuelle, ou Albertine "vicieuse" et homosexuelle] (*R* III, 222)
>
> As soon as we were alone and had started down the corridor, Albertine said to me: "What have you got against me?" Had my severity towards her not been

more painful to myself? Was it only an unconscious stratagem on my part, with a view to inducing in my loved one, vis-à-vis myself, that attitude of fear and entreaty which would enable me to question her and learn perhaps which of the two hypotheses I had long since formed about her was the right one? [i.e., the "good" heterosexual Albertine, or the "bad" homosexual Albertine] (*S* 4, 228)

It is perhaps appropriate that, as the narrator initiates his questioning/torturing of Albertine, the aesthetic dimension of the text fades away and becomes absorbed in a nighttime universe of moral duplicity, in an intricate weaving and unweaving of false narratives, of purely imaginary *récits* told by the narrator to entrap his beloved. Once again, it is useful to quote the seagull description – in this case, the final one – in context, as the narrator leads Albertine to the window to observe the beauty of a natural scene:

J'allai jusqu'à la fenêtre; les mouettes étaient posées de nouveau sur les flots; mais maintenant elles étaient roses. Je le fis remarquer à Albertine. "Ne détournez pas la conversation," me dit-elle, "soyez franc comme moi." *Je mentis.* Je lui déclarai qu'il lui fallait écouter un aveu préalable, celui d'une grande passion que j'avais depuis quelque temps pour Andrée, et je le lui fis avec une simplicité et une franchise dignes du théâtre mais qu'on n'a guère dans la vie que pour les amours qu'on ne ressent pas. (*R* III, 222–23; my emphasis)

I went as far as the window; the gulls had settled again on the waves; but now they were pink. I remarked on this to Albertine: "Don't change the subject," she said, "be open like me." *I lied.* I declared that she would have to listen to a preliminary confession, of a great passion that I had been feeling for some time past for Andrée, and I made it to her with a simplicity and candour worthy of the stage, but which we hardly ever have in life save in the case of a love that we do not feel. (*S* 4, 228; my emphasis)

The contemplation of natural beauty, which had provided an evanescent lyrical conclusion to the *Intermittences of the Heart* episode, turns out, in this context, to be a feint, a ruse within a larger strategy of domination through fiction. What Albertine does not understand is that the expression "Don't change the subject" ("Ne détournez pas la conversation") is, within the Proustian universe, a contradiction in terms. In the vast majority of its occurrences, conversation in the *Recherche* is *détournement*, wherein the imposition of a cultural veneer on nature blots out whatever "simple" beauty nature might be said to possess. The descent into the nocturnal domain of lying, that domain on which both the social conversation on the esplanade and the more intimate questioning in the Grand-Hôtel are grounded, will have been prepared, for some time, by the cultural *détournement* of nature by the person of culture, the narrator himself. As we turn now to the final episode of *Sodome et Gomorrhe*, we begin to enter the claustrophobic world in which a narrator-jailer attempts to imprison a woman who, like the seagulls, is only momentarily to be immobilized but is, in her essence, prone to flight.

Désolation au lever du soleil [Desolation at Break of Day]
*(*R *III, 497–515;* S *4, 505–22)*

The fourth and final chapter of *Sodome et Gomorrhe* begins with the narrator's announcement to his mother that he will not marry Albertine, and concludes with the reversal of this proposition. In a moment characterized not by happiness but by profound distress and anxiety, in the final clipped, seemingly breathless sentences of the volume, the narrator declares to his mother that he must leave Balbec and marry the woman who has caused and will continue to cause him much suffering:

> "Je sais la peine que je vais te faire … Je me suis trompé, je t'ai trompée de bonne foi hier, j'ai réfléchi toute la nuit. Il faut absolument, et décidons-nous tout de suite, parce que je me rends bien compte maintenant, parce que je ne changerai plus, et que je ne pourrais pas vivre sans cela, il faut absolument que j'épouse Albertine." (*R* III, 515)
>
> "I know the pain I'm going to cause you … I was mistaken, I misled you in good faith yesterday, I've been thinking it over all night. I absolutely must, and let that be decided here and now, because I now realize clearly, because I shan't change again, and I couldn't live without it, I absolutely must marry Albertine." (*S* 4, 522)

Between the initial decision not to marry Albertine and its dramatic overturning the narrator has had a second experience of the "intermittences of the heart." Just as the image of his dead grandmother had emerged from the recesses of the past through the fortuitous untying of his boot, in this case, prompted by Albertine's casual allusion to her acquaintance with Mlle Vinteuil and her sister (*R* III, 499; *S* 4, 507), the image of Montjouvain erupts into the narrator's present and becomes for him psychologically more real than his concrete surroundings. At various junctures in the chapter, the image of Montjouvain superimposes itself upon Balbec and, at the end of the volume, as we shall see, succeeds in blotting out exterior reality altogether. The same kind of uncanny, ghostly atmosphere that pervaded the first occurrence of the *Intermittences*, wherein the grandmother's survival, as a strange life-within-death, pervaded the text, is to be found here: Albertine's identity and her potential for inflicting future pain upon the narrator adhere, uncannily, to the identities and to the demonstrated cruelty of which Mlle Vinteuil and her Sapphic friend were capable.

Characterizing the fourth chapter of *Sodome et Gomorrhe* in its entirety is a concatenation or conflation of themes and identities. Not only is the narrator's mother continually compared to his grandmother, to the point of "becoming" the grandmother by assuming her essential identity traits, there is an even more curious conflation of the narrative strand associated with the grandmother with the more recently developed thread woven around Albertine. Both of these converge in the narrator's reflection on his own imagined culpability, which is itself attached to the theme of fiction as lying. When Albertine pronounces the words designating Mlle Vinteuil and her friend, the narrator plunges into a convoluted and multi-faceted reflection which is suffused with guilt:

A ces mots prononcés comme nous entrions en gare de Parville, si loin de Combray et de Montjouvain, si longtemps après la mort de Vinteuil, une image s'agitait dans mon cœur, une image tenue en réserve pendant tant d'années … pour mon supplice, pour mon châtiment, peut-être, qui sait? d'avoir laissé mourir ma grand-mère … peut-être aussi pour faire éclater à mes yeux les funestes conséquences que les actes mauvais engendrent indéfiniment, non pas seulement pour ceux qui les ont commis, mais pour ceux qui n'ont fait, qui n'ont cru, que contempler un spectacle curieux et divertissant, comme moi, hélas! en cette fin de journée lointaine à Montjouvain, caché derrière un buisson, où (comme quand j'avais complaisamment écouté le récit des amours de Swann) j'avais dangereusement laissé s'élargir en moi la voie funeste et destinée à être douloureuse du Savoir. (*R* III, 499–500)

At these words, uttered as we were entering the station in Parville, so far from Combray and from Montjouvain, so long after Vinteuil's death, a picture came to life in my heart, a picture held in reserve during so many years … as my torment, as my punishment perhaps, who knows, for having allowed my grandmother to die … perhaps also to explode before my eyes the fateful consequences to which wicked actions give rise indefinitely, not only for those who have committed them but for those who were no more than, who thought they were merely, onlookers at a curious and diverting spectacle, like me, alas, on that far-off day's end in Montjouvain, hidden behind a bush, where (as when I had listened complaisantly to the account of Swann's amours) I had perilously allowed to broaden out within me the fateful path of Knowledge, destined to become so sorrowful. (*S* 4, 507)

The "rising up" of the image of Montjouvain within the narrator's consciousness constitutes a negative version of the rising up from oblivion of Combray and its inhabitants in the *petite madeleine* episode. Whereas in the early scene, the little cake dipped in tea bridged past and present and allowed for the construction of a narrative line connecting them, here the awakened memory of the scene of sadism and defilement has a retroactive destructive effect. Certainly it is not true, in an objective sense, that the narrator "allowed [his] grandmother to die": the illness, agony, and death of the grandmother unfolded gradually and inevitably in the text. What the narrator is targeting in this phrase where culpability and self-pity intermingle is the more accurate psychological fact that he was, at times – even the most important of times – distant from and indifferent to the suffering of his grandmother. The latter section of the quoted passage is a lucid reflection on what could be called the impossibility of distance (psychological, but also aesthetic) and indifference. Even when one is safely present, by pure chance, at a window observing strange and cruel rituals (Montjouvain), and even when one merely listens comfortably to the tale of someone else's loves (the entirety of *Un Amour de Swann*, as overheard by the well-placed narrator), one is, in fact, deeply engaged *in* those actions, gestures, and words from which a formal theatrical separation is only a matter of appearance, not substance.

It is because the narrator has what he calls, with elegant simplicity, "knowledge" (*le savoir*) of Swann and of Montjouvain (but also now of Charlus, who could have been mentioned in this same passage) that he will be henceforth incapable of not understanding the devious depths of Albertine, henceforth incapable of not deciphering the signs of homosexual discourse and practice. It is because of this knowledge, gained through experience and a sexually inflected *Bildung*, that the realm of nature, in its pure promise of beauty and of happiness, becomes increasingly a mere backdrop for a more profound drama, one which is constructed on the deviousness of desire and superimposed, as an artificial overlay, upon the natural scene it ultimately blots out.

In the final descriptive moment of *Sodome et Gomorrhe*, a natural scene which his grandmother would have appreciated and which his mother shows to him in an effort at consoling him, appears to the narrator as doubly hidden, doubly unavailable to his aesthetic appreciation. Obscured by the image of Montjouvain, but also by a "pure evocation of the sunset" whose *étrangeté* manifests itself in its complete non-relation to the passing of time and to the patterns and rhythms of the natural world, the empty image framed by his hotel window that appears now to the narrator promises nothing but its own artifice, its own inconsistency, its "deserted" and abstract fictitiousness. It is into this truly strange world that the narrator penetrates in the penultimate volumes of the novel, *La Prisonnière* and *Albertine disparue*, a world from which only the redemptive power of art, hinted at in earlier volumes but recently absent, would seem to offer a possible way out. For now, no such egress, no such deliverance can be imagined:

… derrière la plage de Balbec, la mer, le lever du soleil, que maman me montrait, je voyais, avec des mouvements de désespoir qui ne lui échappaient pas, la chambre de Montjouvain où Albertine, rose, pelotonnée comme une grosse chatte, le nez mutin, avait pris la place de l'amie de Mlle Vinteuil … Dans le désordre des brouillard de la nuit qui traînaient encore en loques roses et bleues sur les eaux encombrées des débris de nacre de l'aurore, des bateaux passaient … comme quand ils rentrent le soir: scène imaginaire, grelottante et déserte, pure évocation du couchant qui ne reposait pas, comme le soir, sur la suite des heures du jour que j'avais l'habitude de voir le précéder, déliée, interpolée, plus inconsistante encore que l'image horrible de Montjouvain qu'elle ne parvenait pas à annuler, à couvrir, à cacher – poétique et vaine image du souvenir et du songe. (*R* III, 513–14)

… behind the beach of Balbec, the sea, and the sunrise, to which Mama was pointing, I could see, in a fit of despair that did not escape her, the room in Montjouvain where Albertine, pink, curled up in a ball like a big cat, with her mischievous nose, had taken the place of Mlle Vinteuil's friend … In the disorder of the night mists that still hung in blue and pink shreds over waters littered with the pearly debris of the dawn, boats were passing … as when they return home in the evening: an imaginary scene, shivering and deserted, a pure evocation of the sunset, which did not rest, like the dusk, on the succession of hours of the day that I was in the habit of seeing precede it, slender, interpolated, more insubstantial even than the horrible image of Montjouvain that it had not succeeded in cancelling out, in covering, in concealing – a vain and poetic image of the memory and of the dream. (*S* 4, 521–22)

CHAPTER 5

La Prisonnière [The Prisoner] *and* Albertine disparue [The Fugitive]

The twin penultimate volumes of *A la recherche du temps perdu* were published posthumously, *La Prisonnière* (subtitled *Sodome et Gomorrhe III)* in 1923, and *Albertine disparue* in 1924. This section of the novel presents significant interpretative problems for its reader, in two separate but equally important ways. First, because Proust died before he was able to make final corrections and strategic structural decisions on the length and thematic content of this complex episode, the status of the text – its authenticity as the expression of the author's will and decision-making – remains very much in doubt. Second, the universe in which the action of these two volumes unfolds is significantly reduced in scope from the previous ones. Novelistic verisimilitude is often abandoned in favor of minute and obsessive psychological analysis centered on the claustrophobic arena in which the narrator at first cohabits with Albertine, then agonizes over her disappearance. It is as if, in a sudden discontinuous jump, we were moving from a kaleidoscopic Balzacian social world to strange and spare territories that point to the reduced imaginative space of Samuel Beckett.

At the highest level of generality, *La Prisonnière* and *Albertine disparue* constitute a coherent and symmetrical whole, in that the first volume, as its title implies, describes the "imprisonment" of its female protagonist by the narrator, while its continuation details her escape and death.[1] The original designation of the second volume, *La Fugitive*, drew attention to this dramatic symmetry. Proust changed the title to *Albertine disparue* just four months before his death, when he discovered that the Nobel laureate Rabindranath Tagore (1861–1941) had published a volume of poems that had been recently translated into French as *La Fugitive*. It is at the level of textual detail, and of manuscript edition, however, that critics and editors disagree as to the final design of the twin texts, especially as concerns *Albertine disparue*, which Proust was writing and correcting, with feverish intensity, during the two weeks preceding his death. This was a period of considerable physical suffering in which the writer slept little and ate

6 Marcel Proust in Venice

virtually nothing; whether he himself was the best person, given the circumstances, to make far-reaching editorial decisions on his manuscript has been hotly debated.

What we are now able to reconstruct from a fortuitous discovery made in 1986 by Nathalie Mauriac is that between November 7 and 17, 1922, Proust traced a diagonal line through roughly two-thirds of the typescript of *Albertine disparue.*[2] Concluding that Proust had intended to eliminate these pages, Nathalie Mauriac and Etienne Wolff published a shortened version of the volume in 1987.[3] Their text differs considerably from the 1989 Pléiade edition, which retains the "eliminated" pages while acknowledging, in a lengthy and detailed editor's "Notice," the philological and structural issues raised by the Mauriac–Wolff edition.[4] It is on the Pléiade edition that all recent English translations are based, including the Penguin translation. In 1992, Jean Milly published what he called an "*édition intégrale*" of *Albertine disparue*, which takes into account all existing drafts, notebooks, manuscripts, and typescripts of the episode, and which highlights those sections that Proust had crossed out in the final days of his life. Milly's belief is that the "oblique lines which cross out the suppressed pages are not meant to cancel this portion of the text, but, as is often the case in Proust, indicate that these passages are, or should be, taken up elsewhere."[5] We will never know whether Proust intended to eliminate or to save for later use this considerable portion of the text. The forced interruption of his death leaves the contemporary reader in a quandary from which there is no easy escape. To read *Albertine disparue* in its fragmentary intensity is to bear witness to the writing of the novel as perpetual work-in-progress and to enter the intimacy of the writer's creative process. While I shall be using the Pléiade and Penguin editions for my own purposes here, the reader wishing to deepen his or her knowledge of this major textual question should consult both the Mauriac–Wolff and Milly editions.

LA PRISONNIÈRE

The narrator's anguished decision, at the end of *Sodome et Gomorrhe*, to leave Balbec and marry Albertine against his mother's wishes, results in a considerable narrowing of the subsequent volume's narrative focus. In bringing Albertine to Paris, the narrator wishes to remove her from all temptation – i.e., all possible encounters and relationships with other women – and to do so, he decides to sequester her in his apartment. Most of the plot or action of *La Prisonnière* is reduced to an oscillating psychodrama, in which the narrator alternates between calm and happiness on the one hand (when he senses that he has Albertine within view and under his control), and anxiety and jealousy on the other (when his beloved escapes him, either through the episodes from her past to which he has no access, or through her being physically absent in the present moment). The narrator's universe becomes, increasingly, an interiorized mental landscape, in which the boundaries between the real and the imaginary become blurred. The other characters in the novel appear and reappear sporadically, but, with the exception of the Baron de Charlus, they occupy very little space in the narrative. Whereas her presence had been crucial to the final dramatic conflict in *Sodome et Gomorrhe*, and while she will play a major role in the Venice episode of *Albertine disparue*, the narrator's mother exists only as a distant disapproving voice in *La Prisonnière*, as that person who, along with Françoise, sees Albertine in a critical light. Françoise, the faithful servant who accompanies the narrator on the entirety of his existential and aesthetic quests, is unable to stand in the way of her master's obsessive relationship with a woman whom she profoundly distrusts, and is also only a fleeting presence in this volume. The two principal friends – Bloch and Saint-Loup – depart the scene, only to re-emerge in the two subsequent volumes.

Beyond Albertine and the narrator, the *dramatis personae* have shrunk to three figures, each of whom plays a significant role here: one of them is already dead (the musician Vinteuil), the second dies in the course of the action (the writer Bergotte), and the third, on the contrary, is so full of an exuberant and excessive energy that he would seem to resist and elude all social constraints (Charlus). The baron is the one character in this stretch of the novel who continues to live large and to exert considerable influence beyond the confines of the narrator's room and mind. Having temporarily abandoned Jupien, Charlus is now attached to the young violinist Morel, whose career he is directing. Ever since his providential "conjunction" with Jupien, Charlus has discarded all pretence to a conventional appearance and demeanor, and has taken on the mannerisms and speech of a man who now refuses to hide his homosexuality and any trace of his homoerotic desires. In the only scene from *La Prisonnière* that can compare in length and in descriptive detail to the large-scale dinners and soirées of the previous volumes, a musical evening organized by M. and Mme Verdurin (*R* III, 697–830; *S* 5, 174–302), Charlus's grand entrance is worth quoting:

> Au moment d'arriver chez Mme Verdurin, j'aperçus M. de Charlus naviguant vers nous de tout son corps énorme, traînant sans le vouloir à sa suite un de ces apaches ou mendigots, que son passage faisait maintenant infailliblement surgir même des coins en apparence les plus déserts, et dont ce monstre puissant était bien malgré lui toujours escorté, quoique à quelque distance, comme le requin par son pilote, enfin contrastant tellement avec l'étranger hautain de la première année de Balbec, à l'aspect sévère, à l'affectation de virilité, qu'il me sembla découvrir, accompagné de son satellite, un astre à une tout autre période de sa révolution et qu'on commence à voir dans son plein, ou un malade envahi maintenant

par le mal qui n'était il y a quelques années qu'un léger bouton qu'il dissimulait aisément et dont on ne soupçonnait pas la gravité. (*R* III, 708–09)

As we arrived at Mme Verdurin's, I saw M. de Charlus steering his whole enormous body in our direction, unconsciously drawing along in his wake one of the street-arabs or young gangsters who now invariably sprang from the earth as he passed, even in the most apparently deserted spots, to escort the powerful monster, albeit at a certain distance, as a shark is accompanied by its pilot-fish, and presenting such a contrast with the haughty stranger of my first year at Balbec, with his stern aspect and affectation of manliness, that I felt I was seeing, accompanied by its satellite, a heavenly body at quite a different moment of its orbit and now appearing in its full phase, or a patient now invaded by the illness which a few years ago was a mere pimple, easily concealed and whose gravity no one suspected. (*S* 5, 185)

As we enter the final phase of the *Recherche*, Charlus has evolved from a merely comical or strange (*étrange*) personage to a grotesque figure, a "monster" who has exceeded the bounds of behavior that are permissible in society, and who is made to pay for his arrogance. It could be argued that there are only two actions or events that possess dramatic force in *La Prisonnière*: Albertine's flight from the narrator's apartment at the very end of the volume, and the expulsion of Charlus from the Verdurin *salon* at the conclusion of the musical evening which Charlus has organized and in which Morel has performed. The problem is, precisely, that Charlus, not M. and Mme Verdurin, has been the organizer. In an act of overweening pride which the ancient Greeks called *hubris*, Charlus, without thinking about the possible consequences of his actions, has reversed his role from member of the Verdurin clan (adherent, guest) to social director of that same clan (orchestrator, host). This is why, in the passage quoted above, the expression "powerful monster" is so apt as a descriptive phrase for the baron in his current metamorphosis or planetary "orbit."

Whereas Swann had been excised from the Verdurin *salon* because his hosts had been jealous of his aristocratic connections, Charlus is discharged with similar violence because he has exercised excessive power within the social group. In both cases, there are considerable consequences for the characters' love relationships. As an exile from the Verdurin clan, Swann could only look on as Forcheville became Odette's lover, while, at the end of the musical evening in *La Prisonnière*, the *Patron* and *Patronne* manage to instigate a quarrel between Charlus and Morel which leads to a break-up. Later in this chapter, when we turn to an examination of the musical soirée itself and to the aesthetic revelations it contains, we need to keep in mind that it is framed by an act of social cruelty. It is not art in isolation, or art for art's sake that primarily interests Proust, but rather the often strange and unusual connections between the universe of art and the specific affective context in which or out of which it emerges. As we turn now to three particularly important scenes from *La Prisonnière*, we shall be encountering various ways in which love in its representation as natural expression of human passion and artistic creation as cultural achievement are both differentiated from each other yet also closely intertwined.

Albertine asleep and awake; the naming of "Marcel" *(*R *III, 571–89;* S *5, 53–70)*

Although Proust's ideas on love can be found dispersed throughout the entirety of the *Recherche*, there is one quite concentrated passage, located some fifty pages into *La Prisonnière*, which, in describing the daily rhythm of the narrator's relationship with Albertine, provides a concise and coherent overview of the subject. The passage begins with a general observation that applies not just to Albertine, but also to Andrée, and to all the *jeunes filles en fleurs* – namely, that their elusiveness is such that they can never be "immobilized," never reduced to a stable identity:

> Et, en elles-mêmes, qu'étaient Albertine et Andrée? Pour le savoir il faudrait vous immobiliser, ne plus vivre dans cette attente perpétuelle de vous où vous passez toujours autres, il faudrait ne plus vous aimer, pour vous fixer ne plus connaître votre interminable et toujours déconcertante arrivée, ô jeunes filles, ô rayon successif dans le tourbillon où nous palpitons de vous voir reparaître en ne vous reconnaissant qu'à peine, dans la vitesse vertigineuse de la lumière. (*R* III, 573)
>
> And, in themselves, what were Albertine and Andrée? To know the answer, we should have to be able to arrest your movement, stop our lives being one long wait for you, who when you arrive are always different; to fix your image we should have to stop loving you, no longer experience your endlessly postponed and always disconcerting arrival, O young girls, O successive flashes in the whirlwind where we tremble to see you reappear, barely recognizing you in the dizzying velocity of light. (*S* 5, 54–55)

This thesis statement prepares the reader for the specific and detailed account of the narrator's life with Albertine which follows. Albertine, like all the *jeunes filles*, is in her essence unstable, disseminated through space and time. Because of this, the narrator's love for her cannot be described in affirmative or positive terms, as the simple fulfillment of a desire or as the realization of an amorous plan. Rather, as he puts it succinctly later in the episode: "my pleasure in having Albertine living with me now was much less a positive pleasure than satisfaction at having removed from the world, where everyone could enjoy her in turn, the blossoming young girl who, even if she caused no great joy to me, at least could not offer it to anyone else" (*S* 5, 66). This idiosyncratic, negative, or privative view is quintessentially Proustian and characteristic of his theory of love in general. Yet it is also a bit too general to account for some of the more memorable moments of the episode, moments in which the narrator experiences the closest thing to pure happiness that one can find in the novel. These are privileged, admittedly evanescent occasions in which Albertine becomes metamorphosed, in the imagination of the narrator, into an aesthetically heightened vision which participates both in the layered beauty of artistic creation and in the simplicity of natural phenomena. Because the narrator has known her now for some time, because he has seen her in her variable and contradictory guises (as innocent, childlike girl; as difficult-to-decipher woman who loves other women and whose past is a blank slate), Albertine has taken on the magical aura, the seductive charm of Time itself:

> Je la [Albertine] voyais aux différentes années de ma vie occupant par rapport à moi des positions si différentes qui me faisaient sentir la beauté des espaces interférés, ce long temps révolu, où j'étais resté sans la voir, et sur la diaphane profondeur desquels la rose personne que j'avais devant moi se modelait avec de mystérieuses ombres et un puissant relief. Il était dû, d'ailleurs, à la superposition non seulement des images successives qu'Albertine avait été pour moi, mais encore des grandes qualités d'intelligence et de cœur, des défauts de caractère, les uns et les autres insoupçonnés de moi, qu'Albertine, en une germination, une multiplication d'elle-même, une efflorescence charnue aux sombres couleurs, avait ajoutés à une nature jadis à peu près nulle, maintenant difficile à approfondir. (*R* III, 577)
>
> I saw her [Albertine], in different years of my life, occupying different positions in relation to myself, which made me conscious of the beauty of the intervening spaces, the long periods when I had not been seeing her; against this diaphanous background the rosy person before my eyes took shape, a strongly modelled figure with mysterious shadows. Its three-dimensional character was due to the superposition, not only of the successive images that Albertine had been for me, but also of admirable traits of intelligence and feeling, and grave faults of character, all unsuspected by me, which Albertine, in a kind of germination, a multiplication of herself, a sombre-hued flowering of flesh, had added to a nature almost characterless, but now difficult to know in depth. (*S* 5, 59)

Reading through the dense metaphorical texture of this description, we see Albertine as the beautiful aesthetic object created by the narrator-artist. In and of herself, she is nothing, without intrinsic character or qualities. Yet the passage of time has conferred upon her the equivalent of a patina, such that the series of her appearances and of her encounters with the narrator, when "superposed" upon each other, produces a form of beauty which one usually associates with aesthetic objects. Notable in this rich passage is the balanced combination of imagery derived, on the one hand, from the fine arts, and, on the other, from nature. On the one hand we have terms such as "diaphanous background," "strongly modelled figure," and "superposition," yet on the other we have "germination" and "flowering of the flesh." One is tempted to conclude that one of the reasons underlying the narrator's euphoria in this passage and others like it in this section of the novel is precisely that the domains of nature and art (or culture), often in conflict with each other in the *Recherche*, here relate to each other as complements or benign supplements. Just as in the realm of geometry the superposition of figures is effected in order to demonstrate their congruence, in Proust's imaginary universe the superposition of art upon nature only enhances and makes manifest their points of convergence. It is because of Albertine's capacity to "germinate" and to "flower" that aesthetic depth and the temporal dimension inhabiting "the beauty of the intervening spaces" can be translated from the domain of the intelligible to that of the sensible. Albertine takes on form and color because she is, in her essence, a creature of nature.

The narrator's subsequent development of the "germination" and "flowering" motifs requires scrutiny, however. The delicate equilibrium of nature and art, however powerful in its evocative charm, is achieved at the expense of Albertine's life energy. She becomes beautiful, she becomes malleable for the narrator-artist, only when, under the narcotic effect of sleep, she is motionless and, therefore, no longer threatening or dangerous to him. The most haunting descriptions of Albertine in the entirety of the novel picture her as an inanimate figure that most closely resembles a plant. The young woman's beauty, though depicted here as "natural," might more accurately be characterized as uncanny, *unheimlich*,[6] based upon a strange threshold state between life and death:

> … je trouvais Albertine endormie et ne la réveillais pas. Etendue de la tête aux pieds sur mon lit, dans une attitude d'un naturel qu'on n'aurait pu inventer, je lui trouvais l'air d'une longue tige en fleur qu'on aurait disposée là … Par là son sommeil réalisait dans une certaine mesure, la possibilité de l'amour … En fermant les yeux, en perdant la conscience, Albertine avait dépouillé, l'un après l'autre, ses différents caractères d'humanité qui m'avaient déçu depuis le jour où j'avais fait sa connaissance. Elle n'était plus animée que de la vie inconsciente des végétaux, des arbres, vie plus différente de la mienne, plus étrange, et qui cependant m'appartenait davantage. Son moi ne s'échappait pas à tous moments, comme quand nous causions, par les issues de la pensée inavouée et du regard. (*R* III, 578)
>
> … I would come back to find Albertine sound asleep. I did not wake her. Lying at full length on my bed, in a pose so natural that it could never have been adopted deliberately, she seemed to me like a long, flowering stem that had been laid there … In that way her sleep realized, to a certain degree, the promise of love … By closing her eyes, by losing consciousness, Albertine had put off, one

by one, the various marks of humanity which had so disappointed me in her, from the day that we first met. She was animated only by the unconscious life of plants, of trees, a life more different from my own, stranger and yet which I possessed more securely. Her individuality did not break through at every moment, as it did when we talked, through unconfessed thoughts and unguarded looks. (*S* 5, 59–60)

The problem that lies at the center of this passage, and of the episode as a whole, is that of possession. When awake, when active in a life the entirety of which is not available to the narrator's scrutiny, Albertine is an escape artist, or what the narrator himself, at a later moment, calls an "*être de fuite*" (*R* III, 600). When awake, she cannot be possessed, either physically or imaginatively. It becomes possible for the narrator to possess her neither in her actual absence nor in her real presence, but in the in-between state of sleep, where she has assumed a stranger life than that of the narrator, an uncanny one in which, significantly, she has shed her very humanity. As the passage develops, the narrator refers to "a less pure pleasure" (*S* 5, 62) than day-dreaming which he is able to experience with Albertine, this being masturbation on her sleeping body. The pleasure he has "with" her is actually his own unreciprocated pleasure. When he then says: "It seemed to me at those moments that I had possessed her more completely, like an unconscious and unresisting part of dumb nature [*la muette nature*]" (*S* 5, 62; *R* III, 581), the reader understands that Albertine herself, as human being, has not been possessed, but that a certain image of Albertine-as-plant has been cause for the narrator's private gratification. What guarantees the complete achievement of pleasure for the narrator in these circumstances is that, like the plant kingdom, Albertine is mute (*muette*) or "dumb." Devoid of speech, incapable of dialogue, she is truly his prisoner, his object, his plaything.

For the narrator-jailer to possess his beloved prisoner (according to his narcissistic conception of "possession") she must be asleep and speechless. His mastery of her, his control over her, depends upon the necessary precondition of her having no voice. Given this power relation, it should be of more than passing interest to the reader of Proust that, when Albertine wakes up immediately following this passage, while the narrator once again insists upon his possessive feelings, the young woman's first words can be interpreted against the grain of his proud and secure thoughts:

Mais ce plaisir de la voir dormir, et qui était aussi doux que la sentir vivre, un autre y mettait fin, et qui était celui de la voir s'éveiller … Dans ce premier moment délicieux d'incertitude, il me semblait que je prenais à nouveau plus complètement possession d'elle, puisque au lieu qu'après être sortie elle entrât dans sa chambre, c'était ma chambre, dès qu'elle serait reconnue par Albertine, qui allait l'enserrer, la contenir … Elle retrouvait la parole, elle disait: "Mon" ou "Mon chéri", suivis l'un ou l'autre de mon nom de baptême, ce qui, en donnant au narrateur le même prénom qu'à l'auteur de ce livre, eût fait, "Mon Marcel", "Mon chéri Marcel." (*R* III, 582–83)

But this pleasure of watching her sleep, which was as sweet as that of feeling her live, was soon replaced by another: that of seeing her wake up … In this first delicious moment of uncertainty I felt that I was taking a new, more complete possession of her, for when she came back from outside, she would go first into her room, but now it was my room, as Albertine recognized it, that would enfold her, contain her … Now she began to speak; her first words were "darling" or "my darling", followed by my Christian name, which, if we give the narrator the same name as the author of this book, would produce "darling Marcel" or "my darling Marcel." (*S* 5, 63–64).

It is noteworthy that on one of only two quite brief occasions in a 3,000-page novel in which the narrator is given (albeit conditionally, hypothetically) a name,[7] this should occur in the context of a power struggle. The narrator thinks that because Albertine wakes up in his room, she is his: as he explains it, the room will "enfold" and "contain" her. Yet it would be more precise to say that the room "contains" her up until the moment at which she utters her first words, at which point, precisely because she has regained her voice, she now escapes her lover's control. The terms of affection establish the narrator's identity by naming him, but the initial words, the words that precede the name and frame it, are, of course, possessives: "*Mon* Marcel," "*Mon* chéri Marcel." The narrator gains a name and an identity in a moment of violent dispossession. He may have her in his room, temporarily, but she now has him in her mouth. In order to retain control over what he sees and what he experiences, the narrator has a vested interest in remaining nameless.

The death of Bergotte; the permanence of art *(*R *III, 687–93;* S *5, 165–70)*

Largely absent from *Sodome et Gomorrhe* except in the comical scene with Mme de Cambremer and her daughter-in-law on the esplanade in Balbec, the theme of art returns to center stage in two crucial episodes of *La Prisonnière* that foreshadow the aesthetic revelations of the novel's final volume, *Le Temps retrouvé.* The first of these, quite compact in length, describes the agony and death of Bergotte (*R* III, 687–93; *S* 5, 165–70). The second one, focused on Vinteuil's music, is a bit more extended, and occupies a neatly delimited section of the Verdurin soirée in which Charlus is eventually separated from Morel (*R* III, 753–69; *S* 5, 228–43). I shall be analyzing each of these in turn and shall emphasize their thematic affinities. In both cases, the narrator struggles with the question of the final significance of art, and wonders if individual paintings or writings or musical compositions generally acknowledged as masterpieces are merely the result of technical expertise, or whether they refer to a higher plane than that of our daily existence. Throughout the *Recherche,* the narrator alternates between these two hypotheses, believing in moments of discouragement and depression that even those works possessing the greatest apparent beauty may be nothing more than the products of "illusion" or *trompe-l'oeil* (*S* 5, 179; *R* III, 703), while thinking, at other, more exalted moments, that the artist's devotion to his calling, the sacrifices he makes in the creative act, can ensure the duration, or even the eternity, of what he has produced. Both the scene of Bergotte's death and the later passage on Vinteuil's septet stage the dramatic struggle between these two hypotheses, leaving open the possibility of the triumph of the second one – that of art's perennial dimension – over the first.

The six-page description of Bergotte's final days and death appears quite brusquely in the narrative flow of *La Prisonnière.*[8] In this one respect it is quite different from the longer and much more carefully prepared evocation of the grandmother's agony and death which spans volumes I and II of *Le Côté de Guermantes.* However, the reader senses that Proust wishes him or her to consider these two pivotal textual moments as intimately related to each other, as close variations on the same theme. Both episodes begin by describing medical science in satirical terms. Whereas in the case of the grandmother, there was a multiplication of doctors, each of them morally suspect, in some cases charlatans with contradictory theories about the elderly woman's malady, in the Bergotte scene the narrator keeps a closer focus, and emphasizes one central idea: that medicine essentially prolongs illnesses, and that the artificial addition of drugs and therapies to the course of nature produces nothing less than a "secondary disease." The image used is that of a graft ("la maladie artificiellement *greffée*"):

C'est une grande merveille que la médecine égalant presque la nature puisse forcer à garder le lit, à continuer sous peine de mort l'usage d'un médicament. Dès lors, la maladie artificiellement greffée a pris racine, est devenue une maladie secondaire mais vraie, avec cette seule différence que les maladies naturelles guérissent, mais jamais celles que crée la médecine, car elle ignore le secret de la guérison. (*R* III, 688)

It's a marvelous thing that medicine should be almost as powerful as nature, should force the patient to stay in bed and, under pain of death, to continue a treatment. By this time, the artificially introduced disease has taken root, has become a secondary but true illness, the only difference being that natural diseases can get better, but never medical ones, for medicine knows nothing of the secrets of cure. (*S* 5, 165)

Although the tone of this passage owes as much to Molière as did the extended comical succession of doctors in the scene of the grandmother's death, here the narrator's highlighting of the nature–artifice (or life–art) dichotomy subtends the entirety of the passage and lends it a strong thematic continuity. Not only is there a substantial development on Bergotte's use of narcotics and other drugs toward the end of his career in an effort to counteract the natural evolution of his disease (a development with strong autobiographical overtones given Proust's own alternating abuse of stimulants and opiates in his final years), but the general question of the relation between art as cultural overlay and its basis in life also pervades the episode. In a first section, the narrator depicts Bergotte as a disillusioned man who has written nothing of value for a number of years and who is imprisoned in a largely unproductive existence. Spending much of his time and money luring prepubescent girls (*fillettes*) to his apartment for the satisfaction of his pleasures, Bergotte reasons with a cynicism that piques the interest of the narrator and that raises, albeit negatively and sardonically, the fundamental question of artistic transformation or "transmutation":

Aussi Bergotte se disait-il: "Je dépense plus que des multimillionnaires pour des fillettes, mais les plaisirs ou les déceptions qu'elles me donnent me font écrire un livre qui me rapporte de l'argent". Economiquement ce raisonnement était absurde mais sans doute trouvait-il quelque agrément à transmuter ainsi l'or en caresses et les caresses en or. (*R* III, 689)

So it was that Bergotte said to himself, "I spend more on girls than a multimillionaire, but the pleasures or disappointments they bring me allow me to write a book and make money". On economic grounds this reasoning was absurd, but no doubt he took some pleasure in transmuting gold into caresses in this way, and caresses back into gold. (*S* 5, 166)

In a grand ironical reversal, the final two pages of the passage on Bergotte's death develop this same theme of transformation or transmutation, but in a tone opposite to that of cynicism – with seriousness, exaltation, and aesthetic reverence. Having read a review of a Parisian exhibit of Dutch paintings on loan from the museum of The Hague, and, in particular, an art critic's enthusiastic assessment of the *View of Delft* by Johannes Vermeer (1632–75), Bergotte decides to leave his sickroom and see the assembled paintings. In a scene that is quite closely modeled on Marcel Proust's own life (accompanied by the art critic Jean-Louis Vaudoyer, Proust witnessed such an exhibit of Dutch paintings in May

1921 at the Jeu de Paume museum, including the *View of Delft*),[9] Bergotte experiences an aesthetic revelation just moments before he falls to the museum floor and dies.

Although in passing by the first group of paintings Bergotte "had an impression of the sterility and uselessness of such an artificial form, and how inferior it was to the outdoor breezes and sunlight of a palazzo in Venice, or even an ordinary house at the seaside" (*S* 5, 169), this initial impression of the inferiority of art to nature is dramatically superseded and indeed reversed, as the novelist stands in front of the Vermeer. Having had his attention drawn by the attentive critic (nameless in the novel, but whose model was obviously Vaudoyer) to one particular detail of the work, "un petit pan de mur jaune," or "a little patch of yellow wall" (*R* III, 692; *S* 5, 169), Bergotte realizes that the successful work of art consists in the transmutation of material reality in its utmost simplicity into an aesthetic equivalent which retains this simplicity, but infuses it with a formal rigor and density. The little patch of wall is rendered with such perfection by the Dutch artist that Bergotte is compelled, in the face of this achievement, to place his own work in the balance against that of his predecessor and find it lacking: "That is how I should have written," he said to himself. "My last books are too dry, I should have applied several layers of colour, made my sentences precious in themselves, like that little patch of yellow wall" (*S* 5, 169). The famous novelist falls to the floor and dies, thinking that he has not fully realized his potential or brought to final fruition the imaginative projects that lay dormant within him.

Yet in a dramatic upswing which is quite similar to the movement that structures the scene of the *petite madeleine*, and which uses the same interrogative phrase for this articulation – "Mort à jamais?" ("Dead for ever?") (compare *R* I, 43 to *R* III, 693) – in the same way that he had asked, at the beginning of the novel, whether Combray were truly lost to him in its lived essence, here the narrator wonders whether the writer Bergotte, for all his self-perceived imperfections, is truly dead, or whether, through his works, he might live on. The answer to this question is less emphatically affirmative in the scene of Bergotte's death than in the episode of the *petite madeleine*, in that the very interesting answer is framed by two qualifying statements. At the beginning of the final development we have: "Mort à jamais? Qui peut le dire?" ["Dead for ever? Who can say?"], while the conclusion reads: "De sorte que l'idée que Bergotte n'était pas mort à jamais est sans invraisemblance" ["So that the idea that Bergotte was not dead for ever is not at all implausible"] (*R* III, 693; *S* 5, 170). There is some logical distance between "not at all implausible" and "necessarily true," so that we need to take the narrator's speculations precisely as speculations, but accord them our careful scrutiny.

At the end of the episode's penultimate paragraph, the narrator, using a generalized "nous" ("we"), hypothesizes that all artists owe allegiance to a moral contract to which they were bound in a former life before entering this one. It is only the existence, for the artist, of these prior ethical obligations that can explain the extraordinary efforts he or she expends on individual works of art which might or might not be passed on to posterity. If there should be such a thing as the immortality of the soul, it is not in a traditional religious sense (Proust was not a believer, and his narrator never appears to be), but as a consequence of the existence of those moral obligations contracted in a previous life to which the artist has sworn his fealty, as to the defining parameters of a different "world." It is the intuition that this other world, that of art, exists, that grounds the artist in his creative work, making possible the final short paragraph of the passage, in which the narrator compares the deceased Bergotte's assembled books to "angels with outspread wings" symbolizing his "resurrection." What the narrator says about the different world in which all artists live while also living in our own is worth quoting, with an eye toward the next episode for analysis, that of Vinteuil's posthumous septet:

> Ce qu'on peut dire, c'est que tout se passe dans notre vie comme si nous y entrions avec le faix d'obligations contractées dans une vie antérieure ... Toutes ces obligations qui n'ont pas leur sanction dans la vie présente semblent appartenir à un monde différent, fondé sur la bonté, le scrupule, le sacrifice, un monde entièrement différent de celui-ci, et dont nous sortons pour naître à cette terre, avant peut-être d'y retourner, revivre sous l'empire de ces lois inconnues auxquelles nous avons obéi parce que nous en portions l'enseignement en nous ... De sorte que l'idée que Bergotte n'était pas mort à jamais est sans invraisemblance. (*R* III, 693)
>
> What we can say is that everything in our life happens as if we entered it bearing a burden of obligations contracted in an earlier life ... All these obligations which do not derive their force from the here-and-now seem to belong to a different world founded on goodness, conscientiousness, sacrifice, a world quite different from this one, which we leave to be born on to this earth, and to which we shall perhaps return, to live under those unknown laws which we have obeyed because we carried their teaching within us ... So that the idea that Bergotte was not dead for ever is not at all implausible. (*S* 5, 170)

Vinteuil's septet: unveiling the homeland of the artist *(*R *III, 753–69;* S *5, 228–43)*

At the midpoint of the musical evening organized by the Baron de Charlus and held in the *salon* of M. and Mme Verdurin in order to showcase the virtuosity of the violinist Morel, Proust inserts one of the key passages of his novel, in which the narrator, while listening to the posthumously published septet of Vinteuil, transcribes some of his most moving meditations on the transcendental significance of artistic works. The fifteen-page scene can be divided into two large sections, the first of which deals directly with the narrator's aesthetic reflections as he experiences, for the first time, the masterpiece which had been completed by the same musician who had composed the Sonata for Piano and Violin – the work known to the reader from its dramatic appearance at the soirée hosted by Mme de Saint-Euverte in *Un Amour de Swann*. It is clear that Proust meant his reader to compare and contrast two evenings placed at a textual distance of almost 2,000 pages from each other, the one attended by Swann, the other by the narrator, in which the performance of Vinteuil's music is the pretext for far-reaching theoretical developments on the possibilities and limits of artistic representation.

The second section of the passage on the septet is less directly focused on music *per se*, but is concerned with the vexed human context in which this and other works of art originate. In the final paragraphs of the episode, the narrator introduces an ethical dimension to what had been a discussion with an exclusively aesthetic orientation, and concludes by establishing an analogical relation between the stages of his own life and the evolution of Vinteuil's musical style. Because the passage on the septet is one of the richest in thematic material in the *Recherche* and because my own space is limited, I shall proceed with a concision bordering on the telegraphic, and shall respect the two-part division of the scene.

Vinteuil's septet as aesthetic revelation[10]

The first problem encountered by the narrator as he sits down to listen to the septet is that, having never heard it before, he has trouble situating it: it is as if he were lost in an unknown country. But soon he becomes aware of a familiar presence, that of the *petite phrase,* or "little phrase," which Vinteuil decided to insert, in a different guise, into the new composition as an echo-effect, a thematic reminder of the Sonata for Piano and Violin: "more wonderful than any girl, the little phrase, wrapped, caparisoned in silver, streaming with brilliant sonorities light and soft as scarves, came towards me, still recognizable under these new ornaments" (*S* 5, 228–29). This initial observation allows the narrator to pursue a detailed development on the dialectic between the new and the familiar in the arts, which he then extends as he reflects on the ways in which Vinteuil's musical works all resemble each other at the deepest level while retaining their unmistakable novelty, distinctiveness, and individuality.

Whereas the sonata, according to the narrator's painterly analogy, "opened on a lily-like dawn in the country," the new work seemed, upon a first hearing, to possess a "red light" and "took off on a stormy morning over flat, level surfaces like those of the sea" (*S* 5, 229). The works are thus profoundly different in their tone, or in their "color," but they both possess what the narrator calls the same "accent" (*R* III, 760; *S* 5, 235) – which belongs uniquely to Vinteuil, and which functions in the same way as the signature affixed to a painting, as an unequivocal designation of its creator's imaginative territory. Both the sonata and the septet function not as self-contained aesthetic objects, but as "questions" or "interrogations" (*S* 5, 234) of the world which, despite their particularities, both constitute the same drive for artistic innovation.

Throughout the passage, Vinteuil is presented as an artist endowed with genius according to the classical philosophical conception, whereby, in contradistinction to talent or skill, which can be acquired through learning and imitation, genius is the unique and inimitable possession of one individual.[11] The newness that characterizes Vinteuil's septet, its irreducible distinctiveness which makes it difficult to categorize or to date in the evolution of musical forms, combine, in an apparent paradox, with the quality of duration precisely because Vinteuil is an artistic genius.

In a development that builds upon what had been said in the scene of Bergotte's death, the narrator goes on to affirm that the sign of Vinteuil's distinctive genius, his special style or "accent," points beyond the usual bounds of human communication toward another world or "homeland" (*patrie*) – a world beyond language as such, situated in heavenly reaches, among the "angels" (*S* 5, 235):

> ... c'est bien un accent unique auquel s'élèvent, auquel reviennent malgré eux ces grands chanteurs que sont les musiciens originaux, et qui est une preuve de l'existence irréductiblement individuelle de l'âme ... Ce chant différent de celui des autres, semblable à tous les siens où Vinteuil l'avait-il appris, entendu? Chaque artiste semble ainsi comme le citoyen d'une patrie inconnue, oubliée de lui-même. (*R* III, 760–61)
>
> ... it is to a single, personal voice that those great singers, the original musicians, always return in spite of themselves, a voice which is the living proof of the irreducible individuality of each soul ... This song, so different from everyone else's, so similar in all his own works, where had Vinteuil learnt it? Each great artist seems to be the citizen of an unknown homeland which even he has forgotten. (*S* 5, 235)

These observations lead the narrator to the lyrical conclusion of the episode's first section, in which he postulates that those artists who remain faithful to their respective "homelands" are able to open up to their listening or observing or reading public entire aesthetic territories that this public otherwise never would have entered into. Metaphorically speaking, Bergotte and Vinteuil and Elstir lend us their ears and their eyes so that we can embark upon otherworldly voyages:

> ... cet ineffable qui différencie qualitativement ce que chacun a senti ... l'art d'un Vinteuil comme celui d'un Elstir le fait apparaître, extériorisant dans les couleurs du spectre la composition intime de ces mondes que nous appelons les individus et que sans l'art nous ne connaîtrions jamais ... Le seul véritable voyage, le seul bain de Jouvence, ce ne serait pas d'aller vers de nouveaux paysages, mais d'avoir d'autres yeux, de voir l'univers avec les yeux d'un autre, de cent autres, de voir les cent univers que chacun d'eux voit, que chacun d'eux est; et cela, nous le pouvons avec un Elstir, avec un Vinteuil, avec leurs pareils, nous volons vraiment d'étoiles en étoiles. (*R* III, 762)
>
> ... this inexpressible thing which reveals the qualitative difference between what each of us has felt ... can be expressed through art, the art of a Vinteuil or an Elstir, which makes manifest in the colours of the spectrum the intimate make-up of those worlds we call individuals, and which without art we should never know ... The only real journey, the only Fountain of Youth, would be to travel not towards new landscapes, but with new eyes, to see the universe through the eyes of another, of a hundred others, to see the hundred universes that each of them can see, or can be; and we can do that with the help of an Elstir, a Vinteuil; with them and their like we can truly fly from star to star. (*S* 5, 236–37)

The apparent contrast and profound unity between genius and vice

The rhetorical seductiveness of the narrator's reflections on Vinteuil's music could easily tempt the reader to examine the first section of the musical soirée in abstract isolation, as a series of theoretical propositions that can be linked, quite convincingly, to similar propositions in the conclusion of the novel's last volume, *Le Temps retrouvé.* In the seamless movement whereby a meditation on genius leads to the evocation of an otherworldly domain as the true "homeland" of the artist, it would be easy enough for the reader to lose sight of the here-and-now – or more precisely, of the concrete, quite worldly context in which Vinteuil's septet reaches its audience and is performed, in the specific setting of the Verdurin *salon.* The final pages of the scene detail the various interwoven narrative strands that combine to make the musical evening and its revelations possible.

In the first place, the score of the septet does not appear out of nowhere, but has been patiently and lovingly deciphered by Mlle Vinteuil's Sapphic friend, that same friend who, one early evening in Montjouvain, had participated in a sadistic ritual desecrating the photograph of the deceased musician. In revealing to the reader that it is this morally less than admirable person who has made accessible to the public Vinteuil's nearly illegible masterpiece, the narrator enunciates an interesting economically conceived theory bridging the aesthetic and the ethical in what he calls a law of "compensation": "by spending years sorting out the impenetrable mass of notes he [Vinteuil] left behind, by establishing reliable readings of those unknown hieroglyphs, she [Mlle Vinteuil's friend] had the consolation of ensuring for the composer whose last years she had darkened, a compensating immortality" (*S* 5, 240).

The complex balancing between aesthetics and ethics, between artistic genius and what the narrator calls, quite classically, "vice," extends to the conditions of possibility of the performance itself, which could not have taken place independently of another complicated human relationship – that of Charlus and Morel. This liaison, like that of Mlle Vinteuil and her friend, is outside the bounds of accepted bourgeois behavior and also far from disinterested. Charlus's motives for organizing the soirée have nothing to do with the final revelations of an artistic "homeland" contained in Vinteuil's music, but are uniquely grounded in his desire to please his lover and to launch his lover's career.

What interests the narrator in the final two pages of the scene is not art itself, and certainly not its otherworldly references, but rather what he calls, with admirable concision, the "apparent contrast and profound unity between genius ... and the sheath of vices within which, as had happened for Vinteuil, it is so often contained and protected" (*S* 5, 242). One should not forget, either, that the musical evening made immediately possible by the Baron de Charlus and more distantly possible by Mlle Vinteuil's friend is itself enclosed, as in a "sheath," by an action no less cruel than the spitting on Vinteuil's photograph – namely, the forcible break-up of the Charlus–Morel couple by M. and Mme Verdurin. In the fictional universe created by Marcel Proust, the revelations of art, however majestic in their message and magnificent in their tone, cannot be disengaged from the moral envelope in which they are enclosed. It may be that the true "homeland" of the artist is not to be located in the angelic spheres *or* in the here-and-now, but rather in the space that is created *between* genius and the sheath of vices that encloses it.

ALBERTINE DISPARUE

At the end of *La Prisonnière,* the narrator has reached a state of relative calm in his relations with Albertine and has begun to think of a possible journey to Venice without her. Yet *Albertine disparue* begins with Françoise's breathless announcement, "Mademoiselle Albertine est partie!" ["Miss Albertine has left!"] (*R* IV, 3; *S* 5, 387), which plunges the narrator into an extended period of depression and anxious self-examination. Realizing that his desire to live without Albertine was based upon ignorance of his deepest feelings and needs, the narrator attempts, with every means at his disposal, to find the fugitive woman, the *être de fuite* who will now elude his grasp, both alive and dead. Of all the volumes of the *Recherche, Albertine disparue* is certainly the most introspective, the most psychologically claustrophobic, and the most fraught with dramatic and uncanny turns of events. More than one critic has surmised that, had he lived longer, Proust would have spent considerable effort in rewriting this convoluted and strange episode. This is quite possibly the case, but it does not dispense us from taking it seriously or from reading it as it appears, in the no doubt infelicitous version in which we possess it.

Although, in his race against the clock, Proust did not have time to add finishing touches to a number of the narrative sequences that compose the volume, its overall structure is quite clearly articulated and set out in explicitly defined chapters. In the first of these, entitled "Le chagrin et l'oubli" ("Grieving and Forgetting") (*R* IV, 3–138; *S* 5, 387–523), the narrator enlists the help of friends and acquaintances (principal among them, Saint-Loup and Aimé, the *maître d'hôtel* from the Grand-Hôtel de Balbec) in a futile attempt to locate his beloved. The chapter as a whole is characterized by the use of indirect forms of communication – letters, telegrams, telegraphs, secondhand reports, some of them made after-the-fact – which, taken together, produce a portrait of Albertine as promiscuous seeker of erotic adventure and lover of women both unknown and known to the narrator (the latter group, much to the narrator's chagrin, includes Andrée). Only fifty pages into the volume, a telegraph sent from her mother informs us of Albertine's death. Yet this moment of discovery, which in other novels might constitute the closing of a chapter, serves as a goad to the narrator, who henceforth wishes to find out, retroactively, everything that can be known about his mistress's past. Some of the strangest and most haunting pages of the novel are to be found in the second part of the first chapter, which present with painstaking psychological acuity the evolution of a lover's jealousy *after* his beloved's death.

When a letter from Aimé informs the narrator that Albertine had had numerous liaisons with women in Balbec during the very time at which she was getting to know him, and that she had frequented the dressing-rooms and showers of the beach for her trysts, the images of these surreptitious encounters fill the narrator's mind and superimpose themselves upon the pleasant memories he had had of the same resort, the same beach:

Toutes ces images – échappée sur une vie de mensonges et de fautes telles que je ne l'avais jamais conçue – ma souffrance les avait immédiatement altérées en leur matière même, je ne les voyais pas dans la lumière qui éclaire les spectacles de la terre, c'était le fragment d'un autre monde, d'une planète inconnue et maudite, une vue de l'enfer. L'enfer c'était tout ce Balbec, tous ces pays avoisinants d'où d'après la lettre d'Aimé elle faisait venir souvent les filles plus jeunes qu'elle amenait à la douche. (*R* IV, 99)

Combining with these images – a glimpse of a life of lies and misdeeds of a kind that I had never envisaged – my suffering had immediately eaten into their very substance. I no longer saw them in the light which illuminates earthly visions, it was a fragment of another world, an unknown planet of the damned, a vision of Hell. This Hell comprised the whole of Balbec and all its neighbouring villages where, according to Aimé's letter, she often found younger girls to take into the showers. (*S* 5, 484)

At the end of the first chapter, the narrator realizes that, despite the disturbingly vivid quality of these "hellish" superimposed images, the day will come when he finally forgets Albertine. The second and third chapters of *Albertine disparue* detail three distinct "stages" in the process of mourning and of forgetfulness. Given Proust's theory of the "intermittences of the heart," the reader will not be surprised that these stages do not occur with a metronomic regularity, but in a series of irregular, disruptive moments. As the narrator states it in the opening lines of the second chapter, entitled "Mademoiselle de Forcheville" (*R* IV, 138–202; *S* 5, 523–87), the retracing of one's steps through the labyrinth of a re-experienced past is a chronologically paradoxical journey of fits and starts, an initiation into "the cruelty of memory" (*S* 5, 523):

Et en effet je sentais bien maintenant qu'avant de l'[Albertine] oublier tout à fait, comme un voyageur qui revient par la même route au point d'où il est parti, il me faudrait avant d'atteindre à l'indifférence initiale, traverser en sens inverse tous les sentiments par lesquels j'avais passé avant d'arriver à mon grand amour. (*R* IV, 138–39)

And in fact I now realized that before I could forget her completely, and regain my initial indifference, I would need, like some traveller returning down the same route to his point of departure, to experience in reverse order all the emotions which I had felt on the way out towards my great love. (*S* 5, 523)

As the narrator progressively forgets Albertine, as he emerges from obsessive reflection and retrospection, he is able to undertake projects of his own and begins to reconnect with the outside world. An article of his which appears in the respected and widely circulated Parisian daily newspaper *Le Figaro* is the object of considerable praise, leading him to wonder whether it might not be time for him to abandon his empty social activities and to pursue the literary career about which he had only intermittently dreamed in earlier sections of the novel (*R* IV, 147–52; *S* 5, 531–37). He learns of Gilberte's rise in high society (she is now fully accepted into the *salon* of the Duc and Duchesse de Guermantes) (*R* IV, 153–65; *S* 5, 537–49), and writes of Andrée's planned marriage to a certain Octave, the nephew of M. and Mme Verdurin, whom he had taken for a pretentious imbecile at Balbec, but who, he now finds out, possesses considerable artistic talent (*R* IV, 184–87; *S* 5, 569–72). And, after the voyage he finally undertakes, accompanied by his mother, to Venice, a stay which occupies the entirety of the third chapter and to which I shall return presently (*R* IV, 202–35; *S* 5, 588–620), the narrative takes a new twist with the marriages of Robert de Saint-Loup to Gilberte and of Legrandin's nephew to Jupien's niece (*R* IV, 235–37; *S* 5, 621–23).

The fourth chapter of the volume, situated beyond the narrator's final forgetfulness of Albertine, contains two dramatic revelations at its conclusion, both of which propel us forward toward the universe of *Le Temps retrouvé*. The first is that Saint-Loup, who has just married Gilberte, is homosexual and is pursuing a relationship with Morel, who has by now abandoned the Baron de Charlus (*R* IV, 256–57; *S* 5, 642–43). The second is that the two *côtés*, or "sides," which constituted the paths of the narrator's peregrinations when he was a child, "*le côté de chez Swann*" and "*le côté de Guermantes*," and which provided the titles for the first and third volumes of the novel, are not the separate, mythically divergent territories he had imagined, but can be easily traversed and joined in one easy walk (*R* IV, 266–68; *S* 5, 652–54). The first of the revelations – of Saint-Loup's rather surprising sexual reversal (there had been no obvious hints visible to the reader earlier in the narrative, unlike in Charlus's case) – prepares us for a return to the arena of male homosexuality in the novel's final volume. The second – concerning the possibility of uniting contrary ways or paths, real or symbolic, in a synthetic unity – has an anticipatory value for the theoretical peroration of *Le Temps retrouvé*. The gradual forgetting of Albertine is the prerequisite for the enlivened and renewed forward movement of the narrative. But before turning to the final volume of the *Recherche*, let us pause for a brief moment at the third "stage" of the mourning process – the Venice episode, where beauty and strangeness (*étrangeté*) combine to form an inviting but disquieting fluid universe.

Venice: inhabiting and escaping uncanniness (R IV, 202–35; S 5, 588–620)

The Venice episode of *A la recherche du temps perdu* was originally intended to be far more extensive than the version which was ultimately inserted into the narrative flow of *Albertine disparue.* Constructed on a number of Proust's early writings – not only fragments from *Contre Sainte-Beuve,* but even from the early abortive novel, *Jean Santeuil* – the narrator's stay with his mother in Venice presents, for the literary critic, an archaeological layering of textual strata which reveal, in microcosmic form, the author's evolution as a novelist.[12] For the limited purposes of the present study, however, we can begin with a general thematic observation: the Venice of Proust is not to be confused with the city imagined by so many writers, artists, and musicians, for whom the Queen of the Adriatic represents the exotic *other.*[13] For Proust, Venice is *both* same and other, familiar and unfamiliar; therein resides its charm, in the original sense of that word, in the sense of magic power. The first sentence of the episode reads:

Ma mère m'avait emmené passer quelques semaines à Venise et – comme il peut y avoir de la beauté, aussi bien que dans les choses les plus humbles, dans les plus précieuses – j'y goûtais des impressions analogues à celles que j'avais si souvent ressenties autrefois à Combray, mais transposées selon un mode entièrement différent et plus riche. (*R* IV, 202)

My mother had taken me with her to spend a few weeks in Venice, and – since we can find beauty not only in the humblest but also in the most precious things – I sampled there impressions analogous to those that I had so often felt previously in Combray, but transposed into an entirely different, richer mode. (*S* 5, 588)

The first part of the episode (*R* IV, 202–09; *S* 5, 588–94) is constructed musically, as a series of variations on this fundamental theme of analogical resemblance between Venice and Combray, in which there is a striking repetition of the word *comme* ("like" or "just as," to introduce a simile). As we see Venice for the first time, we see Combray again: Combray reappears as Venice appears. And in the same way that the first pages of *Combray* are evocations of the rooms that will be progressively inhabited by the narrator, in the same way the first part of "Venice" is a series of dwellings viewed from the exterior, from the perspective of a gondola passing by. What adds a sense of strange beauty to the episode as a whole is the permeability of inside and outside. On the one hand, through allusions to one of Proust's favorite texts, the *Arabian Nights,* we have the theme of a mystery to be discovered, a veil to be lifted – that is, of the Orient in its exoticism:

Ma gondole suivait les petits canaux; comme la main mystérieuse d'un génie qui m'aurait conduit dans les détours de cette ville d'Orient, ils semblaient, au fur et à mesure que j'avançais, me pratiquer un chemin, creusé en plein cœur d'un quartier qu'ils divisaient en écartant à peine, d'un mince sillon arbitrairement tracé, les hautes maison aux petites fenêtres mauresques; et comme si le guide magique eût tenu une bougie entre ses doigts et m'eût éclairé au passage, ils faisaient briller devant eux un rayon de soleil à qui ils frayaient sa route. (*R* IV, 206)

My gondola followed the side canals, as if the mysterious hand of a genie were guiding me through the byways of this oriental city, the more I advanced along the canals the more they seemed to show me the way, slicing through a neighbourhood that they divided, as their narrow and arbitrarily traced furrows barely perturbed the tall houses and their small Moorish windows; and like a magical guide holding a candle between his fingers to light my passage, they cast ahead of them a ray of sunlight and opened a pathway for it. (*S* 5, 591)

On the other hand, however, one page later, more fundamentally mysterious than the somewhat facile Orientalist exoticism, beyond a simple sense of mystery considered as otherness, there is an analogy between the inside and the outside, an interpenetration between exteriority and interiority:

J'avais l'impression, qu'augmentait encore mon désir, de ne pas être dehors, mais d'entrer de plus en plus au fond de quelque chose de secret, car à chaque fois je trouvais quelque chose de nouveau qui venait se placer de l'un ou de l'autre côté de moi, petit monument ou campo imprévu, gardant l'air étonné des belles choses qu'on voit pour la première fois et dont on ne comprend pas encore bien la destination et l'utilité. (*R* IV, 207)

I had the impression, further enhanced by my desire, that I was not out of doors, but rather that I was entering some increasingly secret place, for on every occasion I found something new moving into place to one side of me or the other, a small monument or an unsuspected *campo* still endowed with that air of surprise affected by beautiful things which we see for the first time but whose aims and functions we do not yet understand. (*S* 5, 592)

Here, we have a repetition of the initial situation of the novel's Overture, where the narrator, voyager without baggage and without identity, in a state of radical uncertainty, experiences the deepening and hollowing-out of space, before things can assume their proper place and differentiate according to the logic of "aims" and "functions."

The theme of radical uncertainty, which is expressed either by the permeability of the self to external impressions, or by a generalized floating of things between inside and outside, self and other, can be found in the final pages of the episode, after an intercalated fragment describing a political discussion involving M. de Norpois, Mme de Villeparisis, and an Italian prince named Foggi (*R* IV, 209–18; *S* 5, 595–603). The concluding section returns to the dialectic of memory and forgetfulness in relation to

Albertine and describes the narrator's anguish as he faces his imminent departure from Venice (*R* IV, 218–35; *S* 5, 603–20). Once again, this textual block begins with a thematic statement upon which numerous variations will unfold in the subsequent pages:

Parfois au crépuscule en rentrant à l'hôtel je sentais que l'Albertine d'autrefois, invisible à moi-même, était pourtant enfermée au fond de moi comme aux "plombs"[14] d'une Venise intérieure, dont parfois un incident faisait glisser le couvercle durci jusqu'à me donner une ouverture sur ce passé. (*R* IV, 218)

Sometimes at dusk on my return to the hotel I felt that the Albertine of former times, although invisible, was none the less locked deep inside me, as if in the lead-lined cells of some inner Venice, where from time to time an incident would shake the heavy lid enough to give me a glimpse into the past. (*S* 5, 603)

The pages that follow alternate between the narrator's obsessive meditation on the life of an Albertine who is, in fact, already dead (despite her brief and uncanny "resuscitation" in a telegram where the narrator confuses her signature with that of Gilberte – *R* IV, 234–35; *S* 5, 619–20), and lovely descriptions of palaces, churches, and museums in Venice and its environs, notably the baptistery of St. Mark's and the *Virtues and Vices* of Giotto at the Arena Chapel in Padua. This constant coming and going between inside and outside, between a psychological examination of the phenomenon of forgetfulness and an opening upon the visual elegance of a city, forms the narrative rhythm of this portion of the text, a rhythm of suspension or hesitancy. It is only at the very end of the episode that the narrator, himself caught in mental hesitancy, must decide between two options: either remain in Venice to pursue the ever-elusive lady's-maid of Mme Putbus, or depart, to join his mother at the train station. The strangest moment of the passage, the moment in which the narrator is obliged to use the word "*étrange*," occurs as an interruption of the narrative flow. As his mother nears the train station, the protagonist listens to a musician who is singing *Sole mio* (a strange and out-of-place Neapolitan song, a song of the *mezzogiorno* which does not belong, in any sense, to the physical or spiritual geography of the Adriatic):

La ville que j'avais devant moi avait cessé d'être Venise. Sa personnalité, son nom, me paraissaient des fictions mensongères, que je n'avais plus le courage d'inculquer aux pierres. Les palais m'apparaissaient réduits à leurs simples parties et quantités de marbres pareilles à toutes autres, et l'eau comme une combinaison d'hydrogène et d'azote, éternelle, aveugle, antérieur et extérieure à Venise, ignorante des doges et de Turner. Et cependant *ce lieu quelconque était étrange comme un lieu où on vient d'arriver*, qui ne vous connaît pas encore, comme un lieu d'où l'on est parti et qui vous a déjà oublié. (*R* IV, 231; my emphasis)

The city I saw before me had ceased to be Venice.[15] Its personality and its name appeared to me as mendacious fictions that I no longer had the heart to relate to its stones. The palaces appeared reduced to their congruent parts and their portions of indifferent marble, and the waters to a combination of nitrogen[16] and hydrogen, eternal and blind, anterior and exterior to Venice, ignorant of Turner and the Doges. And yet *this unexceptional place was as alien as a place where you have just arrived*, which does not yet know you, or a place that you have left and that has already forgotten you. (*S* 5, 616; my emphasis)

The moment in which the strange, the alien, and the uncanny emerge is thus a moment of interruption and the destruction of appearances in which cultural values and points of reference crumble: this is a Venice before Giotto, Turner, Ruskin, Thomas Mann, and all the others, but also before the name "Venice" itself. The reader of Proust apprehends uncanniness as a moment of unveiling in which he or she discovers the nothingness behind the "mendacious fictions" on which Venice is constructed. This radical strangeness, which has nothing to do with simple exoticism, is the very locus of solitude, a place that reminds all individuals, however sociable they might aspire to be, that they are fundamentally, irremediably alone. Places do not remember us, and forget us as soon as we depart. The moment of uncanniness, or disquieting strangeness (*inquiétante étrangeté*) emerges in an interruption of the narrative flow, in the discovery, or rediscovery, of the thinking subject's solitude.

Yet the Venice episode does not conclude in an atmosphere of dejection or melancholy. Narrative inevitability returns to the fore: the narrator leaves the disenchanted city and joins his mother in the train, in that mechanical mode of transport that so perfectly symbolizes narrative movement. The reader is compelled to appreciate the return of a comic tone at this juncture, especially in the description of the narrator's rather undignified flight:

Mais enfin, d'antres plus obscurs que ceux d'où s'élance la comète qu'on peut prédire – grâce à l'insoupçonnable puissance défensive de l'habitude invétérée, grâce aux réserves cachées que par une impulsion subite elle jette au dernier moment dans la mêlée –, mon action surgit enfin: je pris mes jambes à mon cou et j'arrivai, les portières déjà fermées, mais à temps pour retrouver ma mère rouge d'émotion, se retenant pour ne pas pleurer, car elle croyait que je ne viendrais pas. (*R* IV, 233–34)

But at last, from caverns darker than those from which more predictable comets are launched – thanks to the unsuspected defensive powers of inveterate habit, and the hidden reserves that it can suddenly mobilize and throw into the ring at the very last moment – my action suddenly materialized: I ran for dear life and reached the train after the doors had closed, but still in time to get on board and find my mother, flushed with emotion, holding back her tears, believing that I was not going to come. (*S* 5, 619)

Narrative movement becomes possible once again when the narrator returns to his preference for sociability over isolation, for verisimilitude and the predictability of narrative lawfulness over the strangeness that seizes us when we are no longer protected by our defensive strategies – those of enlightened reason as well as of anesthetizing habit. It is perhaps no coincidence that the episode as a whole concludes on the resolution of an enigma: the deciphering, by mother and son, of the telegram thought to have been sent by Albertine, but which turns out to be from Gilberte, announcing her imminent marriage to Robert de Saint-Loup. It is reassuring to learn that the dead can no longer write; one is tempted, with this knowledge, to breathe a sigh of relief and move on. The problem, however, as we have learned from the psychodrama of *Albertine disparue* in its entirety, is that the dead live *in* us. Our contact with the world is not always reassuring, especially before or until we have decided to insert ourselves into the established social order and allow ourselves to be carried along in the story that constitutes our remembered existence. The resumption of the train's forward movement toward the concluding volume of *Le Temps retrouvé* represents not the clear-cut victory of narrative continuity over the threat of the uncanny, but rather the forgetfulness into which all stories must relegate the wrenching experience of *étrangeté*, in order to continue.

CHAPTER 6

Le Temps retrouvé [Finding Time Again]

First published in 1927, five years after Proust's death, *Le Temps retrouvé* is the capstone of the 3,000-page literary quest to which the writer devoted and eventually sacrificed his life. Having taken great pains, throughout the compositional process, to ensure the architectural unity of his text,[1] in the final volume of the novel Proust not only continues to develop and enrich the thematic material that had predominated in the earlier sections, but he also provides a retrospective, theoretically elaborated aesthetic justification for his work. Despite the considerable editorial problems presented by a text that had to be assembled posthumously from a number of manuscript and typescript sources, the general outline of the volume can be discerned quite clearly.

The first, concisely elaborated episode takes place in Tansonville, and is simply the continuation of the concluding pages of *Albertine disparue* (*R* IV, 275–301; *S* 6, 3–29). In this tranquil environment, the narrator takes walks with Gilberte, his first love now (unhappily) married to Robert de Saint-Loup, and reminisces about the past while also gaining further insight into Robert's homosexual leanings and relationships. These opening pages constitute a repetition of the threshold situation with which Proust had begun the novel, in the Overture of *Du Côté de chez Swann*. The narrator is middle-aged and is poised between the past experiences of his life, which have brought him knowledge of society and human nature without providing him with personal happiness, and the prospect of a future which seems bleak rather than promising.

In the second half of the Tansonville section, the narrator has an experience which seems, on the surface, to confirm suspicions that he had been nurturing at earlier moments in his life – namely, that "literature did not reveal any profound truth; and at the same time it seemed to me sad that literature was not what I had believed it to be" (*S* 6, 15). The demonstration of this proposition unfolds in a wonderful pastiche. The narrator purportedly discovers some pages from the celebrated *Journal* of Jules and Edmond

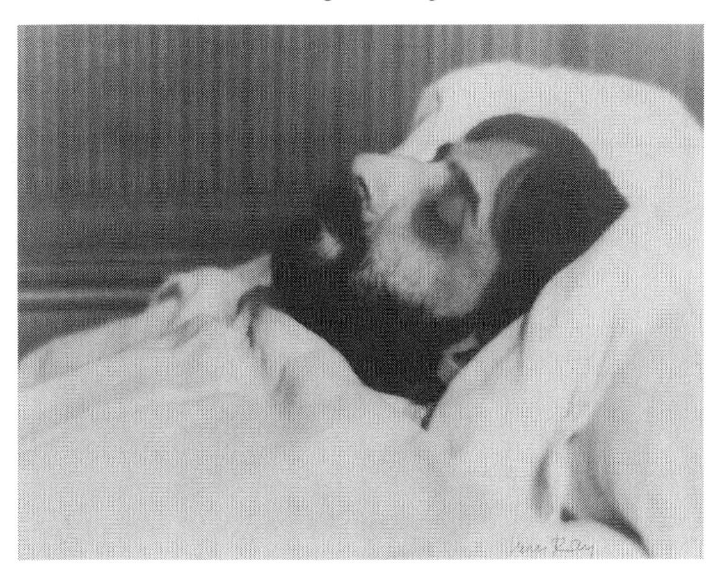

7 Marcel Proust on his deathbed

de Goncourt, which had been published in nine volumes in expurgated form between 1887 and 1896.[2] In fact, the passage excerpted by the narrator for his purposes describes a dinner hosted by the Verdurin clan with portraits of Brichot, Elstir, Swann, and Cottard, which was written, quite brilliantly, in the style of the Goncourt brothers by Proust himself. Upon finishing the "Goncourt" passage, the narrator draws some general conclusions which are of fundamental importance for the expository section on aesthetic theory in the final section of *Le Temps retrouvé.* After remarking upon his own inability to depict surface detail with the minute sense of realism conveyed by the Goncourts, confessing that the "visible, reproducible charm of individuals escaped me" (*S* 6, 25), the narrator reflects upon his own way of seeing things, which might better be characterized as a way of seeing through things:

> Il y avait en moi un personnage qui savait plus ou moins bien regarder, mais c'était un personnage intermittent, ne reprenant vie que quand se manifestait quelque essence générale, commune à plusieurs choses, qui faisait sa nourriture et sa joie … Comme un géomètre qui dépouillant les choses de leurs qualités sensibles ne voit que leur substratum linéaire, ce que racontaient les gens m'échappait, car ce qui m'intéressait, c'était non ce qu'ils voulaient dire mais la manière dont ils le disaient, en tant qu'elle était révélatrice de leur caractère ou de leurs ridicules … J'avais beau dîner en ville, je ne voyais pas les convives, parce que, quand je croyais les regarder, je les radiographiais. (*R* IV, 296–97)

> There was in me a character who knew more or less how to look, but this was an intermittent character, coming to life only when some general essence was revealed, something common to several things, in which it found its nourishment and its delight ... Just as a geometrician, stripping things of their physical qualities, sees only their linear substratum, so what people said escaped me, because what interested me was not what they wanted to say, but the manner in which they said it, in so far as this revealed their character or their absurdities ... How ever often I dined out, I did not see the other guests, because when I thought I was looking at them, I was in fact radiographing them. (*S* 6, 24–25)

At this early moment in *Le Temps retrouvé*, the narrator is consumed by two quite divergent thoughts: first, he recognizes that if literature is to be understood as the mere notational rendition or reproduction of exterior reality, there is no particular reason to devote one's energies to it, which means that the abandonment of a writer's vocation would not entail any particular suffering or sense of loss; second, he reveals to his reader what he considers to be his own special talents, those of a "geometrician" capable of X-raying ("radiographing") reality, locating the "substratum" underlying the world of phenomenal appearances, and finding the "general essence ... common to several things." The problem is, and has always been, that the "character" within the narrator who possesses these considerable talents only reveals himself "intermittently." The reader of the *Recherche* can easily surmise that these intermittent moments are those of the involuntary memory (e.g., the *petite madeleine*) and of aesthetic experience, when works of art act as bridging devices connecting what would otherwise remain distant and disparate planes of reality (e.g., the creations of Bergotte, Elstir, and Vinteuil). But these moments have been few and far between in the narrator's life and in the fictional transposition of that life which we have been reading; they have occurred as haphazard separate illuminations along the narrator's path, but have never been subsumed philosophically or theoretically in a coherent vision that might give a retroactive meaning to the fits and starts that constitute his existence.

The short passage on the "Goncourt" *Journal* should be read as a question pointing to a possible answer: could it be that the ability to discern essences and to uncover the experiential substratum underlying the realm of the sensible is precisely that ability that lends aesthetic specificity to *A la recherche du temps perdu* as a work of art, to the work we have been reading but which, until now, has left unwritten and unrevealed the theoretical base upon which it is constructed? Not having exhausted his thematic material, the novelist Marcel Proust makes his readers wait some

200 pages until the answer emerges, but in the meantime we are meant to wonder whether the capacity to discern essences and uncover the substrata of things is merely a useless gift, or a possible artistic method.

After this expository passage in Tansonville, the text is divided into three large narrative blocks. The first of these is centered on the Baron de Charlus, who, with the disappearance of Albertine, now shares the spotlight with the narrator as one of the two remaining protagonists of the novel. This episode, which takes place during and after World War I, is itself divided into two main sections. The first of these (*R* IV, 301–88; *S* 29–117) possesses a certain narrative complexity, and is based upon a series of temporal jumps. Without entering into any detail, the narrator lets us know that, thanks to his ill health, he has spent prolonged stays in sanatoria during the war, and it is upon his returns from these sanatoria that he encounters the Baron de Charlus in the streets of Paris. It is during his walks with the baron and during his limited stays in Paris at three distinct junctures – in 1914, 1916, and after the war – that the narrator learns of the experiences of the other, by now less visible characters in the novel in indirect ways (one such example being the letters he receives from Gilberte describing the devastating effects of the war on Tansonville, Méséglise, and Combray). The second section devoted to Charlus (*R* IV, 388–433; *S* 118–62) is a focused episode in which the narrator describes his own fortuitous presence in a male brothel run by Jupien but owned by Charlus, in which the baron, surrounded by other homosexuals in search of forbidden pleasures, indulges himself in masochistic rituals (I shall return to this scene presently).

This two-part section focused on Charlus and taking place during and after the war has appeared strange and unsettling to readers ever since the publication of *Le Temps retrouvé*. Although the episode does contain a very rapid overview of the novel's characters as they act and react in the war setting (Bloch is presented as a false patriot in contradistinction to Saint-Loup; the Director of the Grand-Hôtel de Balbec is interned in a concentration camp; Morel first deserts, then, rather improbably, becomes a war hero), it is, for the most part, as if the entirety of the war, and the specificity of Paris as threatened capital of France, were reduced to a stage setting for the theatrical appearances of the increasingly bizarre and outrageous baron. Having become an unabashed Germanophile, Charlus has been consumed by his homosexual yearnings, to the point of losing his personality and his very individuality. Circulating through a city which is described as an exotic "Oriental" space peopled by "a stream of disparate Allied uniforms … among them some Africans in red skirts and

Hindus in white turbans" (*S* 6, 71), the narrator spies Charlus in his final metamorphosis:

Marchant derrière deux zouaves qui ne semblaient guère se préoccuper de lui, j'aperçus un homme grand et gros, en feutre mou, en longue houppelande et sur la figure mauve duquel j'hésitai si je devais mettre le nom d'un acteur ou d'un peintre également connus pour d'innombrables scandales sodomistes … Une seconde je me demandai qui me disait bonjour: c'était M. de Charlus … [Il] était arrivé aussi loin qu'il était possible de soi-même, ou plutôt il était lui-même si parfaitement masqué par ce qu'il était devenu et qui n'appartenait pas à lui seul mais à beaucoup d'autres invertis, qu'à la première minute je l'avais pris pour un autre d'entre eux. (*R* IV, 342–43)

Walking close behind two Zouaves[3] who appeared to be taking almost no notice of him, I noticed a tall, stout man, in a soft felt hat and a long greatcoat, to whose florid features I hesitated whether I should put the name of an actor or a painter, each of whom was well known for numberless sodomitic scandals … For a moment I wondered who was greeting me: it was M. de Charlus … [He] had reached the most distant possible point from himself, or rather he himself was so perfectly disguised by what he had become and which did not belong to himself alone but to many other inverts, that at first I had taken him to be just another one of them. (*S* 6, 71–72)

As we move to the two final episodes of the *Recherche* – an afternoon party held by the Princesse de Guermantes in which the answer to the narrator's artistic self-questioning emerges in a full-blown aesthetic theory (*R* IV, 433–96; *S* 6, 162–226), and the "Bal de têtes" (masked ball) section in which the narrator faces the destructive and transformative process of Time (*R* IV, 496–625; *S* 6, 226–358) – we must keep in mind the vexed ethical background against which the narrator's redemptive theoretical discourse emerges. In the person of the Baron de Charlus, and in the description I have quoted above, we find the eradication of the individual human being under the expanded generality of homosexuality or "inversion." Whatever particular traits the baron may have possessed – his love of art, his knowledge of society and aristocratic genealogy, his generosity toward his lovers – now vanish through the leveling effect of the "vice" (*S* 6, 71) he purportedly shares with all other homosexuals and which has covered him up completely. Whether or not it is fair to see in Charlus a depiction of "the homosexual" as laughable fag (to do so would require a transparent and simplified collapsing of fiction onto reality), at the very least we as readers are compelled to note the *danger* constituted by the eclipsing of the particular by the general. In his final transformation, Charlus as individual *no longer exists*: he has become a caricature, a puppet, a grotesque.

It is precisely against the background of this ethical nullity (Charlus has been consumed by the "vice" that he shares with others; as fictional figure, he is reduced to the simple manifestation of his desires) that the pages detailing the triumph of art which conclude the novel emerge in an atmosphere of joy and affirmation. As we read these pages and yield, inevitably, to their charm, we should not allow ourselves to forget that they too present the victory of the general over the particular in a final, harmonizing vision whose logical underpinnings deserve our scrutiny. As we move now to the reading of specific passages from *Le Temps retrouvé*, we may wish to ask ourselves whether the mere location of the elevated, atemporal discourse on aesthetic theory *after* the passage devoted to the cruel specificity of the war and the masochistic excesses of Charlus constitutes an overcoming of or redemption from what merely *precedes* it. I am suggesting that there is a powerful effect in *Bildungsromane* or quest narratives such as *A la recherche du temps perdu* whereby what follows in the flow of narrative temporality tends to efface what precedes it. Perhaps the act of reading is based as much on forgetfulness as on memory.[4] We shall return to this curious (*étrange*) notion as we examine, in succession, three large episodes from *Le Temps retrouvé* which, in quite diverse ways, stage the struggle of artistic creation and of aesthetic beauty against the constraints of mortality and against the ethically grounded conditions in which human beings pursue their goals and realize their desires.

CHARLUS IN CHAINS, OR THE THEATRICALITY OF EVIL (*R* IV, 388–413; *S* 6, 118–43)

The scene devoted to a depiction of Jupien's male brothel in wartime Paris is the final episode in the *Recherche* preceding the narrator's exposition of the aesthetic theory on which he plans to base his forthcoming novel – this novel being presumably, or at least hypothetically, the one we have just read. The scene's importance derives not only from its strategic placement at the end of the narrator's often anguished and frustrating quest for the connectedness or interrelatedness of his life experiences, but also from the obvious resemblance it shares with two similar passages that precede it: the episode of ritualistic sadism and desecration at Montjouvain in *Du Côté de chez Swann,* in which the daughter and friend of the recently deceased musician Vinteuil spit on the composer's photographic image; and the "conjunction" of Charlus and Jupien at the beginning of *Sodome et Gomorrhe.*

Each of these episodes can be considered a variation on the theme of homosexuality or, more precisely, homoerotic rituals and practices meant to be performed in secret, but which, through rather extraordinary coincidence or chance, are observed by a well-placed narrator who can see everything and everyone but is himself safely distant, in the position of a voyeur.

As I have suggested earlier in this study, the aesthetic distance enjoyed by a heterosexual narrator who remains essentially untouched and unaffected by the psychodrama of homosexuality, given the use of first-person narrative by a figure who bears a strong resemblance, and at times a very strong resemblance, to a real person, a homosexual named Marcel Proust, deserves fuller scrutiny than is possible in these pages. Suffice it to say here that the use of the same narrative staging, or *mise-en-scène*, in each of the three key passages draws the reader's attention to the theatricality of homosexual desire as it is expressed in the Proustian novel. Proust never wrote a single play, but his oeuvre contains a strong theatrical element.

As was the case in the Montjouvain scene, the homoerotic practices that take place in Jupien's brothel occupy the sado-masochistic register, in which the production and reception of acts of cruelty provide an occasion for the narrator and the reader to ponder the relation between the appearance and the reality of evil. In the Montjouvain episode, sharing the privileged distant position of the narrator, we first observed dramatically staged acts of cruelty and desecration, then read the narrator's retroactive interpretation of these acts, in which he drew a fundamental conclusion that is also relevant to the brothel scene in *Le Temps retrouvé*. Speaking of Mlle Vinteuil, the narrator remarked: "A sadist of her sort is an artist of evil, something that an entirely bad creature could not be, for then evil would not be exterior to her, it would seem to her quite natural, would not even be distinguishable from her" (*S* 1, 164). Both the Montjouvain and the wartime brothel scenes are based upon a distance or disjunction between the theatrical appearance of evil and evil itself, and both scenes implicitly pose very interesting questions. In the human world, a world in which we manifest our desires theatrically, that is, indirectly and via the aesthetic distance of representation, is such a thing as "pure" or unmediated evil possible? Could it be that evil is an unattainable absolute? Is there really such a thing as a "bad creature" for whom evil is "natural" and not distinguishable from her essential individuality and personality? These questions constitute the ethical backdrop of both passages.

The shock value of the brothel episode equals or perhaps surpasses that of the Montjouvain segment. While walking through Paris at night, the narrator, becoming thirsty, comes upon a hotel and decides to enter it, seeking both a drink and a room (the necessity of a private room for the consumption of a glass of *cassis* might seem to fly in the face of conventional literary verisimilitude, but this would not be the first time that Proust sacrifices verisimilitude to high drama). The narrator first spies a furtive individual leaving the place; this individual turns out to be

Saint-Loup, who, we learn later, loses his military decoration, his *croix de guerre*, that very evening in Jupien's establishment. Thereupon follows a description of working-class men (one of them is called Maurice) who service the needs of a disparate male clientele. Finally, spurred on by his curiosity upon hearing "stifled moans" (*S* 6, 123) at the end of a corridor, the narrator finds a room with a window from which he catches fragments of a dialogue between two men, one of whom seems to be striking the other and ignoring his pleas for mercy:

Alors je m'aperçus qu'il y avait dans cette chambre un œil-de-bœuf latéral dont on avait oublié de tirer le rideau; cheminant à pas de loup dans l'ombre, je me glissai jusqu'à cet œil-de-bœuf, et là, enchaîné sur un lit comme Prométhée sur son rocher, recevant les coups d'un martinet en effet planté de clous que lui infligeait Maurice, je vis, déjà tout en sang, et couvert d'ecchymoses qui prouvaient que le supplice n'avait pas lieu pour la première fois, je vis devant moi M. de Charlus. (*R* IV, 394)

Then I noticed that the room had a small round side-window and that somebody had forgotten to draw the curtain behind it; advancing stealthily through the darkness, I slid up to the window and there, chained to a bed like Prometheus to his rock, receiving the blows which Maurice was delivering with a whip which was indeed studded with nails, I saw, already running with blood, and covered in bruises which proved that the flogging was not happening for the first time, there, right in front of me, I saw M. de Charlus. (*S* 6, 123)

As was the case in the "conjunction" scene, the narrator is able to observe Charlus at an unguarded moment and witness the baron giving himself over to his desires. Whereas at the beginning of *Sodome et Gomorrhe*, the initial (or initiatory) ritual in which Charlus and Jupien engaged was an artistically choreographed dance that eventually led to sexual consummation, here we find the baron indulging in what is traditionally called "perverse" behavior, where the search for pleasure becomes deviated through the experience of pain. But the problem, for Charlus, is that this bundle of pleasure/pain does not simply materialize: it is delivered by a human being named Maurice. What Charlus *wants*, in fact, is not some particular dose of pleasure/pain, but rather the knowledge that this sensation comes to him from an evil man, from a person who, being evil, is capable of visiting evil upon him. As was the case in the Montjouvain episode, however, where the two young women were performing a sadistic ritual without being themselves consumed by evil, in Jupien's brothel the working-class men who play their roles in exchange for money are essentially bad actors possessing limited imaginations. If Charlus is disappointed in them, it is not because they strike him with insufficient violence or inflict insufficient pain, but rather because, behind their forced attempts at depravity lies a fundamental, undeniable innocence. When one of the men tries to impress the baron with obviously invented "perversity," the narrator reflects upon the matter in much the same way as he had at the conclusion of the Montjouvain episode:

> Et M. de Charlus était à la fois désespéré et exaspéré par cet effort factice vers la perversité qui n'aboutissait qu'à révéler tant de sottise et tant d'innocence. Et même le voleur, l'assassin le plus déterminés ne l'eussent pas contenté, car ils ne parlent pas leur crime; et il y a d'ailleurs chez le sadique – si bon qu'il puisse être, bien plus, d'autant meilleur qu'il est – une soif de mal que les méchants agissant dans d'autres buts ne peuvent contenter. (*R* IV, 406)
>
> And M. de Charlus would be driven both to despair and to exasperation by this contrived attempt at perversity, which resulted only in revealing so much stupidity and so much innocence. In fact even the most determined thief or murderer would not have satisfied him, for they do not talk about their crimes; and anyway sadists – however kind they may be, in fact the kinder they are – have a thirst for evil which villains acting in pursuit of other goals are incapable of satisfying. (*S* 6, 135)

Once again, the distinction is between truly evil people – people for whom evil is indistinguishable from their person – and sadists, who are the artists of evil, who stage and represent evil without ever becoming one with its power and effects. It is noteworthy that Proust's vast novelistic universe contains no major characters who are criminals, no protagonists who, like Balzac's Vautrin, have served time and represent a threat to society. The characters of the *Recherche* do not engage in evil activity or commit crimes. Rather, their minds are the stages on which desire projects its fantasies, fantasies that test the limits of the ethical. If there is perversion in Proust's novel, it is to be understood not in the narrow or strict moral sense, but in the larger sense of an imaginary detour or deviation that is inherent in a restless mind which, despite all its efforts, continually comes up against the incapacity of the world to meet its insatiable appetites. As the narrator puts it quite succinctly: "There is nothing more limited than pleasure and vice. In that sense, changing the meaning of the phrase slightly, it can truly be said that we are always going round in the same vicious circle" (*S* 6, 135).

The more Charlus insists upon being flogged, the more men he asks to do the flogging, the more he will be disappointed in the experience. Not only is there no Maurice in Paris or elsewhere who can perform his role to the level of the baron's expectations, but even real criminals don't think enough and don't talk enough about their crimes to be of interest to the sadist, the artist of evil. And this sadist is, in fact, nothing but a dreamer; it's just that his dreams, in being perverted and diverted from their initial course, have taken on a strange appearance. At the apparent disenchanted end of the narrator's quest stands the stark and unpleasant image of Charlus in chains, a Prometheus devoured not by vultures sent by the gods, but by his love for men, an aesthetically mediated love that knows no limits and can find no ultimate satisfaction. The substratum of what the narrator has been calling Charlus's "vice" is an unassuaged desire clothed in ugliness.

As we turn now to the triumphant passage in which the narrator professes an aesthetic theory that would ground his work-to-be in the beauty of a rigorous style, we should neither forget nor abandon the Baron de Charlus. In the obscurity of wartime Paris, during air raids, Charlus dreams of hiding in the corridors of the pitch-black Métro and of mingling anonymously with other men. The narrator is sensitive to the strange beauty of this dream, which, in its very deviousness, in its false illusion of reality, may possess as much poetry as a beautiful theory:

En somme, son désir [celui de Charlus] d'être enchaîné, d'être frappé, trahissait, dans sa laideur, un rêve aussi poétique que, chez d'autres, le désir d'aller à Venise ou d'entretenir des danseuses. Et M. de Charlus tenait tellement à ce que ce rêve lui donnât l'illusion de la réalité, que Jupien dut vendre le lit de bois qui était dans la chambre 43 et le remplacer par un lit de fer qui allait mieux avec les chaînes. (*R* IV, 419)

In short, his [Charlus's] desire to be chained and beaten betrayed, in its ugliness, a dream just as poetic as other men's desire to go to Venice or to keep a mistress. And M. de Charlus clung so tenaciously to the illusion of reality created by his dream that Jupien had to sell the wooden bed that used to be in Room 43 and replace it with an iron bed that was better suited to the chains. (*S* 6, 148)

PERPETUAL ADORATION: PROUST'S AESTHETIC THEORY (*R* IV, 433–96; *S* 6, 162–226)

As the episode centered on Charlus in wartime Paris comes to a conclusion, the narrator seems to have reached an impasse in his life. He has lost Albertine; he no longer believes in the prestige of names and places; he has no plans for the future. It is in this atmosphere of disillusionment that the large narrative block devoted to aesthetic theory and entitled "L'Adoration perpétuelle" begins. Making use of the same Flaubertian temporal device he had employed in establishing a two-year separation between the Paris and Balbec sections of *A l'Ombre des jeunes filles en fleurs*,[5] Proust inserts a blank space consisting of several years between the passage devoted to World War I and the narrator's return to post-war Parisian society.

What remain undescribed in the text are the prolonged fruitless stays in sanatoria which occupy the blank space; we are made to understand, simply, that these years amounted to lost time, or, in Proustian language, *du temps perdu*. As he returns to Paris by train, the narrator sees a row of trees illuminated by the sun; but not only does this vision fail to provoke any feelings in him, it seems to confirm his lack of artistic talent – i.e., his inability to convey to a reader the depth of his impressions:

> Si j'avais vraiment une âme d'artiste, quel plaisir n'éprouverais-je pas devant ce rideau d'arbres éclairé par le soleil couchant, devant ces petites fleurs du talus qui se haussent presque jusqu'au marchepied du wagon, dont je pourrais compter les pétales, et dont je me garderais bien de décrire la couleur comme feraient tant de bons lettrés, car peut-on espérer transmettre au lecteur un plaisir qu'on n'a pas ressenti? (*R* IV, 434)
>
> If I truly had the soul of an artist, what pleasure should I not experience at the sight of this screen of trees lit by the setting sun, these little flowers on the embankment that reached almost up to the carriage step, whose petals I could count, and whose colours I was careful not to describe, as so many good men of letters would, for could one hope to transmit to the reader a pleasure one has not felt oneself? (*S* 6, 163)

The remainder of the "Perpetual Adoration" episode is devoted to an exposition of the narrator's transition from disillusionment to joy as he first re-experiences the profound and life-altering pleasure of involuntary memory, then gradually discovers an artistic method that would permit him to transmit this pleasure to others – these others being the readers of the literary work upon which he is about to embark. Having received an invitation to an afternoon party hosted by the Prince de Guermantes, who has changed dwellings and is now living in a grand private hotel on the avenue du Bois (present-day avenue Foch), the narrator, having nothing better to do, hires a cab and proceeds to the social event. On his way, however, as the vehicle strikes uneven pavement, the narrator has the agreeable sensation of "extreme smoothness" as well as an intuitive impression that obstacles are being overcome, that the present-day moment is beginning to open toward the lost realm of the past:

> … je sentis tout d'un coup la suppression des obstacles extérieurs … les rues par lesquelles je passais en ce moment étaient celles, oubliées depuis si longtemps, que je prenais jadis avec Françoise pour aller aux Champs-Elysées. Le sol de lui-même savait où il devait aller; sa résistance était vaincue. Et, comme un aviateur qui a jusque-là péniblement roulé à terre, "décollant" brusquement, je m'élevais lentement vers les hauteurs silencieuses du souvenir. (*R* IV, 437)
>
> … I suddenly felt the elimination of those external obstacles … the streets through which I was now passing were those, forgotten for so long, through

which I had walked with Françoise on the way to the Champs-Elysées. The ground knew of its own accord where it had to lead; its resistance was overcome. And, like an aviator, who has up to that point travelled laboriously along the ground, suddenly "taking off", I rose up slowly towards the silent heights of memory. (*S* 6, 166)

At this juncture in the episode, the narrator is merely noting his impressions without submitting them to reflection or analysis. He observes that the roads he is taking, despite their new names and superficial new appearance, are in fact the same ones that he had taken with Françoise when he was a child (when he was playing with Gilberte on the Champs-Elysées in the first part of *A l'Ombre des jeunes filles en fleurs*, many years ago). The past is thus linked to the present, or can be linked to it, given the right circumstances – which means, implicitly, that a person's life is not necessarily a series of fragmentary experiences, but might possess some coherence. One senses, upon reading the final sentence of the passage, with the striking image of the narrator's "taking off" toward the "silent heights of memory," that it is the act of opening, or, perhaps, *unlocking* of memory, that is capable of providing aesthetic pleasure in the deepest sense.

It is precisely to this image of opening or unlocking (which Proust, borrowing from the "Open Sesame" motif of the *Arabian Nights*, had evoked on several key occasions earlier in the novel) that he turns at the single most dramatic moment of the narrator's quest – the moment at which, miraculously, negative turns to positive, failure yields to intimations of triumph. Following immediately upon disabused reflections concerning his purported "sterile lucidity," the narrator writes:

Mais c'est quelquefois au moment où tout nous semble perdu que l'avertissement arrive qui peut nous sauver, on a frappé à toutes les portes qui ne donnent sur rien, et la seule par où on peut entrer et qu'on aurait cherchée en vain pendant cent ans, on y heurte sans le savoir, et elle s'ouvre. (*R* IV, 445)

But sometimes it is just when everything seems to be lost that we experience a presentment that may save us; one has knocked on all the doors which lead nowhere, and then, unwittingly, one pushes against the only one through which one may enter and for which one would have searched in vain for a hundred years, and it opens. (*S* 6, 174)

The pages that follow this assertion consist, first, of a multiplication of involuntary memory experiences, then of the narrator's attempts to clarify the meaning of these revelations, and, especially, to explain to himself as well as to his reader why the triggering of involuntary memory seems inevitably to be accompanied by a strong sense of certainty as well as joy. In the first of these experiences, having tripped on an uneven paving stone in the courtyard of the Prince de Guermantes's hotel, the narrator finds himself transported to Venice, where he had also stumbled, but that time in the darkened interior of St. Mark's baptistery, as related in *Albertine disparue*. In a second instance, when a clumsy servant at the afternoon party knocks a spoon against a plate, the narrator, now imagining that he is surrounded by the smell of smoke in a forest, recognizes the similarity between what he has just heard and the "sound of a workman's hammer doing something to one of the wheels of the train while we were halted beside the little wood" (*S* 6, 176) upon his return to Paris after his final stay in a sanatorium. And in a third moment it is Balbec in its essence that emerges from oblivion when the narrator, upon wiping his mouth with a napkin at the afternoon party, recognizes in it "the same stiffness and the same degree of starch" (*S* 6, 177) as a towel with which he had had difficulty drying himself on the first day after his arrival at the seaside resort, at the beginning of *Noms de pays: le pays*. In commenting upon the flood of sensations – sounds, odors, and colors – that are now overwhelming him as he vacillates or hesitates between his present reality and a past he thought was forever closed to him, the narrator draws a first conclusion:

> Et je ne jouissais pas que de ces couleurs, mais de tout un instant de ma vie qui les soulevait, qui avait été sans doute aspiration vers elles, dont quelque sentiment de fatigue ou de tristesse m'avait peut-être empêché de jouir à Balbec, et qui maintenant, débarrassé de ce qu'il y a d'imparfait dans la perception extérieure, pur et désincarné, me gonflait d'allégresse. (*R* IV, 447)
>
> And it was not just these colours which filled me with joy, but a whole moment of my life which aroused them, which had probably been an aspiration towards them, which some sense of fatigue or of sadness had perhaps prevented me from enjoying at Balbec, and which now, freed of whatever was imperfect in the external perception, pure and disembodied, filled me with delight. (*S* 6, 177)

What emerges here is the logical basis upon which the subsequent aesthetic revelations in the passage are constructed: namely, that the unmediated experiences one has in life at the very moment of their occurrence can never be fully absorbed because there is always some affective residue – of "fatigue or of sadness" for example – that stands in the way of our enjoyment and understanding. It is in the retroactive synthetic moment of involuntary memory that one discovers that the manifold world of sensation in which we are enfolded is, in fact, "an aspiration towards" something meaningful. According to Proust, meaning emerges, in its "pure and disembodied" state, when we have been freed from the contingencies of everyday reality and from the constraints of habit.

A consequence of this philosophical stance is the apparently paradoxical but profoundly logical result that the ecstatically revealed truth of recuperated Time, established by a link between present and past in a "pure and disembodied state," is itself atemporal or extra-temporal. It is when the narrator searches for the cause of the happiness that fills him while re-experiencing his past that he draws a second, far-reaching conclusion upon which many of the passage's later celebrated pronouncements are based:

Or cette cause [la cause de ma félicité], je la devinais en comparant entre elles ces diverses impressions bien-heureuses et qui avaient entre elles ceci de commun que j'éprouvais à la fois dans le moment actuel et dans un moment éloigné le bruit de la cuiller sur l'assiette, l'inégalité des dalles, le goût de la madeleine, jusqu'à faire empiéter le passé sur le présent, à me faire hésiter à savoir dans lequel des deux je me trouvais; au vrai, l'être qui alors goûtait en moi cette impression la goûtait en ce qu'elle avait de commun dans un jour ancien et maintenant, *dans ce qu'elle avait d'extra-temporel* ... Cet être-là n'était jamais venu à moi, ne s'était jamais manifesté, qu'en dehors de l'action, de la jouissance immédiate, chaque fois que le miracle d'une analogie m'avait fait échapper au présent. Seul, il avait le pouvoir de me faire retrouver les jours anciens, le temps perdu, devant quoi les efforts de ma mémoire [volontaire] et de mon intelligence échouaient toujours. (*R* IV, 449–50; my emphasis)

And I began to divine this cause [the cause of my happiness] as I compared these varied impressions of well-being with each other, all of which, the sound of the spoon on the plate, the uneven flagstones, the taste of the madeleine, had something in common, which I was experiencing in the present moment at the same time in a moment far away, so that the past was made to encroach upon the present and make me uncertain about which of the two I was in; the truth was that the being within me who was enjoying this impression was enjoying it because of something shared between a day in the past and the present moment, *something extra-temporal* ... This being had only ever come to me, only ever manifested itself to me on the occasions, outside of action and immediate pleasure, when the miracle of an analogy had made me escape from the present. It alone had the power to make me find the old days again, the lost time, in the face of which the efforts of my [voluntary] memory and my intellect always failed. (*S* 6, 179–80; my emphasis)

We can consider this passage to be the summation of the narrator's philosophical argument. In it, he makes several points that deserve emphasis. The first of these is that the particular pleasure he feels in moments of involuntary memory association depends upon an "encroachment" of the past upon the present, that is, upon a hesitation or initial uncertainty as to where exactly he is located in time and space. But this initial uncertainty yields to a more profound and theoretically justified certainty when he realizes that there exists a being within himself capable of enjoying the linkage between past and present, a linkage that can only be established outside of time. It is as if there were a subject-within-a-subject in Proust's universe, an inner being that manifests itself only on those occasions in which time itself is bridged and therefore negated or conquered. This realization allows the narrator to establish a link of a different sort – between the episode of the *petite madeleine* at the beginning of *Du Côté de chez Swann* and the aesthetic revelations of *Le Temps retrouvé* at the end of the novel – thus providing an illustration of the philosophical inner coherence of the work we have been reading. The multiplication of involuntary memory experiences in the final volume of the novel serves to retroactively ground the beautiful but isolated scene of the *petite madeleine*, and especially to explain, after the fact, why it was, in those early pages, that the narrator, *as* extra-temporal being, could be "unconcerned with the vicissitudes of the future" (*S* 6, 179).

The final two sentences of the passage serve both as a philosophical conclusion and as a bridge toward the properly literary considerations that follow in the text. We are reminded of the central premise on which Proust had founded his writing ever since the earliest embryonic fragments of the novel as found in *Contre Sainte-Beuve* – namely the insufficiency of rational thought (or "intelligence") and of voluntary memory in contradistinction to the possibilities of involuntary memory. And we are told, in a phrase referring to the title of the novel, that only the involuntary memory opens up the past in its essence, allowing the narrator to "find the old days again, the lost time [*le temps perdu*]." The extra-temporal being whose theoretical basis has been revealed to us in this passage is that being capable of searching for, and finding, lost time. What remains to be explained, however, is the way in which or the method by which this theory of the extra-temporal self recuperating the essence of the past can convert or translate an ecstatic, philosophically formulated experience into a literary equivalent. What kind of writing, what literary style, might be capable of rendering "the miracle of an analogy?" The answer, or variously phrased answers, to this question, often expressed not as fully-fledged arguments but as aphoristic declarations, make up the final section of "L'Adoration perpétuelle" and constitute some of the most memorable (and quotable) passages of the *Recherche*.

The first of these concisely formulated statements, and perhaps the best-known of all of Proust's theoretical utterances, begins with a definition of "reality" and moves on to a description of the particular or unique style that is adequate to that reality. The way to render "the miracle of an analogy," according to the narrator, is to adopt a style based upon metaphor – or, in his (metaphorical) description, a figural discourse capable of establishing "necessary links" between and among disparate objects in space or moments in time. The necessary character of the metaphorical relations thus established removes the compared objects or moments from their habitual surroundings and from the "contingencies of time": once again, we find ourselves in an extra-temporal realm, the realm of truth toward which all artists aspire:

Une heure n'est pas qu'une heure, c'est un vase rempli de parfums, de sons, de projets et de climats. Ce que nous appelons la réalité est un certain rapport entre ces sensations et ces souvenirs qui nous entourent simultanément – rapport que supprime une simple vision cinématographique, laquelle s'éloigne par là d'autant plus du vrai qu'elle prétend se borner à lui – rapport unique que l'écrivain doit retrouver pour en enchaîner à jamais dans sa phrase les deux termes différents. On peut faire se succéder indéfiniment dans une description les objets qui figuraient dans le lieu décrit, la vérité ne commencera qu'au moment où l'écrivain prendra deux objets différents, posera leur rapport, analogue dans le monde de l'art à celui qu'est le rapport unique de la loi causale dans le monde de la science, et les enfermera dans les anneaux nécessaires d'un beau style. Même, ainsi que la vie, quand en rapprochant une qualité commune à deux sensations, il dégagera leur essence commune en les réunissant l'une et l'autre pour les soustraire aux contingences du temps, dans une métaphore. (*R* IV, 467–68)

An hour is not just an hour, it is a vessel full of perfumes, sounds, plans and atmospheres. What we call reality is a certain relationship between these sensations and the memories which surround us simultaneously – a relationship which is suppressed in a simple cinematographic vision, which actually moves further away from truth the more it professes to be confined to it – a unique relationship which the writer has to rediscover in order to bring its two different terms together permanently in his sentence. One can list indefinitely in a description all the objects that figured in the place described, but the truth will begin only when the writer takes two different objects, establishes their relationship, the analogue in the world of art of the unique relation created in the world of science by the laws of causality, and encloses them within the necessary armature of a beautiful style. Indeed, just as in life, it begins at the moment when, by bringing together a quality shared by two sensations, he draws out their common essence by uniting them with each other, in order to protect them from the contingencies of time, in a metaphor. (*S* 6, 197–98)

Proust's aesthetic theory is based upon certain fundamental premises that are crucial for an understanding of his novelistic project as a whole and for an appreciation of his personal literary style. A moment taken from the totality of our lives – what the narrator here calls "an hour" among the many hours we have lived – is not confined to its evanescent appearance along a straight chronological line, but is a "vessel" containing the sensual and existential depths of our experience, depths which we can explore by establishing links and relations *between* this and that, here and now. The narrator's critique of what he calls "a simple cinematographic vision" is certainly not to be understood in the narrow sense as a polemic against the cinema or the visual arts in general, but is to be taken metaphorically, as a critique of any mode of artistic representation that would limit itself to the mere depiction of objects in space or simple temporal succession.

Proust's view of the world and his theory of literary style are grounded in a *relational* perspective: things, places, and persons are never truly isolated, but call out for our active interpretation and for our exploration of the relations they entertain among themselves. If the world appears flat and insignificant at times, it is because, at those moments of disillusionment, one's capacity to make relations and weave a narrative from those relations is temporarily dormant. What exists within all readers as well as all writers is the depth of experience from which to structure an understanding of the world: the question is simply whether we can make ourselves attuned to this depth, to this "vessel full of perfumes, sounds, plans and atmospheres."

Proust's view of the world and his conception of literary style are thus not esoteric. A talented writer, or even a writer possessed of genius, like Proust, has not necessarily had unusual or exotic experiences. What any of us chooses to write about can be common or uncommon, but in either case, the subject-matter for the work of art does not lie outside of us, but within us, within our reach. This is why, in a second memorable statement, the narrator distinguishes between "invention" and "translation," asserting that the writer conscious of his craft and devoted to the creation of an individual style does not have to create his fictions out of nothing, but rather give form to what already exists within his interiority, that is, *to translate*:

> ... je m'apercevais que ce livre essentiel, le seul livre vrai, un grand écrivain n'a pas, dans le sens courant, à l'inventer puisqu'il existe déjà en chacun de nous, mais à le traduire. Le devoir et la tâche d'un écrivain sont ceux d'un traducteur. (*R* IV, 469)
>
> ... I slowly became aware that the essential book, the only true book, was not something the writer needs to invent, in the usual sense of the word, so much as to translate, because it already exists within each of us. The writer's task and duty are those of a translator. (*S* 6, 199)

The thread that unifies the two theoretical assertions I have just quoted is the strong semantic similarity, conveyed by etymology, between metaphor and translation. Deriving from the Greek word *metaphora*, meaning a transferring to one word the sense of another, the English word "metaphor" designates a figure of speech in which one thing is likened to another, different thing by being spoken of as if it were that other. The English verb "to translate" comes from the Latin *transferre*, meaning to carry over or across, to transfer, transport, or convey.[6] What metaphorical discourse and translation have in common, via their etymological origins, is the common notion of transfer or transport. When I engage in metaphorical language, when I liken one thing to another, different thing, I transfer meaning from one location to another; when I translate, I transport a constellation of meanings originally uttered or written in one linguistic system to another.

One could say that the entirety of Proust's aesthetic project, as contained in the seven volumes of the *Recherche* we have just read, is a vast, continually renewed exercise in translation conveyed in metaphorical terms. Whether it is the narrator attempting to translate his sensual impressions into an evocative descriptive language; whether it is Elstir, through the "metaphors" of his seascapes attempting to connect the disparate realms of water and land; or whether it is the reader attempting to find, underlying the human comedy of the *Recherche*, the general social laws upon which it is based – in each case, the efforts to uncover relations and to bridge gaps depend upon a properly translational movement, whereby the evidence of our senses and the meanings we impute to the world are transported from one place to another.

The indirect poetic revelations of metaphorical language permit not only the bridging of gaps between levels of sense and reality, but also communication between writer and reader. Just as Proust does not use the word "translation" in a narrow mechanical sense in his theoretical exposition, so he does not think of a writer's style as something uniquely or essentially technical. Style is what opens up universes; style is, in fact, vision. Literary art, founded in a beautiful style, because it reveals otherwise unexplored worlds to its readers, is not a pleasant diversion from life, but life itself:

La vraie vie, la vie enfin découverte et éclaircie, la seule vie par conséquent pleinement vécue, c'est la littérature ... Notre vie; et aussi la vie des autres; car le style pour l'écrivain aussi bien que la couleur pour le peintre est une question non de technique mais de vision. Il est la révélation, qui serait impossible par des moyens directs et conscients, de la différence qualitative qu'il y a dans la façon dont nous apparaît le monde, différence qui, s'il n'y avait pas l'art resterait le secret éternel de chacun. (*R* IV, 474)

Real life, life finally uncovered and clarified, the only life in consequence lived to the full, is literature ... Our lives; and the lives of other people, too; because style for a writer, like colour for a painter, is a question not of technique but of vision. It is the revelation, which would be impossible by direct or conscious means, of the qualitative difference in the ways we perceive the world, a difference which, if there were no art, would remain the eternal secret of each individual. (*S* 6, 204)

The strong assertion of the equivalency between life and literature allows the narrator to make one more explicit move in his theoretical argument – a move that should not surprise those readers who have been attuned to the continual emphasis on aesthetic truths that punctuates the novel (the repeated allusions to the efforts, achievements, and performances of the imaginary artists inhabiting the *Recherche* – Bergotte, La Berma, Elstir, Vinteuil). He goes on to analyze the retroactive discovery, in the library of the Prince de Guermantes, that his entire life, including all its disappointments and failures, contains the unconsciously stored material for a work-to-be. Viewed from the perspective of its potential aesthetic transformation, the narrator's existence in all its dimensions can be considered a *vocation*:

Et je compris que tous ces matériaux de l'oeuvre littéraire, c'était ma vie passée; je compris qu'ils étaient venus à moi, dans les plaisirs frivoles, dans la paresse, dans la tendresse, dans la douleur, emmagasinés par moi sans que je devinasse plus leur destination, leur survivance même, que la graine mettant en réserve tous les aliments qui nourriront la plante. Comme la graine, je pourrais mourir quand la plante se serait développée ... Ainsi toute ma vie jusqu'à ce jour aurait pu et n'aurait pas pu être résumée sous ce titre: une vocation. (*R* IV, 478)

And I understood that all these raw materials for a literary work were actually my past life; I understood that they had come to me, in frivolous pleasures, in idleness, in tenderness, in sorrow, that they had been stored up by me without my divining their ultimate purpose, even their survival, any more than a seed does as it lays up a reserve of all the nutrients which will feed the plant. Like the seed, I would be able to die when the plant had developed ... So all my life up to that day could, and at the same time could not, have been summed up under the title: A vocation. (*S* 6, 207–08)

What appears, from the perspective of concrete achievement, *not* to have constituted a vocation (a life spent largely in idleness with no books to "show" for the time he has dreamed of writing books), is, in fact, a vocation, when viewed from the perspective of its potential, when conceived of metaphorically as the growth of a plant. In this case, all of the narrator's life experiences have been stored up for use in the book-to-come and form its nourishment. This particularly seductive metaphor – that of the developing plant, which evokes the conception of the work of art as organic whole – is not without its darker connotations, however. The evolution from seed to growth to death occurs quite rapidly in the botanical sphere. The narrator states quite explicitly: "Like the seed, I would be able to die when the plant had developed." But the question is this: having wasted so much of his time on frivolous social pursuits and on love relationships which brought more psychological insight than happiness, will the narrator have enough time to recapture Time in his book? The work of art may be conceptualized as an extra-temporal essence, but the human being who composes it is constrained by his mortality. It is to the contradiction between these two divergent temporal dimensions and to the drama of the artist in his race against death that the narrator returns in the final large narrative block of the *Recherche*, entitled "Le Bal de têtes."

"Le Bal de têtes" ("The Masked Ball"): the novel reaches its end (R IV, 496–625; S 6, 226–358)

As the narrator leaves the seclusion of the Prince de Guermantes's library and descends the staircase to the great drawing-room, his ambitious literary project runs up against what he calls "the gravest of objections" (*S* 6, 229) – namely, the ageing of the cast of characters that has peopled the *Recherche* from its earliest pages. The reason this section is called "The Masked Ball" is that the ambitious bourgeois and complacent aristocrats we have met along the narrator's path have become so ancient as to be unrecognizable: it is as if, hiding the faces with which we readers have become familiar, fanciful and grotesque masks had been superimposed upon them. On the one hand, the narrator is obliged to reflect upon "this destructive action of Time at the very moment when I wanted to begin to clarify, to intellectualize within a work of art, realities whose nature was extra-temporal" (*S* 6, 239). On the other hand – and herein resides the originality of this final episode as a whole – Time is not uniquely a destructive force: it is an agent of transformation, of metamorphosis. A large section of the episode is devoted to minute and often amusing descriptions of the quite diverse ways in which the characters have taken on new and unusual forms. Whereas Odette's surprisingly youthful appearance (the narrator at first takes her for her daughter, Gilberte) "seemed a more miraculous defiance of the laws of chronology than the conservation of radium was of the laws of nature" (*S* 6, 256), Bloch, who now calls himself Jacques du Rozier, has become difficult to identify under a veneer of English fashion which has nearly effaced what the narrator characterizes as his Jewish traits:

> J'eus de la peine à reconnaître mon camarade Bloch, lequel d'ailleurs maintenant avait pris non seulement le pseudonyme, mais le nom de Jacques du Rozier, sous lequel il eût fallu le flair de mon grand-père pour reconnaître la "douce vallée" de l'Hébron et les "chaînes d'Israël" que mon ami semblait avoir définitivement rompues. Un chic anglais avait en effet complètement transformé sa figure et passé au rabot tout ce qui se pouvait effacer. (*R* IV, 530–31)

I had some difficulty recognizing my friend Bloch, who in fact had now permanently adopted his pseudonym of Jacques du Rozier as his own name, behind which it would have needed my grandfather's flair to detect the "sweet valley" of Hebron and the "bonds of Israel"[7] which my friend seemed definitively to have broken. His face had been completely transformed in accordance with the latest English fashion, and every unevenness seemed to have been smoothed away, as with a plane. (*S* 6, 261)

The transformations to which the characters are subject in this final enchanted scene are not limited to physical appearance or to individual traits of temperament and character, but extend to their rank and status within society. The vulgar bourgeois aesthete *arriviste* Mme Verdurin, the amusing but vicious *Patronne* who first appeared in *Un Amour de Swann*, has metamorphosed into the Princesse de Guermantes (*R* IV, 532–34; *S* 6, 262–64) thanks to the elevation of a particularly well-arranged third marriage. The Faubourg Saint-Germain as a whole has degenerated and become *déclassé* (*R* IV, 535–36; *S* 6, 266–67); both the Duchesse de Guermantes and Mme de Villeparisis are part of a general decadence within the transformations of post-war aristocratic society (*R* IV, 581–83; *S* 6, 313–15). Charlus, now in physical and mental decline, spends his time chasing after young men and has no more interest in society, while the senile but sexually unrepentant Duc de Guermantes is involved in a highly visible liaison with Odette, the current Mme de Forcheville and erstwhile courtesan pursued by the young Swann. What Time has wrought crystallizes in a large portrait of momentous change and unforeseen upheaval, which, despite the fanciful character of its varied manifestations, leads the narrator to the following disenchanted reflections:

Ainsi, dans le faubourg Saint-Germain, ces positions en apparence imprenables du duc et de la duchesse de Guermantes, du baron de Charlus, avaient perdu leur inviolabilité ... Ainsi change la figure des choses de ce monde; ainsi le centre des empires, et le cadastre des fortunes, et la charte des situations, tout ce qui semblait définitif est-il perpétuellement remanié, et les yeux d'un homme qui a vécu peuvent-ils contempler le changement le plus complet là où justement il lui paraissait le plus impossible. (*R* IV, 596)

Thus in the Faubourg Saint-Germain, the apparently impregnable positions of the Duc and the Duchesse de Guermantes and of Baron de Charlus had lost their inviolability ... This is how the pattern of things changes in this world; how the focus of empires, registers of wealth, and titles to social positions, everything that seemed permanent is perpetually recast, and the eyes of a man may over the course of a lifetime contemplate the most complete change precisely in those places where it had appeared most impossible. (*S* 6, 328)

Yet precisely at the moment when it seems to the narrator that the exterior world, in constant flux, escapes his control and eludes his understanding, Gilberte fortuitously introduces him to her young daughter, Mlle de Saint-Loup, in whom the narrator recognizes a principle of coherence, or, as he calls it, a "point of convergence" of the various paths he has taken in his life. He sees that she stands at the center of a vast thematic network whose complexity, worthy of the closest scrutiny, in constituting the rich fabric of his existence, weaves threads from past to present, thus bypassing and overcoming the destructive fragmentation of passing time. What the narrator discovers here is, in fact, the thematic coherence of the novel we have been reading, with its repetitions, its echo-effects, its variations on common motifs, and the "connecting roads" bridging and uniting people and places:

Comme la plupart des êtres, d'ailleurs, n'était-elle [Mlle de Saint-Loup] pas comme sont dans les forêts les "étoiles" des carrefours où viennent converger des routes venues, pour notre vie aussi, des points les plus différents? Elles étaient nombreuses pour moi, celles qui aboutissaient à Mlle de Saint-Loup et qui rayonnaient autour d'elle. Et avant tout venaient aboutir à elle les deux grands "côtés" où j'avais fait tant de promenades et de rêves – par son père Robert de Saint-Loup le côté de Guermantes, par Gilberte sa mère le côté de Méséglise, qui était le "côté de chez Swann" … Et n'était-ce pas le grand-père de Mlle de Saint-Loup, Swann, qui m'avait le premier parlé de la musique de Vinteuil, de même que Gilberte m'avait la première parlé d'Albertine? Or, c'est en parlant de la musique de Vinteuil à Albertine que j'avais découvert qui était sa grande amie et commencé avec elle cette vie qui l'avait conduite à la mort et m'avait causé tant de chagrins … Certes, s'il s'agit uniquement de nos cœurs, le poète a eu raison de parler des "fils mystérieux" que la vie brise. Mais il est encore plus vrai qu'elle en tisse sans cesse entre les êtres … si bien qu'entre le moindre point de notre passé et tous les autres un riche réseau de souvenirs ne laisse que le choix des communications. (*R* IV, 606–07)

Was she [Mlle de Saint-Loup] not, as indeed most human beings are, like one of those "stars" in forests, cross-roads where roads converge which have come, as they do in our lives, from the most diverse starting-points? They were numerous enough, in my case, the roads leading to Mlle de Saint-Loup and radiating out again from her. Above all it was the two great "ways" which had led to her, along which I had had so many walks and so many dreams – through her father, Robert de Saint-Loup, the Guermantes way, through her mother, Gilberte, the Méséglise way which was the "way by Swann's" … And was it not the grandfather of Mlle de Saint-Loup, Swann, who had first mentioned the music of Vinteuil to me, just as it was Gilberte who had first spoken to me of Albertine? And it was by talking about the music of Vinteuil to Albertine that I had discovered who her great friend was and thus had begun that part of my life with her which led to her death and caused me so much pain … If it were only a matter of our hearts, the poet would have been right to speak of the "mysterious threads" that are broken by life.[8] But it is even more true to say that life is ceaselessly weaving these threads between individuals … to such an extent finally that between the least significant point in our past and all the others a rich network of memories gives us in fact a choice about which connection to make. (*S* 6, 338–40)

More strikingly and more explicitly than ever before, we are now in a position to appreciate the admirable narrative sleight of hand whereby the novel which we have enjoyed and with which we have struggled during our hours of reading is, by an anticipatory form of circularity, the novel the narrator is about to write. The narrator as novelist-to-be has just demonstrated, in advance of his writing, the forthcoming structural solidity of the work which will presumably absorb his energies for years to come. And all of the interwoven threads, all of the radiating pathways, move through the element of Time. The book the narrator plans to write is bathed in Time; and it is his analytical reflection on Time as incentive or as "spur" (*S* 6, 342) toward the act of writing that allows the narrator to deliver to us some of his most beautiful and moving metaphorical statements on the renewed efforts that will be necessary in his quest to render, in a work of art, the essence of his past experience. To be able to write a book steeped in Time is no mere technical achievement; it constitutes a justification of one's life, a proof that life has value:

Que celui qui pourrait écrire un tel livre serait heureux, pensais-je, quel labeur devant lui! Pour en donner une idée, c'est aux arts les plus élevés et les plus différents qu'il faudrait emprunter des comparaisons; car cet écrivain, qui d'ailleurs pour chaque caractère en ferait apparaître les faces opposées, pour montrer son volume, devrait préparer son livre, minutieusement, avec de perpétuels regroupements de forces, comme une offensive, le supporter comme une fatigue, l'accepter comme une règle, le construire comme une église, le suivre comme un régime, le vaincre comme un obstacle, le conquérir comme une amitié, le suralimenter comme un enfant, le créer comme un monde. (*R* IV, 609–10)

How happy the writer of a book like that would be, I thought, what a labour awaited him! To give some idea of it, one would have to go to the most elevated and divergent arts for comparisons; for this writer, who would also need to show the contrasting aspects of each character to create depth, would have to prepare his book scrupulously, perpetually regrouping his forces as in an offensive, and putting up with the work like tiredness, accepting it like a rule, constructing it like a church, following it like a regime, overcoming it like an obstacle, winning it like a friendship, feeding it up like a child, creating it like a world. (*S* 6, 342)

As the novel reaches its concluding pages, the exterior reality surrounding the narrator begins to fade; it has ceased being a "masked ball" occupying its own limited moment in present time to become the material out of which the observer-turned-writer will weave his own text. In taking a final look at the eighty-three-year-old Duc de Guermantes, who, in wavering on trembling legs, appears to be perched on stilts, the narrator sees in the pathetic old man's stance not so much a concession to age and the destructiveness of time, as the very condition we humans share – we creatures elevated beyond the constraints of physical space who, precisely because our lives touch so many distant locations in Time, appear unnatural or even "monstrous" as we move, hesitatingly but with a strange and awkward grace, along the paths each of us has chosen to take:

... comme si les hommes étaient juchés sur de vivantes échasses, grandissant sans cesse, parfois plus hautes que des clochers, finissant par leur rendre la marche difficile et périlleuse, et d'où tout d'un coup ils tombaient ... Aussi, si elle m'était laissée assez longtemps pour accomplir mon œuvre, ne manquerais-je pas d'abord d'y décrire les hommes, cela dût-il les faire ressembler à des êtres monstrueux, comme occupant une place si considérable, à côté de celle si restreinte qui leur est réservée dans l'espace, une place au contraire prolongée sans mesure puisqu'ils touchent simultanément, comme des géants plongés dans les années à des époques, vécues par eux si distantes, entre lesquelles tant de jours sont venus se placer – dans le Temps. (*R* IV, 625)

... as if all men are perched on top of living stilts which never stop growing, sometimes becoming taller than church steeples, until eventually they make walking difficult and dangerous, and down from which, all of a sudden, they fall ... Therefore, if enough time was left to me to complete my work, my first concern would be to describe the people in it, even at the risk of making them seem colossal and unnatural creatures, as occupying a place far larger than the very limited one reserved for them in space, a place in fact almost infinitely extended, since they are in simultaneous contact, like giants immersed in the years, with such distant periods of their lives, between which so many days have taken up their place – in Time. (*S* 6, 357–58)

Notes

INTRODUCTION: AT THE THRESHOLD OF PROUST'S NOVEL

1 Quoted in Hermione Lee, *Virginia Woolf* (New York: Knopf, 1997), p. 404.
2 Walter Benjamin, "On the Image of Proust," in *Walter Benjamin, Selected Writings*, vol. II, 1927–34, trans. Rodney Livingstone *et al.*, ed. Michael W. Jennings, Howard Eiland, and Gary Smith (Cambridge, MA and London: Harvard University Press, 1999), p. 237.
3 Interview with Hubert Fichte (December 19, 20, and 21, 1975) included in *L'Ennemi déclaré: textes et entretiens*, ed. Albert Dichy, *Oeuvres complètes de Jean Genet*, vol. VI (Paris: Gallimard, 1991), pp. 165–66. The English translation of the passage which I am quoting here is from Edmund White, *Genet: A Biography* (New York: Knopf, 1993), p. 169.
4 Marcel Proust, "A propos du 'style' de Flaubert," in *Contre Sainte-Beuve, précédé de Pastiches et mélanges et suivi de Essais et articles* (Paris: Gallimard, 1971), p. 944, note 2; my translation.
5 "A propos du 'style' de Flaubert," p. 586, my emphasis.
6 When quoting the French original, I shall refer to: Marcel Proust, *A la recherche du temps perdu*, 4 vols., ed. Jean-Yves Tadié (Paris: Gallimard [Pléiade], 1987–89).
7 When quoting in English, I shall refer to: Marcel Proust, *In Search of Lost Time*, 6 vols., ed. Christopher Prendergast (London: Penguin Classics, 2003).
8 For a discussion of Sainte-Beuve's continued relevance to the practice of literary criticism in France until the advent of structuralism and the "theoretical turn," see David R. Ellison, "Proust and Posterity," in *The Cambridge Companion to Proust*, ed. Richard Bales (Cambridge: Cambridge University Press, 2001), pp. 200–15. For an important assessment of the development of Sainte-Beuve's critical philosophy in its evolution from a cosmopolitan to an increasingly nationalist conception, as set against the background of the question "What is a classic?" (a question Sainte-Beuve himself had examined in his 1850 essay "Qu'est-ce qu'un classique?"), see Christopher Prendergast, *The Classic: Sainte-Beuve and the Nineteenth-century Culture Wars* (Oxford: Oxford University Press, 2007).
9 For a detailed and amusing depiction of Proust's ploys to avoid being physically present at the Bibliothèque Mazarine, see William C. Carter, *Marcel Proust: A Life* (New Haven and London: Yale University Press, 2000), pp. 214–15.

10 For a thorough discussion of the appropriation and "kitschification" of Proust in contemporary cultural representations, see Margaret E. Gray, *Postmodern Proust* (Philadelphia: University of Pennsylvania Press, 1992).
11 See Jean-Yves Tadié, *Marcel Proust: A Biography*, trans. Euan Cameron (London: Viking, 2000), p. 301. (All subsequent references are to Cameron's translation.)
12 I shall be quoting the English translation of "John Ruskin" and "Sur la lecture" as contained in *Marcel Proust: On Reading Ruskin*, trans. and ed. Jean Autret *et al.*, intro. Richard Macksey (New Haven: Yale University Press, 1987). When citing the French original of "John Ruskin," I shall refer to the 1971 Pléiade edition of *Contre Sainte-Beuve*. When citing the French original of "Sur la lecture," I shall refer to *Sésame et les lys, précédé de Sur la lecture*, intro. Antoine Compagnon (Paris: Editions Complexe, 1987).
13 Tadié, *Marcel Proust*, p. 513.
14 Tadié, *Marcel Proust*, pp. 579–80.

CHAPTER I *DU CÔTÉ DE CHEZ SWANN* [*THE WAY BY SWANN'S*]

1 As I stated in the Introduction, when quoting from *A la recherche du temps perdu* in the original French, I shall refer to the four-volume Pléiade edition (1987–89). I shall abbreviate the novel's title as *R*, following it by volume number in Roman numerals, then page number. Hence, a quoted passage from p. 10 of *Du Côté de chez Swann*, which is contained in the first volume of the Pléiade edition, would be: *R* I, 10. When quoting from the 2003 six-volume Penguin translation, *In Search of Lost Time*, I shall abbreviate the novel's title as *S*, following it by volume number in Arabic numerals, then page number. Hence a quoted passage from p. 10 of *The Way by Swann's*, which is the first volume of the Penguin edition, would be: *S* 1, 10.
2 Quoted in Antoine Compagnon, *Proust entre deux siècles* (Paris: Seuil, 1989), p. 9; my translation.
3 For a detailed and erudite study of Proust's novel in its multiple thematic and structural references to medieval architecture, see Luc Fraisse, *L'Oeuvre cathédrale: Proust et l'architecture médiévale* (Paris: Corti, 1990).
4 For a concise and analytically brilliant account of the convergences between Freud and Proust, see Malcolm Bowie, "Freud and Proust," in *Freud, Proust and Lacan: Theory as Fiction* (Cambridge: Cambridge University Press, 1987), pp. 68–97.
5 The Pléiade editors point out that an allusion to this Celtic legend can be found in Michelet's *Histoire de France*, in the paragraphs of his "Tableau de la France" devoted to Brittany (*A la recherche du temps perdu*, vol. I [Paris: Gallimard [Pléiade], 1987], p. 1122).
6 On the capacity of the narrator to sense stimuli at a great distance from himself and to "devour" objects that would seem, on the surface, to lie far removed from his purview, see the striking comparison Gilles Deleuze makes of Proust to a spider: "Indeed the narrator is an enormous body without

organs ... But what is a body without organs? The spider too sees nothing, remembers nothing. She receives only the slightest vibration at the edge of her web, which propagates itself in her body as an intensive wave and sends her leaping to the necessary place. Without eyes, without nose, without mouth, she answers only to signs, the merest sign surging through her body and causing her to spring upon her prey" (*Proust and Signs*, trans. Richard Howard [Minneapolis: University of Minnesota Press, 2000], pp. 181–82).

7 For the narrative consequences of the split between the "remembering I" ("das erinnernde ich") and the "remembered I" ("das erinnerte ich"), see Hans Robert Jauss, *Zeit und Erinnerung in Marcel Prousts "A la recherche du temps perdu"* (Heidelberg: Carl Winter, 1970).

8 See Sigmund Freud, "Die Verneinung," *Gesammelte Werke Chronologisch Geordnet*, vol. XIV, 1925–31 (London: Imago Publishing Co., 1946–55), pp. 11–15. This remarkably concise article, first published in 1925, centers on an interesting linguistic phenomenon which emerges from time to time in the dialogue between the analyst and his patient. Freud describes a situation in which a patient states: "'You ask who this person in the dream can be. It's *not* my mother.' We [analysts] emend this to: 'So it *is* his mother'" (Sigmund Freud, "Negation," in *The Standard Edition of the Complete Psychological Works of Sigmund Freud*, trans. and ed. James Strachey in collaboration with Anna Freud, vol. XIX, 1923–25 [London: The Hogarth Press and the Institute of Psychoanalysis], p. 235). Freud's major point is that "the content of a repressed image or idea can make its way into consciousness on condition that it is *negated*. Negation is a way of taking cognizance of what is repressed; indeed it is already a lifting of the repression, though not, of course, an acceptance of what is repressed" (pp. 235–36). Legrandin, in constantly stating that he is the opposite of a snob, reveals to the psychologically attuned reader that he is precisely that, a snob. The reader is thus placed in the position of the analyst who discovers an affirmation underneath the apparent negation.

9 The poet Francis Jammes (1868–1938) was particularly offended by the episode in question. For a discussion of this reaction, and for Proust's aesthetic justification of the scene, see Marcel Proust, *Du Côté de chez Swann* (Paris: Garnier-Flammarion, 1987), pp. 605–06, note 178.

10 For a theoretically grounded reading of Proust's "dreaming" on names in this section, see Roland Barthes, "Proust et les noms propres," in *To Honor Roman Jakobson* (The Hague: Mouton, 1967), pp. 150–58. Gérard Genette contextualizes Barthes's reading within a larger meditation on Proust's theory of language in "Proust et le langage indirect," in *Figures II* (Paris: Seuil, 1969), pp. 223–94.

CHAPTER 2 *A L'OMBRE DES JEUNES FILLES EN FLEURS* [*IN THE SHADOW OF YOUNG GIRLS IN FLOWER*]

1 Gérard Genette, *Figures III* (Paris: Seuil, 1972), p. 75.

2 Allusions to the tales contained in the *Arabian Nights* as well as to the text's death-defying narrator, Scheherazade, abound in the *Recherche*. Proust

discovered an allegorical development of the "Open Sesame" motif in the works of Ruskin and commented upon it in the first lengthy footnote to his translation of *Sesame and Lilies*. See Proust, *Sésame et les lys, précédé de Sur la lecture*, intro. Antoine Compagnon (Paris: Editions Complexe, 1987), pp. 101–04.

3 The complex linguistic movement by which an innovative figure of discourse passes from its original force, via usage or *usure*, into cliché, forms the basis of an extensive development in Jacques Derrida's "La Mythologie blanche," an essay contained in *Marges de la philosophie* (Paris: Minuit, 1972), pp. 249–324.

4 The narrator alludes to Leonardo's expression in his analysis of the purely mental dimension of happiness: "Happiness, happiness from Gilberte, was something I had constantly thought about, something that existed only in thought, something which was like what Leonardo da Vinci said about painting, *cosa mentale*" (*S* 2, 75). The phrase *cosa mentale* used in relation to painting is to be found in Leonardo's *Treatise on Painting*, which first appeared in Paris in 1656. For a discussion of this phrase, its origin, and its significance, see *A la recherche du temps perdu*, vol. I (Paris: Gallimard [Pléiade], 1987), p. 1364, note 2.

5 See Proust's assessment of Flaubert's ability to convey a sense of time in his narratives: "He [Flaubert] is a master at rendering a sense of Time in his works. In my opinion the most beautiful feature of *L'Education sentimentale* is not a sentence, but an empty space (*un blanc*)" ("A propos du 'style' de Flaubert," in *Contre Sainte-Beuve, précédé de Pastiches et mélanges et suivi de Essais et articles* [Paris: Gallimard, 1971], p. 595; my translation).

6 For a further development of the various ways in which Proust incorporated Ruskin's meditations on the theme of "custom" or habit into his novel, see David Ellison, *The Reading of Proust* (Baltimore: The Johns Hopkins University Press, 1984; Oxford: Blackwell, 1984), pp. 50–55.

7 In this episode and subsequent passages in the current chapter, I am indebted to the magisterial study by Deleuze, *Proust et les signes*.

8 Proust's use of the expression "une petite vieille de pierre" to describe La Vierge du porche points to Baudelaire's "Les petites vieilles," one of three ironical and uncanny poems dedicated to Victor Hugo in the "Tableaux parisiens" section of the second edition (1861) of *Les Fleurs du Mal*.

9 For a development of this point, see Ellison, *The Reading of Proust*, p. 10 and p. 191, note 13.

10 In *L'Influence de Ruskin sur la vie, les idées et l'oeuvre de Marcel Proust* (Geneva: Drost, 1955), Jean Autret noted that for his description of the porch of Balbec church, Proust had borrowed heavily from Emile Mâle's *L'Art religieux du XIIIe siècle en France* (1898). For a detailed listing of these borrowings, see *A la recherche du temps perdu*, vol. II (Paris: Gallimard [Pléiade], 1988), editor's note 1, pp. 1438–40.

11 There is an autobiographical dimension to this detail. In the later years of his life, when he seldom left his cork-lined bedroom, Proust would summon musicians to his apartment in the late hours of the evening or early hours of the morning to play chamber music for him, often Beethoven's late quartets. For a lively description of the origin of these curious evenings, see Jean-Yves Tadié, *Marcel Proust: A Biography*, trans. Euan Cameron (London: Viking, 2000), pp. 638–39.

CHAPTER 3 *LE CÔTÉ DE GUERMANTES* [*THE GUERMANTES WAY*]

1 Eugène de Rastignac is the young protagonist of Honoré de Balzac's *Le Père Goriot* (1834). Like Rastignac, the narrator of *A la recherche du temps perdu* is fascinated by the Parisian aristocracy of his time, but his social ambition is more refined and less aggressive than that of his predecessor.

2 Charlus's apartment is described as a place both threatening and mysteriously beautiful. The *salon* in which the narrator waits for the baron is *verdâtre*, or "greenish" (*R* II, 841, 849; *S* 3, 552, 561) and contains a gallery of portraits which guest and host examine at the end of the scene. There is a metaphorical correspondence between the baron and his dwelling: both are characterized by the color green, which in the Proustian scheme of things connotes that which is slimy and snake-like. Charlus is compared to "an ageing Apollo; but it is as if an olive-greenish, bilious juice was about to seep out of his malevolent mouth" (*S* 3, 555). At the same time, the apartment also echoes with beautiful music – Beethoven's "Pastoral" Symphony – which seems to waft down from the second floor of Charlus's building, although Charlus refuses to explain why such music can be heard in the early morning (*R* II, 850; *S* 3, 562). For the autobiographical dimension of this reference to the playing of music in the early morning hours, see note 11 of the previous chapter.

3 For a description of the various manuscripts and typescripts from which Proust constructed the episode of the grandmother's illness and death, see *A la recherche du temps perdu*, vol. II (Paris: Gallimard [Pléiade], 1988), editor's notes, pp. 1666–67.

4 In trying to convince the narrator's grandmother that she is not suffering from a physical disorder, but that her suffering is purely imaginary, Dr. du Boulbon alleges that nervous disorders "have a genius for mimicry. They will produce lifelike imitations of dyspeptic swelling, morning sickness, irregular heartbeat, tubercular fever. If this can deceive the doctor, how much the more so the patient?" (*S* 3, 301–02). No doubt wishing to make the grandmother feel better about being a member of that class of beings called "neurotics," Dr. du Boulbon says: "Feel comfortable to be called a neurotic. You belong to that splendid, pitiable family, which is the salt of the earth. Everything we think of as great has come to us from neurotics. They and they alone are the ones who have founded religions and created great works of art" (*S* 3, 301). One wonders whether there is not a sly autobiographical aside here on the part of a writer whose neuroses became the stuff of legend.

5 For a concise account of Fliess's career, his professional relationship with Freud, and his theory that the nose is the dominant organ in the human body, influencing all aspects of human physical life, including sexuality, see Peter Gay, *Freud: A Life for Our Time* (New York: Norton, 1988), pp. 56–58.

6 The Pléiade editors suggest that Dieulafoy could be a conflation of two characters' names from *Le Malade imaginaire*: the doctor, Diafoirus, and the solicitor, Bonnefoy (see *A la recherche du temps perdu*, vol. II [Paris: Gallimard [Pléiade], 1988], editor's notes, p. 1706).

7 In an early development of the first part of *A l'Ombre des jeunes filles en fleurs* immediately preceding the "tussling" scene, the narrator accompanies his family's maid, Françoise, to "a little green-trellissed pavilion that looked rather like one of the disused Paris toll-booths from former times, in which had recently been installed what the English call a *lavabo* and the French, in their misguided anglomania, water closets" (*S* 2, 67). When the woman who oversees the pavilion graciously offers the narrator a cubicle free of charge, the latter wonders if she might be attracted to young men, but concludes: "But if the fancy of Françoise's countess did run to youths for whom she opened the hypogean portal into her stone cubes, where men crouch like sphinxes, the aim of this kindness towards them must have been less the chance of seducing them than the unrequited pleasure of being indulgent towards a loved one, as I never saw her being visited by anyone other than one of the old park-keepers" (*S* 2, 68).

8 It is appropriate that the grandmother's last literary allusion should be to Marie de Rabutin-Chantal, the Marquise de Sévigné (1626–96), whose vivid and witty letters are considered to be a model of French classical style, and whose thirty-year correspondence with her daughter, Madame de Grignan, was always a source of amusement and instruction to the grandmother (and to Proust himself, a great admirer of the marquise's memorably cryptic descriptions). The Pléiade editors think that the cited passage, "En les écoutant je pensais qu'ils me préparaient les délices d'un adieu," is a slightly modified quotation of Mme de Sévigné's letter of June 21, 1680, to Mme de Grignan, in which the marquise complains of having to endure a boring visit from Mme de La Hamelinière – "les délices d'un adieu" referring to the wished-for imminent departure of her tedious guest (*A la recherche du temps perdu*, vol. II [Paris: Gallimard [Pléiade], 1988], editor's notes, p. 1670).

CHAPTER 4 *SODOME ET GOMORRHE* [*SODOM AND GOMORRAH*]

1 The episode of Sodom and Gomorrah, the Cities of the Plain, extends from Genesis 18:16 to Genesis 19:29. The inhabitants of these cities are destroyed in fire and brimstone for the sinfulness of their homosexual practices.

2 Proust was an avid reader of Balzac and an admirer of the character Vautrin, who appears in several volumes of the vast novelistic cycle *La Comédie humaine* (1831–50), beginning with *Le Père Goriot*, where he assumes a kind of diabolical mentor-role vis-à-vis the young hero, Eugène de Rastignac. Whereas Vautrin's tenderness for Rastignac in that volume has homoerotic overtones, it would be an exaggeration to equate it with a fully expressed homosexual passion, as Proust does, in his essays and early drafts of the *Recherche*. Vautrin's homosexual desire will find its outlet in another character of the cycle, Lucien de Rubempré. Proust was particularly interested in the moment, in *Illusions perdues* (1836–43), when Vautrin, alias Carlos Herrera, having intervened to save Lucien from his plan to drown himself, passes in front of Rastignac's country residence and pauses for a moment of reflection. In his *Carnet* of 1908, a

preparatory notebook for the *Recherche*, Proust calls this moment a "'Tristesse d'Olympio' de la péderastie," alluding to one of Victor Hugo's most famous poems. Charlus makes this same comparison in a conversation with the "faithful" of the Verdurin circle at La Raspelière (*R* III, 437; *S* 4, 444). For a detailed discussion of these points, see the editor's notes in *A la recherche du temps perdu*, vol. III (Paris: Gallimard [Pléiade], 1988), pp. 1587–88.

3 The reader meets Jupien for the first time in the very early pages of *Combray*, when the narrator's grandmother pays a visit to Mme de Villeparisis and finds the tailor (*giletier*, or "waist-coat maker") who has his shop in her courtyard to be "the most distinguished, the finest man she had ever seen" (*S* 1, 24; *R* I, 20). Making only sporadic appearances before the *conjonction* scene, Jupien as character becomes more developed in the second half of the *Recherche*, his moral attributes far more complex in their mode of expression. Possessing equally impressive doses of loyalty, shrewdness, and deviousness, in the final volume, *Le Temps retrouvé*, he runs a male bordello which Charlus and other homosexuals frequent during the dark nights of wartime Paris.

4 For an excellent analysis of the *conjonction* episode which takes into account the complex association between the strange and the natural that underlies the scene as a whole, see Marcel Muller, "Etrangeté ou, si l'on veut, naturel," in *Recherche de Proust*, ed. Gérard Genette and Tzvetan Todorov (Paris: Seuil "Points," 1980), pp. 55–67. For a reading of this scene as it relates to earlier moments in the novel, when the narrator has yet to fully recognize Charlus's homosexual identity, see David Ellison, "Comedy and Significance in Proust's *Recherche*: Freud and the Baron de Charlus," *MLN*, 98:4 (May 1983), 657–74.

5 Originally intended to be a major character in the *Recherche*, "la femme de chambre de Mme Putbus" [Mme Putbus's lady's-maid] was eventually made unnecessary by the expanding role of Albertine. As the Pléaide editors express it in an apt comparison, she was like "one of the supporting walls which one places in a building under construction and which one removes when the edifice has been completed" (*A la recherche du temps perdu*, vol. IV [Paris: Gallimard [Pléiade], 1989], p. 710; my translation).

6 It should be noted that the second stay in Balbec, like the first, is constructed upon the large theme of habit (*habitude*) and the undermining or destruction of habitual actions by aesthetic and experiential novelty.

7 In his retroactive understanding of the ways in which he had been cruel and indifferent to the sufferings of his grandmother, the narrator remembers one particular episode from the first stay at Balbec with particular intensity: the sequence of the photograph that was taken of his grandmother on a day in which she was in acute physical pain. The experience of the "intermittences of the heart" allows the narrator to understand, when it is too late, why his grandmother had acted with such apparent and, for her, unusual coyness as she dressed for her session with the photographer. In its ambiguous status as permanent reminder of the evanescence of things, the photograph as such can be viewed as an uncanny or ghostly artistic form, a "strange contradiction between survival and oblivion." For an expanded development of this point,

and for a highly personal view of the polyvalent aesthetic and psychological dimensions of photography, see Roland Barthes, *La Chambre claire: Essai sur la photographie* (Paris: Seuil, 1980), translated by Richard Howard as *Camera Lucida: Reflections on Photography* (New York: Hill and Wang, 1981).

8 In his novel *Le Jardin des plantes* (Paris: Minuit, 1997), the Nobel-prize-winning writer Claude Simon was particularly interested in this use of descriptive pauses for narrative (rhythmical and temporal) purposes, and quoted extensively from both the scene on the esplanade and its surrounding frame in Part II of his text.

9 See Proust's essay "La Méthode de Sainte-Beuve," in which the future author of the *Recherche* begins a sustained polemic against the Beuvian critical method with the topic sentence: "At no time in his life did Sainte-Beuve conceive of literature in a truly profound way. He placed it at the same level as conversation" ("La Méthode de Sainte-Beuve," in *Contre Sainte-Beuve, précédé de Pastiches et mélanges et suivi de Essais et articles* [Paris: Gallimard, 1971], p. 225; my translation).

CHAPTER 5 *LA PRISONNIÈRE* [*THE PRISONER*] AND *ALBERTINE DISPARUE* [*THE FUGITIVE*]

1 Because *La Prisonnière* and *Albertine disparue* are shorter in length than the other volumes of the novel, and because they are related so closely to each other thematically, the decision of the Penguin editors to publish them together, as volume 5 of *In Search of Lost Time*, makes sense.

2 For a clear and concise account of this apparently drastic editorial decision and the way it has been interpreted by Proust critics, see Marion Schmid, "The Birth and Development of *A la recherche du temps perdu*," in *The Cambridge Companion to Proust*, ed. Richard Bales (Cambridge: Cambridge University Press, 2001), pp. 70–73.

3 Marcel Proust, *Albertine disparue*, ed. Nathalie Mauriac and Etienne Wolff (Paris: Grasset, 1987).

4 See the "Notice" written by Anne Chevalier for *Albertine disparue*, pp. 993–1038 of *A la recherche du temps perdu*, vol. IV (Paris: Gallimard [Pléiade], 1989).

5 Jean Milly, "Introduction," in Marcel Proust, *Albertine disparue* (Paris: Champion, 1992), p. 57; my translation.

6 Throughout the present chapter I shall be analyzing passages in *La Prisonnière* and *Albertine disparue* in which one finds a strange interplay, as well as moments of overlap, between polar opposites such as: familiar and unfamiliar; life and death. The haunting or ghostly quality of these passages owes a great deal to their threshold or in-between status: the scenes and events they portray seem to hover *between* the familiar and the unfamiliar, life and death. It is at these moments of the novel that Proust's writing practice converges with the theoretical observations enunciated by Sigmund Freud in his essay "Das Unheimliche" ("The Uncanny"). In his initial definition of the term, Freud writes: "the uncanny is that species of the frightening that goes

back to what was once well known and had long been familiar." But as his essay develops, Freud describes the peculiar movement whereby what was once (originally) familiar becomes its opposite, the unfamiliar or disquieting. At the conclusion of his argument, Freud states: "*Heimlich* thus becomes increasingly ambivalent, until it finally merges with its antonym *unheimlich*" (Sigmund Freud, *The Uncanny*, trans. David McLintock, intro. Hugh Haughton [New York: Penguin Books, 2003], pp. 124, 134). Perhaps the most *unheimlich* of all episodes in the *Recherche* is the stay in Venice in *Albertine disparue*, which I discuss in the final pages of the present chapter.

7 For a more detailed reading of this passage on naming and its narrative as well as psychological ramifications, see David Ellison, "The Named Self," in *The Reading of Proust* (Baltimore: The Johns Hopkins University Press, 1984; Oxford: Blackwell, 1984), pp. 178–88.

8 For a detailed description of the editorial difficulties presented by the scene of Bergotte's death (its fragmentary character, the textual strata of manuscripts and typescripts on which it is built), see the editor's comments in *A la recherche du temps perdu*, vol. III (Paris: Gallimard [Pléiade], 1988), "Notes et variantes," pp. 1737–38.

9 For an account of Proust's museum excursion with Vaudoyer, see Tadié, *Marcel Proust: A Biography*, trans. Euan Cameron (London: Viking, 2000), pp. 872–74.

10 Two of Vinteuil's compositions – the Sonata for Piano and Violin (*Un Amour de Swann*) and the septet (*La Prisonnière*) – play a crucial role in the exposition of Proust's ideas about the transcendental or otherwordly significance of achieved works of art. Proust's aesthetic theory holds that the work of art in its highest form can lift the human being above his or her daily existence, and can constitute, in the best of cases, an aesthetic revelation, or even a "redemption" from the travails of human life in its concrete reality. For the best (most literarily and musically sound) account of Proust's interest in and knowledge of music, see Jean-Jacques Nattiez, *Proust as Musician* (Cambridge: Cambridge University Press, 1989). Nattiez makes short work of the perennial and fruitless attempts to "identify" Vinteuil's imaginary compositions and establish one-to-one correspondences between them and real musical works written by a host of composers: Franck, Fauré, and Saint-Saëns for the sonata; Schumann, Franck, Beethoven, and even Ravel for the septet. As Nattiez writes: "In fact, the [identification] game quickly proves fruitless, first because all the evidence suggests that Proust was inspired by a multitude of specific musical data in composing his imaginary works of music, and secondly because, as previous critics have noted, his technical descriptions of the little phrase are few and far between, thus leaving the field open to the most diverse interpretations" (p. 5). What interests Nattiez is the deeper question of music as "redemptive model for literature," which he pursues in a subtle and multi-faceted argument, via Wagner (in particular, *Parsifal*) and Beethoven, as well as the philosophical meditations of Schopenhauer.

11 See Immanuel Kant, Paragraph 49 of the *Critique of Judgment* (1790): "genius is the exemplary originality of a subject's natural endowment in the *free* use of his cognitive powers. Accordingly, the product of a genius (as regards what

is attributable to genius in it rather than to possible learning or academic instruction) is an example that is meant not to be imitated, but to be followed by another genius. (For in mere imitation the element of genius in the work – what constitutes its spirit – would be lost)" (*The Critique of Judgment*, trans. Werner S. Pluhar [Indianapolis: Hackett, 1987], pp. 186–87).

12 For a detailed analysis of the "Venice" episode that includes a survey of the early drafts, or *avant-textes* on which it is constructed, see David Ellison, "Proust's 'Venice': The Reinscription of Textual Sources," *Style*, 22 (Fall 1988), 432–49.

13 This is perhaps most obviously and dramatically the case in Thomas Mann's novella, *Death in Venice* (1912), in which the city of the Doges is the exotic place in which unconscious desires and erotic passion are unleashed, in contradistinction to the stultifying and reason-bound northern climes of Germany, which the protagonist, Gustav von Aschenbach, flees.

14 The *plombs* to which Proust refers here are the *piombi*, or lead-lined cells located in the attics of the Doges' palace in Venice in which political prisoners were held. In fact, Proust may have confused the *piombi* with the *pozzi*, which were basement dungeons, often compared to wells, in the same palace. On this point, see *A la recherche du temps perdu*, vol. IV (Paris: Gallimard [Pléiade], 1989), "Notes et variantes," p. 1118.

15 The Penguin translator erroneously rendered "La ville que j'avais devant moi avait cessé d'être Venise" as: "The city I saw before me was still Venice." I have corrected the translation to: "The city I saw before me had ceased to be Venice."

16 Here Proust would seem to be confusing nitrogen and oxygen.

CHAPTER 6 *LE TEMPS RETROUVÉ* [*FINDING TIME AGAIN*]

1 In the latter years of his life, Proust often pointed out this unity to readers and critics alike. For one example among others, see his letter of November 10, 1919, to the critic Paul Souday, in which Proust justifies the inclusion, within the pages of *Du Côté de chez Swann*, of the Montjouvain episode, which had shocked a number of his first readers. Proust explains that later sections of the novel, and later developments on the related themes of homosexuality, sado-masochism, and jealousy, would be incomprehensible if this episode had been removed (see Marcel Proust to Paul Souday, pp. 289–91 of *Proust: Correspondance*, ed. Jérôme Picon [Paris: Garnier-Flammarion, 2007]).

2 The brothers Jules (1830–70) and Edmond (1822–96) de Goncourt were associated with the late nineteenth-century literary current of naturalism, whose most famous exponents were Emile Zola (1840–1902) and Guy de Maupassant (1850–93). The Goncourt brothers wrote all of their works together, including a novel entitled *Germinie Lacerteux* (1865), based upon the life of their own maidservant, and the multi-volume *Journal*, which provides an often gossipy overview of the literary figures and social events of their time. One of

Proust's "pastiches" in his *Pastiches et mélanges* (see the Introduction to the present book) had targeted the Goncourt brothers. For a brief account of the circumstances surrounding the expurgated original publication of the *Journal*, see the editor's notes to Marcel Proust, *A la recherche du temps perdu*, vol. IV (Paris: Gallimard [Pléiade], 1989), p. 1188.

3 The word "Zouave" first entered the French language in 1830 and is of Berber/ Arabic origin. The word originally designated Algerian soldiers belonging to the infantry of the French army as of 1830, but later referred to French colonial regiments whose soldiers wore colorful, "Oriental" uniforms.

4 A prime example of this effect whereby what succeeds in the narrative order effaces what has preceded it can be seen if one juxtaposes the narrator's theoretical affirmations on the "necessary" quality of a literary style based upon metaphor (upon the "chaining" together of divergent objects in a rigorous metaphorical discourse – *R* IV 467; *S 6, 197*), to a scene that took place only seventy-five pages earlier, in which the Baron de Charlus finds himself in chains of an altogether different sort (*R* IV, 394; *S* 6, 123). The tendency has been for readers and critics to forget the literal thrust of the earlier, sado-masochistic scene in favor of the lofty, metaphorically expressed theoretical declaration.

5 See note 5 to Chapter 2 of the present study for Proust's appreciation of Flaubert's use of temporal *blancs* or empty spaces.

6 *Webster's New Universal Unabridged Dictionary*, 2nd edn. (New York: Simon & Schuster, 1983). For "metaphor" see p. 1132, and for "translation," see p. 1939.

7 In the early pages of *Combray*, the narrator's grandfather had amused himself by "detecting" Bloch's Jewish traits and by referring to them, *sotto voce*, through allusions to musical dramas based upon Jewish themes. The "sweet valley" (*douce vallée*) of the Hebron comes from Joseph's aria in the first act of the opera *Joseph* by Etienne-Nicolas Méhul (1763–1817). A revised version of the work had been performed at the Paris Opéra in 1899. The phrase "bonds of Israel" (*les chaînes d'Israël*) is taken from Samson's aria in the second act of *Samson et Dalila*, a rather more famous and musically impressive opera by Camille Saint-Saëns (1835–1921). *Samson et Dalila* was created in 1877 and was performed on the stage of the Paris Opéra in 1892 (see editor's notes to *A la recherche du temps perdu*, vol. I [Paris: Gallimard [Pléiade], 1987], p. 1146).

8 The poet in question is Victor Hugo, and the poem from which the expression "mysterious threads" (*fils mystérieux*) is taken is one of Hugo's most famous melancholy meditations on love lost, "Tristesse d'Olympio." The relevant verses are: "Que peu de temps suffit pour changer toutes choses! / Nature au front serein, comme vous oubliez! / Et comme vous brisez dans vos métamorphoses / Les fils mystérieux où nos cœurs sont liés" (see *A la recherche du temps perdu*, vol. IV [Paris: Gallimard [Pléiade], 1989], editor's notes, p. 1308).

Select bibliography

Thousands of critical studies devoted to Proust have appeared since the author's death in 1922. Only a selection of those considered by consensus to be among the most useful and the most influential can be included here.

A LA RECHERCHE DU TEMPS PERDU

IN FRENCH

Proust, Marcel, *A la recherche du temps perdu*, 4 vols., ed. Jean-Yves Tadié (Paris: Gallimard [Pléiade], 1987–89).

The best French paperback editions are those published by Folio (ed. Jean-Yves Tadié) and by Garnier-Flammarion (ed. Jean Milly). They both provide full critical apparatus.

IN ENGLISH

Proust, Marcel, *In Search of Lost Time*, 6 vols., ed. Christopher Prendergast (London: Penguin Classics, 2003). This is the translation chosen for use in the present study.

Proust, Marcel, *In Search of Lost Time,* 6 vols. (London: Vintage, 1992).

Proust, Marcel, *In Search of Lost Time,* 6 vols. (New York: The Modern Library, 1993).

(The text of the Vintage and Modern Library editions is identical, but the pagination varies.)

OTHER WORKS BY PROUST

Le Carnet de 1908, ed. Philip Kolb (Paris: Gallimard, 1976).

Contre Sainte-Beuve, précédé de Pastiches et mélanges et suivi de Essais et articles (Paris: Gallimard, 1971).

Contre Sainte-Beuve, suivi de Nouveaux mélanges, ed. Bernard de Fallois (Paris: Gallimard, 1954).

Ecrits de jeunesse (Paris: Institut Marcel Proust International, 1991).

Jean Santeuil, précédé de Les Plaisirs et les jours (Paris: Gallimard [Pléiade], 1971).

Textes retrouvés, ed. Philip Kolb (Paris: Gallimard, 1971).

TRANSLATIONS OF RUSKIN

La Bible d'Amiens (Paris: Mercure de France, 1904).
Sésame et les lys (Paris: Mercure de France, 1906).
Sésame et les lys, précédé de Sur la lecture, intro. Antoine Compagnon (Paris: Editions Complexe, 1987).

AVAILABLE IN ENGLISH TRANSLATION

Against Sainte-Beuve and Other Essays, trans. and ed. J. Sturrock (Harmondsworth: Penguin, 1988); see also *On Art and Literature*, trans. S.T. Warner (New York: Carroll and Graf, 1997).
Jean Santeuil, trans. G. Hopkins (New York: Simon & Schuster, 1956; Harmondsworth: Penguin, 1985).
Marcel Proust: On Reading Ruskin, trans. and ed. Jean Autret *et al.*, intro. Richard Macksey (New Haven: Yale University Press, 1987).
Pleasures and Regrets, trans. L. Varese (New York: Crown, 1948).

CORRESPONDENCE

IN FRENCH

Correspondance de Marcel Proust, 21 vols., ed. Philip Kolb (Paris: Plon, 1970–93).
(See also Kazuyoshi Yoshikawa *et al.*, eds., *Index général de la Correspondance de Marcel Proust* [Presses de l'Université de Kyoto, 1998].)

IN ENGLISH

Selected Letters, 4 vols. (London: Collins, then HarperCollins, 1983–2000).

BIOGRAPHY

Carter, William C., *Marcel Proust: A Life* (New Haven and London: Yale University Press, 2000).
Diesbach, Ghislain de, *Proust* (Paris: Perrin, 1991).
Hayman, Ronald, *Proust: A Biography* (New York: HarperCollins, 1990).
Maurois, André, *A la recherche de Marcel Proust* (Paris: Hachette, 1949). The English translation by Gerard Hopkins is available as *The Quest for Proust* (Harmondsworth: Penguin, 1962) and as *Proust: Portrait of a Genius* (New York: Harper and Brothers, 1950).
Painter, George D., *Marcel Proust: A Biography*, 2 vols. (London: Chatto and Windus, 1959, 1965; New York: Random House, 1959, 1965).
Tadié, Jean-Yves, *Marcel Proust: Biographie* (Paris: Gallimard, 1996). Available in English as *Marcel Proust: A Biography*, trans. Euan Cameron (London: Viking, 2000).

White, Edmund, *Proust* (London: Weidenfeld and Nicolson, 1999; New York: Viking, 1999).

JOURNALS

Bulletin d'informations proustiennes.
Bulletin de la Société des amis de Marcel Proust et des amis de Combray.

CRITICAL WORKS

Album Proust (Paris: Gallimard [Pléiade], 1965).
Alden, Douglas W., *Marcel Proust and His French Critics* (Los Angeles: Lymanhouse, 1940).
Autret, Jean, *L'Influence de Ruskin sur la vie, les idées et l'oeuvre de Marcel Proust* (Geneva: Droz, 1955).
Bal, Mieke, *The Mottled Screen: Reading Proust Visually* (Stanford University Press, 1997).
Bales, Richard, *Proust: "A la recherche du temps perdu"* (London: Grant and Cutler, 1995).
Proust and the Middle Ages (Geneva: Droz, 1975).
Bardèche, Maurice, *Marcel Proust romancier*, 2 vols. (Paris: Les Sept Couleurs, 1971).
Barthes, Roland, "Proust et les noms propres," in *To Honor Roman Jakobson* (The Hague: Mouton, 1967), pp. 150–58.
Baudry, Jean-Louis, *Proust, Freud et l'autre* (Paris: Les Editions de Minuit, 1984).
Beckett, Samuel, *Proust* (London: John Calder, 1965). (Other editions available.)
Benhaïm, André, *Panim: Visages de Proust* (Lille: Presses Universitaires du Septentrion, 2006).
Benjamin, Walter, "The Image of Proust," in *Illuminations*, ed. Hannah Arendt, trans. Harry Zohn (New York: Schocken Books, 1968), pp. 201–15.
Bersani, Leo, *Marcel Proust: The Fictions of Life and Art* (New York and London: Oxford University Press, 1965).
Bizub, Edward, *Proust et le moi divisé* (Geneva: Droz, 2006).
La Venise intérieure: Proust et la poétique de la traduction (Neuchâtel: Les Editions de la Baconnière, 1991).
Bonnet, Henri, *Marcel Proust de 1907 à 1914*, 2 vols. (Paris: Nizet, 1971, 1976).
Botton, Alain de, *How Proust Can Change Your Life* (New York: Pantheon, 1997).
Bouillaguet, Annick, *L'Imitation Cryptée: Proust lecteur de Balzac et de Flaubert* (Paris: Champion, 2000).
Marcel Proust: bilan critique (Paris: Nathan, 1994).
Bowie, Malcolm, *Freud, Proust and Lacan: Theory as Fiction* (Cambridge: Cambridge University Press, 1987).
Proust among the Stars (London: HarperCollins, 1998; New York: Columbia University Press, 1998).

Brée, Germaine, *Du Temps perdu au temps retrouvé* (Paris: Les Belles Lettres, 1969). Available in English as *Marcel Proust and Deliverance from Time*, trans. C.J. Richards and A.D. Truitt (New Brunswick: Rutgers University Press, 1969).

Brun, Bernard, "*Le Temps retrouvé* dans les avant-textes de *Combray*," *Bulletin d'informations proustiennes*, 12 (1981), 7–23.

Brunel, Patrick, *Le Rire de Proust* (Paris: Champion, 1997).

Brunet, Etienne, *Le Vocabulaire de Proust*, 3 vols. (Geneva: Slatkine; Paris: Champion, 1983).

Bucknall, Barbara, *The Religion of Art in Proust* (Urbana: University of Illinois Press, 1969).

Butor, Michel, "Les Oeuvres d'art imaginaires chez Proust," in *Répertoire II* (Paris: Minuit, 1964), pp. 252–92.

Canavaggia, J., *Proust et la politique* (Paris: Nizet, 1986).

Carter, William C., *Proust in Love* (New Haven: Yale University Press, 2006).

The Proustian Quest (New York University Press, 1992).

Carter, William C., ed., *The UAB Marcel Proust Symposium* (Birmingham, AL: Summa Publications, 1989).

Chantal, René de, *Marcel Proust critique littéraire*, 2 vols. (Presses de l'Université de Montréal, 1967).

Citati, Pietro, *La Colombe poignardée*, trans. Brigitte Pérol (Paris: Gallimard/Folio, 1997).

Cocking, J.M., *Proust: Collected Essays on the Writer and His Art* (Cambridge: Cambridge University Press, 1982).

Collier, Peter, *Proust and Venice* (Cambridge: Cambridge University Press, 1989).

Compagnon, Antoine, *Proust entre deux siècles* (Paris: Seuil, 1989). Available in English as *Proust between Two Centuries*, trans. Richard E. Goodkin (New York: Columbia University Press, 1992).

Coudert, Raymonde, *Proust au féminin* (Paris: Grasset, 1998).

Curtius, Ernst Robert, *Marcel Proust*, trans. Armand Pierhal (Paris: *La Revue nouvelle*, 1928 [1925]).

Davenport-Hines, Richard, *Proust at the Majestic: The Last Days of the Author Whose Book Changed Paris* (New York and London: Bloomsbury, 2006).

Deleuze, Gilles, *Proust et les signes*, 5th edn. (Paris: Presses Universitaires de France, 1979). Available in English as *Proust and Signs*, trans. Richard Howard (Minneapolis: University of Minnesota Press, 2000).

De Man, Paul, "Reading (Proust)," in *Allegories of Reading* (New Haven and London: Yale University Press, 1979), pp. 57–78.

Descombes, Vincent, *Proust: philosophie du roman* (Paris: Minuit, 1987). Available in English as *Proust: Philosophy of the Novel*, trans. Catherine Chance Macksey (Stanford University Press, 1992).

Doubrovsky, Serge, *La Place de la Madeleine: Ecriture et fantasme chez Proust* (Paris: Mercure de France, 1974). Available in English as *Writing and Fantasy in Proust: La Place de la Madeleine*, trans. Carol Mastrangelo Bové and Paul A. Bové (Lincoln: University of Nebraska Press, 1986).

Dyer, Nathalie Mauriac, *Proust inachevé: le dossier "Albertine disparue"* (Paris: Champion, 2005).
Eells, Emily, *Proust's Cup of Tea: Homoeroticism and Victorian Culture* (Aldershot; Burlington, USA: Ashgate, 2002).
Ellison, David, "Proust and Posterity," in *The Cambridge Companion to Proust* (Cambridge: Cambridge University Press, 2001), pp. 200–15.
The Reading of Proust (Baltimore: The Johns Hopkins University Press, 1984; Oxford: Blackwell, 1984).
Ferré, André, *Les Années de collège de Marcel Proust* (Paris: Gallimard, 1959).
Géographie de Marcel Proust (Paris: Sagittaire, 1939).
Finn, Michael R., *Proust, the Body and Literary Form* (Cambridge: Cambridge University Press, 1999).
Fraisse, Luc, *L'Oeuvre cathédrale: Proust et l'architecture médiévale* (Paris: Corti, 1990).
Le Processus de la création chez Marcel Proust: le fragment expérimental (Paris: Corti, 1988).
Gamble, Cynthia J., *Proust as Interpreter of Ruskin: The Seven Lamps of Translation* (Birmingham, AL: Summa Publications, 2002).
Genette, Gérard, *Figures III* (Paris: Seuil, 1972). Available in English as *Narrative Discourse: An Essay in Method*, trans. Jane E. Lewin (Ithaca: Cornell University Press, 1980).
Nouveau discours du récit (Paris: Seuil, 1983). Available in English as *Narrative Discourse Revisited*, trans. Jane E. Lewin (Ithaca: Cornell University Press, 1990).
"Proust et le langage indirect," in *Figures II* (Paris: Seuil, 1969), pp. 223–94.
"Proust palimpseste," in *Figures I* (Paris: Seuil, 1966), pp. 39–67.
Graham, Victor, *The Imagery of Proust* (Oxford: Blackwell, 1966).
Gray, Margaret E., *Postmodern Proust* (Philadelphia: University of Pennsylvania Press, 1992).
Hassine, Juliette, *Marranisme et hébraïsme dans l'oeuvre de Proust* (Paris: Minard, 1994).
Hayes, Jarrod, "Proust in the Tearoom," *PMLA*, 110 (1995), 992–1005.
Henry, Anne, *Marcel Proust: théories pour une esthétique* (Paris: Klincksieck, 1981).
Proust romancier: le tombeau égyptien (Paris: Flammarion, 1983).
Hindus, Milton, *The Proustian Vision* (New York: Columbia University Press, 1954).
Hodson, Leighton, *Marcel Proust: The Critical Heritage* (London and New York: Routledge, 1989).
Houston, John Porter, *The Shape and Style of Proust's Novel* (Detroit: Wayne State University Press, 1982).
Hughes, Edward J., *Marcel Proust: A Study in the Quality of Awareness* (Cambridge: Cambridge University Press, 1983).
Jauss, Hans Robert, *Zeit und Erinnerung in Marcel Prousts "A la recherche du temps perdu"* (Heidelberg: Carl Winter, 1970).

Jordan, Jack Louis, *Marcel Proust's "A la recherche du temps perdu": A Search for Certainty* (Birmingham, AL: Summa Publications, 1993).

Kasell, Walter, *Marcel Proust and the Strategy of Reading* (Amsterdam: John Benjamins, 1980).

Kilmartin, Terence, *A Guide to Proust* (Harmondsworth: Penguin, 1985 [1983]).

Kolb, Philip, "Historique du premier roman de Proust," *Saggi e ricerche di letteratura francese*, IV (1963), 217–77.

Kristeva, Julia, *Proust and the Sense of Time*, trans. Stephen Bann (New York: Columbia University Press, 1993).

Le Temps sensible: Proust et l'expérience littéraire (Paris: Gallimard, 1994). Available in English as *Time and Sense: Proust and the Experience of Literature*, trans. Ross Guberman (New York: Columbia University Press, 1996).

Ladenson, Elisabeth, *Proust's Lesbianism* (Ithaca: Cornell University Press, 1999).

Lehrer, Jonah, *Proust Was a Neuroscientist* (Boston: Houghton Mifflin, 2007).

McDonald, Christie, *The Proustian Fabric: Associations of Memory* (Lincoln: University of Nebraska Press, 1991).

Mendelson, David, *Le Verre et les objets de verre dans l'univers imaginaire de Marcel Proust* (Paris: Corti, 1968).

Milly, Jean, *La Phrase de Proust* (Paris: Larousse, 1975; reprinted Geneva: Slatkine, 1983).

Proust et le style (Paris: Minard, 1970).

Moss, Howard, *The Magic Lantern of Marcel Proust* (London: Faber and Faber, 1963).

Muller, Marcel, *Les Voix narratives dans "A la recherche du temps perdu"* (Geneva: Droz, 1965).

Nabokov, Vladimir, "The Walk by Swann's Place," in *Lectures on Literature* (New York and London: Harcourt, Brace, Jovanovich, 1980), pp. 206–49.

Nattiez, J-J., *Proust musicien* (Paris: Christian Bourgois, 1984). Available in English as *Proust as Musician*, trans. Derrick Puffett (Cambridge University Press, 1989).

Péchenard, Christian, *Proust à Cabourg* (Paris: Quai Voltaire, 1992).

Picon, Gaëtan, *Lecture de Proust* (Paris: Gallimard, 1995 [1963]).

Pierre-Quint, Léon, *Marcel Proust: sa vie, son œuvre* (Paris: Editions du Sagittaire, 1946 [1925]).

Piette, Adam, *Remembering and the Sound of Words: Mallarmé, Proust, Joyce, Beckett* (Oxford: Clarendon Press, 1996).

Poulet, Georges, *L'espace proustien* (Paris: Gallimard, 1963). Available in English as *Proustian Space*, trans. Elliott Coleman (Baltimore: The Johns Hopkins University Press, 1977).

Pugh, Anthony R., *The Birth of "A la recherche du temps perdu"* (Lexington, KY: French Forum, 1987).

Quémar, Claudine, "Autour de trois avant-textes de l''Ouverture' de la *Recherche*: Nouvelles approches des problèmes du *Contre Sainte-Beuve*," *Bulletin d'informations proustiennes*, 3 (1976), 7–39.

"Rêveries onomastiques proustiennes à la lumière des avant-textes," in Almuth Grésillon, ed., *Essais de critique génétique* (Paris: Flammarion, 1979), pp. 69–102.

Reid, James H., *Proust, Beckett, and Narration* (Cambridge: Cambridge University Press, 2003).

Richard, Jean-Pierre, *Proust et le monde sensible* (Paris: Seuil, 1974).

Rivers, J.E., *Proust and the Art of Love: The Aesthetics of Sexuality in the Life, Times and Art of Marcel Proust* (New York: Columbia University Press, 1981).

Rivière, Jacques, *Quelques progrès dans l'étude du coeur humain* (Paris: Librairie de France, 1926).

Rogers, Brian G., *Le Dessous des cartes: Proust et Barbey d'Aurevilly* (Paris: Champion, 2000).

Proust's Narrative Techniques (Geneva: Droz, 1965).

Rorty, Richard, "Self-creation and Affiliation: Proust, Nietzsche and Heidegger," in *Contingency, Irony, and Solidarity* (Cambridge University Press, 1989), pp. 96–121.

Schmid, Marion, *Processes of Literary Creation: Flaubert and Proust* (Oxford: Legenda, 1998).

Shattuck, Roger, *A Field Guide to Proust* (New York: Norton; London: Penguin/The Allen Lane Press, 2000).

Proust (London: Fontana, 1974).

Proust's Binoculars: A Study of Memory, Time, and Recognition in "A la recherche du temps perdu" (New York: Random House, 1963; London: Chatto and Windus, 1964).

"The Threat to Proust," *New York Review of Books*, March 18, 1999, pp. 10–12.

Simon, Anne, *Proust ou le réel retrouvé* (Paris: Presses Universitaires de France, 2000).

Slater, Maya, *Humour in the Works of Proust* (Oxford University Press, 1979).

Splitter, Randolph, *Proust's "Recherche": A Psychoanalytic Interpretation* (Boston: Routledge and Kegan Paul, 1981).

Sprinker, Michael, *History and Ideology in Proust: "A la recherche du temps perdu" and the Third Republic* (Cambridge: Cambridge University Press, 1994; London: Verso, 1998).

Steel, Gareth H., *Chronology and Time in "A la recherche du temps perdu"* (Geneva: Droz, 1979).

Straus, Walter, *Proust and Literature: The Novelist as Critic* (Cambridge, MA: Harvard University Press, 1957).

Tadié, Jean-Yves, ed., *Marcel Proust: l'écriture et les arts* (Paris: Gallimard/Bibliothèque nationale de France/Réunion des musées nationaux, 1999).

Proust et le roman (Paris: Gallimard, 1971; reprinted 1986).

Proust, le dossier (Paris: Belfond, 1983).

Terdiman, Richard, *The Dialectics of Isolation: Self and Society in the French Novel from the Realists to Proust* (New Haven: Yale University Press, 1976).

Wimmers, Inge Crosman, *Proust and Emotion: The Importance of Affect in "A la recherche du temps perdu"* (University of Toronto Press, 2003).

Winton, Alison [Alison Finch], *Proust's Additions: The Making of "A la recherche du temps perdu,"* 2 vols. (Cambridge: Cambridge University Press, 1977).
Yoshida, Jo, "Proust contre Ruskin: la genèse de deux voyages dans la *Recherche* d'après des brouillons inédits," 2 vols. Unpublished dissertation, Université de Paris IV-Sorbonne, 1978.

Index

Note: Personal and place names in italic indicate characters and places in the novel. Page references in italic indicate illustrations.